LIBRARY OF NEW TESTAMENT STUDIES

635

Formerly the Journal for the Study of the New Testament Supplement series

Editor
Chris Keith

Editorial Board
Dale C. Allison, John M.G. Barclay, Lynn H. Cohick, R. Alan Culpepper,
Craig A. Evans, Robert Fowler, Simon J. Gathercole, Juan Hernández
Jr., John S. Kloppenborg, Michael Labahn, Matthew V. Novenson,
Love L. Sechrest, Robert Wall, Catrin H. Williams, Brittany E. Wilson

The Divine-Human Relationship in Romans 1–8 in the Light of Interdependence Theory

Yoonjong Kim

LONDON • NEW YORK • OXFORD • NEW DELHI • SYDNEY

T&T CLARK
Bloomsbury Publishing Plc
50 Bedford Square, London, WC1B 3DP, UK
1385 Broadway, New York, NY 10018, USA
29 Earlsfort Terrace, Dublin 2, Ireland

BLOOMSBURY, T&T CLARK and the T&T Clark logo are trademarks of Bloomsbury Publishing Plc

First published in Great Britain 2020
This paperback edition published in 2022

Copyright © Yoonjong Kim, 2020

Yoonjong Kim has asserted his right under the Copyright, Designs and Patents Act, 1988, to be identified as Author of this work.

For legal purposes the Acknowledgements on p. xii constitute an extension of this copyright page.

All rights reserved. No part of this publication may be reproduced or transmitted in any form or by any means, electronic or mechanical, including photocopying, recording, or any information storage or retrieval system, without prior permission in writing from the publishers.

Bloomsbury Publishing Plc does not have any control over, or responsibility for, any third-party websites referred to or in this book. All internet addresses given in this book were correct at the time of going to press. The author and publisher regret any inconvenience caused if addresses have changed or sites have ceased to exist, but can accept no responsibility for any such changes.

A catalogue record for this book is available from the British Library.

Library of Congress Cataloging-in-Publication Data

Names: Kim, Yoonjong, author.
Title: The divine-human relationship in Romans 1–8 in the light of interdependence theory / Yoonjong Kim.
Description: London ; New York : T&T Clark, 2020. | Series: The library of New Testament studies, 2513-8790 ; 635 | Includes bibliographical references and index. | Summary: "Yoonjong Kim aims to analyse the divine-human relationship in Paul's theology, focusing on Paul's portrayal of the relationship in Romans 1–8. Kim stresses that previous studies of this relationship have not paid sufficient attention to the fact that it is not static, but rather exhibits progression and development towards a goal. To address the significance of the human agent's role in the relationship, Kim employs a social psychological theory – interdependence theory – offering a consistent analytic framework for diagnosing the interactions in a dyadic relationship in terms of the dependency created by each partner's expectations of outcomes"– Provided by publisher.
Identifiers: LCCN 2020030086 (print) | LCCN 2020030087 (ebook) | ISBN 9780567695772 (hb) | ISBN 9780567696823 (paperback) | ISBN 9780567695789 (epdf) | ISBN 9780567695802 (epub)
Subjects: LCSH: Bible. Romans, I-VIII–Criticism, interpretation, etc. | Spirituality–Biblical teaching.
Classification: LCC BS2665.52 .K465 2020 (print) | LCC BS2665.52 (ebook) | DDC 227/.106—dc23
LC record available at https://lccn.loc.gov/2020030086
LC ebook record available at https://lccn.loc.gov/2020030087

ISBN:	HB:	978-0-5676-9577-2
	PB:	978-0-5676-9682-3
	ePDF:	978-0-5676-9578-9
	ePUB:	978-0-5676-9580-2

Series: Library of New Testament Studies, volume 635
ISSN 2513-8790

Typeset by RefineCatch Limited, Bungay, Suffolk

To find out more about our authors and books visit www.bloomsbury.com
and sign up for our newsletters.

Contents

List of Figures ... ix
List of Abbreviations ... x
Abstract ... xi
Acknowledgements ... xii

1 Introduction ... 1
  1.1 Introduction ... 1
  1.2 Scholarship on the divine-human relationship in Romans 1–8 ... 2
    1.2.1 Divine and human agency ... 3
    1.2.2 Apocalyptic Paul ... 7
    1.2.3 Χάρις in Paul ... 10
    1.2.4 Covenantal relationship (N. T. Wright) ... 16
    1.2.5 Summary and prospect ... 17
  1.3 The procedure of the study ... 18

2 Methodology ... 21
  2.1 Introduction ... 21
  2.2 An outline of IT ... 21
    2.2.1 Reward and cost ... 22
    2.2.2 Comparison level and comparison level for alternatives ... 23
    2.2.3 Outcome table ... 23
    2.2.4 Various powers in the relationship: Partner control, joint control and actor control ... 24
    2.2.5 Four features of interdependence ... 26
      2.2.5.1 Degree of dependence ... 26
      2.2.5.2 Mutuality of dependence ... 26
      2.2.5.3 Basis of dependence ... 27
      2.2.5.4 Covariation of interests (correspondence of outcomes) ... 27
    2.2.6 Transformation of motivation: From "given situation" to "effective situation" ... 28
  2.3 Why do we need IT? ... 30
  2.4 Methodological considerations: Toward a use of IT for the interpretation of Romans 1–8 ... 31

	2.4.1 On historical-cultural validity: The issue of the individual and IT	32
	2.4.1.1 Understanding the individual in antiquity	34
	2.4.1.2 Paul's understanding of the individual	36
	2.4.1.3 The concept of "outcome" and self-interest	38
	2.4.2 Placing the divine-human relationship into the framework of a dyadic relationship	44
	2.4.2.1 Human beings: As group and as single entity	44
	2.4.2.2 Can God be like a human actor?	45
	2.4.3 Using text as source	49
	2.5 Conclusion	52
3	Diagnosing Human Corruption: Human Sinfulness as Betrayal (Rom. 1:18–3:20)	53
	3.1 Introduction	53
	3.2 The broken relationship between God and humanity (1): Betrayal by the wrong calculation (Gentiles) (Rom. 1:18–32)	54
	3.2.1 Betrayal in IT	54
	3.2.2 The relational characteristic of human sin: Subversion and animosity (Rom. 1:21–32)	56
	3.2.3 The reason for betrayal: Different calculations of "outcomes" (humanity's perspective vs. Paul's perspective)	58
	3.2.3.1 The calculation by humanity: The reason for leaving	58
	3.2.3.2 The calculation by Paul: The reason for remaining	61
	3.2.4 Summary	62
	3.3 The broken relationship between God and humanity (2): Breaking "social norms" (Jews) (Rom. 2:1–3:8)	63
	3.3.1 The function of "social norms" in IT	63
	3.3.2 Aspects of brokenness: Unfaithfulness to the law and circumcision as "social norms" (Rom. 2:1–5; 2:17–3:8)	64
	3.4 The universality of brokenness (Rom. 3:9–20)	68
	3.5 Conclusion	69
4	The Relational Significance of Jesus' Death (1)—"Making Amends for Sins": Jesus as ἱλαστήριον and the Process of Forgiveness (Rom. 3:21–26)	71
	4.1 Introduction	71
	4.2 The process of forgiveness in IT	72
	4.3 Recompense and forgiveness (and reconciliation) according to ancient perspectives	74

	4.4 Forgiveness in Rom. 3:21–26: From an interpersonal perspective	76
	4.5 Situating Rom. 3:21–26 within the process of forgiveness in IT: God as "victim," humanity as "perpetrators," sin as "betrayal" and ἱλαστήριον as "amends"	79
	4.5.1 Three different outlooks on ἱλαστήριον: Expiation, propitiation and the mercy seat	80
	4.5.2 Suggesting an alternative way to understand ἱλαστήριον: ἱλαστήριον and "amends"	83
	4.5.2.1 "Amends" and expiation	85
	4.5.2.2 "Amends" and propitiation	87
	4.5.2.3 "Amends" and the mercy seat	89
	4.5.2.4 Summary	91
	4.6 "Through faith" (διὰ [τῆς] πίστεως) and mutual participation	91
	4.7 Conclusion	94
5	The Relational Significance of Jesus' Death (2)—The Meaning of God's Self-Sacrifice in Christ's Death (Rom. 5:1–11)	97
	5.1 Introduction	97
	5.2 Understanding God's self-sacrifice in Christ from an interpersonal perspective	99
	5.2.1 The pattern of "martyrdom"	101
	5.3 "Self-presentation" and "attribution": The process of communication for "transformation"	102
	5.3.1 Self-presentation	102
	5.3.2 Attribution	103
	5.4 The results from the transformation: Positive outcomes for God and for the (long-term) relationship	107
	5.5 Contextual evidence: Christ's death as a gift	109
	5.6 Conclusion	111
6	History of Slavery and History of Salvation: An Investigation of the Sin-Human Relationship (Rom. 5:12–8:11)	113
	6.1 Introduction	113
	6.2 The identity of Sin in Romans 5–8	113
	6.2.1 Sin as a personified cosmic power	114
	6.2.2 Sin as a malicious slave master	116
	6.3 Romans 7 in the light of IT – The issue of the "I" (Rom. 7:7–25)	118
	6.3.1 "Non-voluntary relationship" in IT	120
	6.3.2 Reading the monologue of the "I" in the light of "non-voluntary relationship" in IT	122

		6.3.2.1 An alternative option for the "I" and the required cost: The reason for remaining in the abusive relationship with Sin (Rom. 7:1–6)	123
		6.3.2.2 The solution for the abusive relationship – The implication of the Christ-event for the termination of the Sin-human relationship (Rom. 6:1–11; 8:1–11)	126
	6.4	Conclusion	128
7	Investment for the Future: The Meaning of Endurance throughout Suffering (Rom. 8:12–39)		131
	7.1	Introduction	131
	7.2	Framing suffering and glory: Suffering as "cost" and glory as "reward" (Rom. 8:17–18)	132
	7.3	Relational implication of enduring suffering (1): An expression of fidelity	135
	7.4	Relational implication of enduring suffering (2): In the light of the "investment situation" in IT (Rom. 8:12–30)	137
		7.4.1 Forgoing immediate interests (Rom. 8:12–17)	138
		7.4.2 Necessity of mutual commitment (Rom. 8:18–30)	140
		7.4.2.1 The use of familial language	141
		7.4.2.2 The use of συν- compounds	143
	7.5	Strategies for sustaining the relationship	150
		7.5.1 Persistence objectively warranted by a goal (Rom. 8:26–27, 31–39)	150
		7.5.2 Persistence promoted by proximity (Rom. 8:18)	150
		7.5.3 Persistence promoted by mounting exit vosts (Rom. 8:6, 13)	151
		7.5.4 Persistence promoted by trust and commitment (Rom. 8:31–39)	151
		7.5.5 Relationship maintenance mechanisms (Rom. 8:14–17)	153
		7.5.6 Increasing locomotion (Rom. 8:13–14, 18, 24–25)	153
	7.6	Conclusion	154
8	Conclusion		157
	8.1	Summary of the study	157
	8.2	Implications of the study	160
Bibliography			163
Index of References			179
Index of Authors			191

Figures

2.1	Illustration of 2 X 2 table	24
2.2	Illustration of A's partner control over B	25
2.3	Illustration of A's joint control over B	25
2.4	Outcome tables of corresponding situation vs conflicting situation	28
2.5	Transformation process	29
3.1	Humanity's calculation	59
3.2	Paul's calculation	62
5.1	Expected outcomes for God by his self-sacrificial act (conventional point of view)	100
5.2	Outcome tables for the pattern of "martyrdom"	101
5.3	Transformation process and the influence of the communication process	104
6.1	Patterns of voluntary versus non-voluntary dependence	122
6.2	Pattern of the "non-voluntary dependence" of the "I" upon Sin	125

Abbreviations

All abbreviations of ancient literature, academic journals and monograph series follow the forms indicated in the *SBL Handbook of Style: For Biblical Studies and Related Disciplines*, Second Edition (Atlanta: SBL Press, 2014), with the following exceptions, which are not included in the *SBL Handbook of Style*:

Academic journals

APSR	American Political Science Review
APsy	American Psychologist
ARP	Annual Review of Psychology
BASP	Basic and Applied Social Psychology
CV	Counselling and Values
EC	Early Christianity
IntS	Interaction Studies
JPSP	Journal of Personality and Social Psychology
JSCP	Journal of Social and Clinical Psychology
JSPHL	Journal for the Study of Paul and His Letters
PR	Personal Relationships
PSPB	Personality and Social Psychology Bulletin
SPPC	Social and Personality Psychology Compass

Interdependence theory

IT	Interdependence Theory
CL	Comparison Level
CL-alt	Comparison Level for Alternatives
PC	Partner Control
JC	Joint Control
AC	Actor Control
MPC	Mutual Partner Control
MJC	Mutual Joint Control

Abstract

The present project aims to analyze the divine-human relationship in Paul's theology, focusing on Paul's portrayal of the relationship in Romans 1–8. The issue of the divine-human relationship has been treated by multiple Pauline studies with various foci, for instance, the issues of agency, the apocalyptic character of Paul's gospel, the concept of χάρις and the covenantal relationship. Nevertheless, these approaches often do not pay sufficient attention to the fact that the divine-human relationship in Romans is not static but exhibits progression and development towards a goal. As a result of this, such studies cannot effectively address the significance of the human agent's role in the relationship, a role which changes at each stage of the relationship's development.

In order to offer a different perspective, the present study utilizes a social psychological theory, namely, interdependence theory (IT). IT offers a consistent analytic framework for diagnosing the interactions in a dyadic relationship in terms of the dependency created by each partner's expectations of outcomes. By deploying IT, we explore several key stages of the divine-human relationship and the direction in which the relationship develops throughout Romans 1–8 in order to highlight the significance of the human partners in the course of the development. The key stages include: betrayal (1:18–3:20), restoration (3:21–26; 5:1–11), the oppressive relationship with Sin (5:12–8:11) and the investment for the future (8:12–39). From our investigation, we conclude that although the foundation of the relationship rests on God's initiative, the divine outworking guides the relationship so that it facilitates mutual participation of the human partners in the restoration and development of the relationship toward the ultimate goal. Another contribution of the present study can be found in our attempt to introduce IT to the field of NT studies through our methodological considerations.

Acknowledgements

This book is a slightly revised version of my PhD thesis accepted by the University of Manchester in 2017. It is a pleasant task to express my gratefulness to those who supported me in various ways to carry out this project. Firstly, I thank my primary supervisor Professor Peter Oakes who supervised this project from beginning to end. He has always been supportive and carefully gave his attention to what I wanted to say. He has continuously challenged me to express my ideas in better shape with great patience and encouragement. I am also thankful to Janet Oakes for her concern for my wife and daughters. Thanks are also due to my secondary supervisor Dr Todd Klutz. He has been generous with sharing his thoughts and gave helpful comments to sharpen my ideas.

I am also deeply thankful for fellowship with colleagues in Manchester. It was a weekly joy to gather for a PhD class with Benedict Kent, Sam Rogers, Rosie Jackson, Justin Daneshmand, Alex Potts, David Bell and Heiner Georgi. Benedict, as a same year postgraduate student, became not only a good academic peer but also a good friend to my family. I am also thankful for my friendship with Peter Choi, Mija Wi and Eunho Kim. Robert and Janet Nettleton require special mention, they warmly welcomed my family to their home and took care of us with great love and hospitality.

This project would have been impossible without the help and sacrifice of Yulbang Church in Korea, which helped me to carry out my research abroad. It provided consistent financial support and unceasing prayer and encouragement. Whenever my family visited Korea, they received us with great kindness and love. I hope that my time in England made me a better person in my work for Yulbang Church. Rev. Minho Kim and his wife Hyunkyung Cho have been a great source of love and encouragement. They have always been considerate and put their trust in me. As exemplary Christians, they inspired me to experience the depth and width of the Bible. I would also like to express my gratefulness to Sungoh Jung, Hyekyung Cho, Sangwon Yoo, Sungmi Son, Suyoung Lee and Juhee Kim who shared my joy and struggles. I deeply thank Judy Kim who willingly spent her time carefully reading this manuscript and helped me to present this study in more readable English. Nevertheless, all remaining errors are my responsibility. My thanks also go to all my colleagues and students at All Nations Bible Institute.

My family has always walked alongside me, and I cannot measure their love for me. My parents, Changyoung Kim and Gwija Park, have always been supportive. Their parcels from Korea that contained nice Korean things not available in Manchester, always brought great happiness to my family and I. My in-laws, Jongsup Kim and Myungja Lee, have always made themselves available to help us too, especially when we had our second baby.

I must express my immeasurable thanks and deep love to my immediate family: Hyunjin, Shinhye (Faith) and Seunghye (Vicky). We have been through this journey together and endured toil, making us "interdependent." Shinhye and Seunghye are two of the best girls a Daddy could ever ask for. They have tolerated my busyness and have always tried to make me happy and surprised by their ingenuity, from their drawings to their (incomplete) somersaults! They painted my monotonous life with beautiful colours. I love you so much! I would also like to mention my third child Younghye (Lucy) who was born while the publication process was going on. She has brought extra joy to my family! My wife Hyunjin has put up with the hardships of being a wife of a PhD student, away from family and friends. She always enjoyed listening to what I was working on and tried to help me clarify my thoughts. Her endless love, encouragement, self-sacrifice and prayer made me carry on with my research. Throughout this journey we have grown little by little, as partners, parents and Christians, and we have come to love each other more than before.

Finally, all these thanks ultimately go to God, who steered our journey throughout these past few years. I cannot help confessing that what I had and experienced are all his gifts, even the things that were unexpected. Although my life and my studies are very small, just like a small drop in the ocean, I hope I can serve him humbly with my life as he has always been faithful to me.

1

Introduction

1.1 Introduction

The issue of the divine-human relationship has long been a significant topic in studies of Paul's theology, and scholars have reached various conclusions through different routes of interpretation. In particular, the differences in position derive from how important and influential one thinks the role of each party in the relationship is. Some scholars perceive human beings to be totally dependent upon God; therefore, the human role cannot make any significant difference in the relationship, particularly with regard to salvation. Other scholars, although acknowledging the special quality of the divine action, have attempted to give weight to the meaning of human action. Although a few Pauline studies discuss the issue of the divine-human relationship with various foci, a full-scale study on the question of how the relational dynamics can vary according to the development of the relationship has not been thoroughly attempted. The present study aims to map the geography of the relational dynamics between God and human beings in the course of the relationship's development, examining to what extent both partners' roles are significant in each situation and how the relationship is characterized in terms of dependence between the partners. As will be argued, although the divine-human relationship is fundamentally contingent upon God's initiative, Paul indicates the importance of the mutual engagement of the human actors as the relationship progresses and develops in order to achieve a shared ultimate goal. For our study, we will deploy an analytic framework from social psychology that focuses on relational dynamics in a dyadic relationship, namely "interdependence theory."

Before delving into discussion, it should be noted that we will limit our primary focus to Romans 1–8. Although we can find Paul's description of the divine-human relationship in several places throughout his letters, Paul puts more effort into this topic in Romans 1–8 than in his other letters. Since Romans 1–8 contains rich information about the different stages of the divine-human relationship at a universal level, these chapters can be considered the most appropriate field for our discussion of Paul's view on the divine-human relationship in general.[1] Although Paul's view on the

---

[1] This is because one of the purposes behind Paul's epistle to the Romans was to explain his theological outlook (cf. Rom. 1:15) to a people whom he had not yet met, thereby obtaining their support, and also to encourage them to cooperate with him (cf. 15:22–24) by presenting his universal plan according to his gospel, along with his apostolic authority, which springs from what he says. Cf. Jeffery A.D. Weima, "The Reason for Romans: The Evidence of Its Epistolary Framework (1:1–15; 15:14–16:27)," *R&E* 100

issue of the divine-human relationship can be expressed variously throughout his letters, given the importance recognized by scholars of Romans in Paul's theology, even called a "template,"[2] what we observe in Romans 1–8 can provide grounds for further discussion later on. As will be shown, various stages of the divine-human relationship constitute the flow of Romans 1–8. For instance, the broken state (1:18–3:20), the restorative moments (3:21–26; 5:1–11) and a high degree of intimacy (8:12–39), along with the depiction of an antithetical type of relationship (5:12–8:11). Therefore, in Romans 1–8 our focus will primarily be on the passages related to the aforementioned key stages. Another crucial portion of Romans that also discusses the issue of the divine-human relationship, Romans 9–11, is not dealt with in our research. Although Paul speaks of the divine-human relationship at a universal level in Romans 9–11, because of the particular interest of Romans 9–11 in the relationship between Jews and Gentiles, these chapters will need independent treatment, though this is not to weaken the link between Romans 9–11 and other chapters in Romans. In a similar vein, Romans 12–15, which mainly concentrates on the relationship between believers, is not our main focus, though we will refer to several passages from these chapters that reflect how believers' relationships with God can be related to their lifestyle in practical ways regarding the relationship with others.

In pursuing this aim, we will firstly review several seminal works of Pauline scholarship on the issue of the divine-human relationship mainly in Romans 1–8, elucidating the differences between perspectives as well as the areas for further development. In dealing with the scholars, we will classify them according to their primary orientation of approach to Paul.

1.2 Scholarship on the divine-human relationship in Romans 1–8

In this section, we will critically survey several crucial clusters of Pauline scholarship. The topics of "agency," "apocalyptic" interpretation of Paul, the concept of χάρις

(2003): 17–33. Also, from a pastoral point of view, to spell out the universally meaningful history of the divine-human relationship has the effect of inviting everyone in the community into a single story in which the distinctions between ethnic groups are blurred (cf. 3:9, 23, 29; 14:1–15:13), which will consequently strengthen the community to become a partner for his missionary work. As noted by a few scholars, despite the different degrees of emphasis on each opinion, the two broad aims should not be regarded as mutually exclusive. Cf. F.F. Bruce, "The Romans Debate—Continued," *BJRL* 64 (1981): 334–59; James D.G. Dunn, *Romans 1–8* (Dallas: Word Books, 1988), liv–lvii; A.J.M. Wedderburn, *The Reasons for Romans* (London: T&T Clark, 2004); Klaus Haacker, *The Theology of Paul's Letter to the Romans* (Cambridge: Cambridge University Press, 2003), 16–20; A. Andrew Das, *Solving the Romans Debate* (Minneapolis: Fortress, 2007), 52; Richard N. Longenecker, *Introducing Romans: Critical Issues in Paul's Most Famous Letter* (Grand Rapids: Eerdmans, 2011), 92–3; *The Epistle to the Romans* (Grand Rapids: Eerdmans, 2016), 10. Therefore, it appears necessary for Paul to give a detailed description about the divine-human relationship as one of the crucial elements that constitute his theological outlook to deal with several practical issues that he faces for his ministry in relation to the Roman believers. For various suggestions regarding the purpose of Romans, see Karl P. Donfried, ed., *The Romans Debate* (Peabody: Hendrickson, 1991).

[2] Cf. James D.G. Dunn, *The Theology of Paul the Apostle* (Grand Rapids: Eerdmans, 1998), 25–6. See also, Sheila E. McGinn, ed., *Celebrating Romans: Template for Pauline Theology* (Grand Rapids: Eerdmans, 2004).

(gift) and "covenantal relationship" provide entry points for our discussion on the divine-human relationship.[3] As will be shown, one of the main points commonly considered is the possibility of human beings' active involvement in the relationship.

1.2.1 Divine and human agency

A crucial aspect in discussions about the divine-human relationship is the issue of "agency." John Barclay's categorization of different perspectives on divine and human agency summarizes what is at issue among scholars. The three categories are as follows: 1) the "competitive relationship" model in which "the more that one is to be effective, the less can be attributed to the other," while both agencies remain separated—thus "divine sovereignty and human freedom" would be treated as "mutually exclusive" from this viewpoint;[4] 2) the "kinship" model in which "the agency of one is shared with the other, rather than standing in competition"—thus, in this shared agency, what can make human agency "most effective" is what is "shared with God";[5] 3) the "non-contrastive transcendence" model, which sees the transcendence of divine agency as not necessarily conflicting with human agency, while distinguishing one from the other—thus "created human agencies are founded in, and constituted by, the divine creative agency, while remaining distinctive from God."[6] Two questions are embedded in such categorization. On the one hand, it considers the matter of independence of agency; on the other, it considers the matter of competitiveness between agencies.

Francis Watson's interpretation of Paul appears to fall into Barclay's first category when he examines Paul's interpretative work on the OT in light of the Christ-event. Watson argues that Paul, in contrast to other contemporary Jewish interpreters, prioritizes divine agency in his interpretation of the Torah:

> Paul's controversy with "Judaism" (Christian or otherwise) is in fact a conflict about the interpretation of the Torah.... [T]he question at issue is whether interpretative priority is to be given to a particular mode of divine agency (the making of an unconditional promise) or of human agency (the observance of the commandments).[7]

Watson argues that Paul, in his reading of Gen. 15:6, prioritizes and acknowledges divine agency in terms of salvation over the counter principle based on the reading

---

[3] The Πίστις Χριστοῦ debate is not dealt with as one of the main categories, because 1) this issue will be dealt with in more detail when we discuss some of the key texts for the issue (e.g. Rom. 3:21–26), and 2) the issue will be referenced when we discuss other categories (e.g. Francis Watson; "apocalyptic Paul"; "covenantal relationship" [N.T. Wright]).
[4] John M.G. Barclay, "Introduction," in *Divine and Human Agency in Paul and His Cultural Environment*, ed. John M.G. Barclay and Simon J. Gathercole (London: T&T Clark, 2006), 6.
[5] Ibid., 6–7.
[6] Ibid., 7.
[7] Francis Watson, *Paul and the Hermeneutics of Faith*, Second Edition. (London: Bloomsbury, 2016), 486.

of passages such as Lev. 18:5 (cf. 4 Maccabees; 4QMMT),[8] which reflects Paul's distinctive grammar of hermeneutics, i.e. "the hermeneutics of faith."

However, Watson does not merely stress the passivity of human beings, but appears to acknowledge the importance of human response. Regarding the meaning of faith as human "acceptance," Watson states that "'faith' is foundational to the divine-human relationship because faith alone is the human act that corresponds to the prior divine communicative action and is intended in it."[9] Responding to Hays' critique that Watson's interpretation of faith makes the divine-human relationship contingent upon the human act,[10] Watson spells out the nature of faith as something intended in the divine promise. According to Watson, "if divine speech is to be effective, it must evoke a human response."[11] Therefore, as a human response, faith still points toward God's initiative. In this sense, Watson argues that in Paul "gracious divine initiative and human activity are not mutually exclusive after all,"[12] which touches upon Barclay's third category.

However, Watson's position becomes somewhat obscure when he also thinks that Paul views human agency as "incorporated within the transformative divine agency (cf. Phil. 2:12–13)" in his ethical discourses.[13] This might require another type of category (i.e. the second one), and is also the same when he contends that the implication of the antithesis of agency is meaningful in the context of "scriptural controversy."[14] In a positive sense, Watson's readings could represent the divine-human relationship according to Paul as dynamic in specific contexts. However, such an observation also indicates the need for extra clarity, which could be provided by a consistent framework that explicates why Paul is making such different points.

A similar interpretative strategy can be found in other recent works. Jason Maston attempts to understand Romans 7–8 in the context of Second Temple Judaism, in which the issue of agency is a crucial topic among the contemporary writings.[15] Maston presents two opposing points of view that emphasize either human agency for earning salvation (Sirach) or the decisiveness of divine agency (Hodayot), arguing that Paul is making a critique of the former view (i.e. the "two-ways theology") in Romans 7–8 by showing the inability of human beings to obey the Torah. According to Maston, in Rom. 7:7–25 Paul is describing the person "who thinks that he possesses the moral capacity to obey" the law, an epitomized model of the "two-way tradition," but ends up

---

[8] See Francis Watson, "Constructing an Antithesis: Pauline and Other Jewish Perspectives on Divine and Human Agency," in *Divine and Human Agency in Paul and His Cultural Environment*, ed. John M.G. Barclay and Simon J. Gathercole (London: T&T Clark, 2006), 99–102.
[9] Watson, *Hermeneutics*, 177 (see n. 37). In this sense, Watson sympathizes with Bultmann who signifies the meaning of faith as the acceptance of the *kerygma*. Cf. Rudolf Bultmann, *Theology of the New Testament*, trans. by Kendrick Grobel (Waco: Baylor University Press, 2007), Vol. 1, 314 ("'faith' is the acceptance of the Christian message"); 318–19.
[10] Cf. Richard B. Hays, "Paul's Hermeneutics and the Question of Truth," *ProEccl* 16 (2007): 126–33.
[11] Watson, *Hermeneutics*, xl.
[12] Ibid., xxxviii.
[13] Watson, "Constructing," 102.
[14] Ibid.
[15] Jason Maston, *Divine and Human Agency in Second Temple Judaism and Paul: A Comparative Study* (Tübingen: Mohr Siebeck, 2010).

failing because of the power of Sin.¹⁶ Hence, Paul offers an alternative view in 8:1–13 showing that it is the divine act that enables the human agents to obey, similar to how Hodayot sees divine action as the solution to the "human dilemma."¹⁷

Maston argues that it is divine agency that "creates human agency," and "the divine and human do not stand opposed to one another."¹⁸ However, Maston's point of view appears to be drawn toward Barclay's second category when he explicates the nature of human obedience. Maston argues that human obedience cannot be understood as a sort of "response" but rather is "a continuation of God's gracious work in the believer's life,"¹⁹ and that Paul does not describe human agency as "independent of divine action."²⁰ Such a viewpoint becomes clearer when he interprets Rom. 8:4 as saying that "the obedience required for life arises from a unification between the divine and human agents."²¹ In this sense, for Maston, it seems natural to ascribe the failure of believers to obey to the fact that "one does not possess the Spirit and therefore is outside the bounds of God's grace."²² Nevertheless, such an explanation makes some of Paul's exhortations about obedience confusing, as they appear to admit the possibility for believers to fall away from Christ (cf. Rom. 8:13), thereby acknowledging the independence of human agency to some extent.

Preston Sprinkle attempts to understand the issue of agency in Paul, comparing Paul's letters with the Dead Sea Scrolls.²³ In five issues related to soteriology, Sprinkle finds similarity/dissimilarity between the two perspectives, and consistently observes that Paul's soteriology has a unique emphasis on divine agency: 1) In terms of the rescue from the curse of the law, Paul, like a few of his contemporaries, depends upon OT prophetic texts in prioritizing God's unilateral intervention;²⁴ 2) Paul highlights the agency of the eschatological spirit for the transformation of human beings (cf. Rom. 8:1–13),²⁵ and human obedience "flows from God's prior work and is underwritten by the spirit's agency;"²⁶ 3) Paul holds comprehensive anthropological pessimism, and this is true even when human capacity is not compared with God (cf. Rom. 1:18–3:26);²⁷ 4) Paul's idea that God justifies the ungodly is unprecedented (cf. Rom. 3:23–24; 4:2–5; 5:6–9) in the Scrolls;²⁸ and 5) regarding the final judgement according to works, Paul puts greater emphasis on divine agency than is found in the Scrolls, showing that Christ will advocate believers at the final judgment. Believers'

---

[16] Ibid., 20; 127–40. I use the capital "S" throughout this study to point out Sin as a personified cosmic power.
[17] Ibid., 153–70.
[18] Ibid., 168.
[19] Ibid., 169.
[20] Ibid., 170.
[21] Ibid., 167.
[22] Ibid., 170.
[23] Preston M. Sprinkle, *Paul and Judaism Revisited: A Study of Divine and Human Agency in Salvation* (Downers Grove: IVP Academic Press, 2013).
[24] Ibid., 68–94.
[25] Ibid., 95–121.
[26] Ibid., 241.
[27] Ibid., 125–44.
[28] Ibid., 145–71.

obedience that is necessary for "a positive verdict" is also divinely empowered (cf. Rom. 8:1–13).[29]

Sprinkle's work appropriately underscores the importance of divine initiative in Paul's soteriology. However, since Sprinkle's discussion of agency is restricted to a rubric of "soteriology," which he defines as "the restoration God brings to those who belong to his covenant community,"[30] it seems to be inevitable for him to pay extra attention to divine agency, overlooking the matter of how human agency changes in response to the works of divine agency. Although Sprinkle recognizes that Paul's anthropological outlook becomes rather optimistic when the believers' life is at issue in Romans 6 (cf. 6:1–11), Sprinkle's emphasis is still on divine agency in claiming that the empowered human agency is "bound up 'in Christ' and infused with the divine spirit";[31] thus, "obedience in Paul is not just made possible but *inevitable*."[32] However, similar to Maston's case, this type of interpretation has difficulty in accounting for the subtle tension in Paul's warning about falling away as well as his exhortation about obedience (cf. 6:12–23). Consequently, Sprinkle's approach might result in an incomplete understanding of human agency.

In contrast, Colin Miller is keen to vivify the significance of human agency in Romans. Miller locates Paul within "a classical model" by Alasdair MacIntyre, which insists on an indissoluble connection between human action and virtues. Miller argues that MacIntyre's concept of virtue as "a quality which tends towards achieving goods internal to a practice and the lack of which prevents us from attaining such goods," can explain Paul better than the modern philosophical strands that tend to detach practice from human agency (e.g. Kant).[33] Unlike some threads of thought that downplay the meaning of human agency by emphasizing either the "forensic" aspect of justification or "magical transformation," Miller claims that obedience is a "genuine human action" and simultaneously a "gift" of God:

> In Rom. 5 Paul argues that Christ makes possible for the church a just practice. Christ's obedience unto death, his "just act" (δικαίωμα) is what makes an obedient life possible. This act, however, comes to the world entirely as God's gift (ἡ χάρις, ἡ δωρεά) … [and] creates a community of just practice (δικαίωμα).[34]

Miller interprets Romans 6–8 as requiring "a strong notion of realistic participation," i.e. "participation by practice." For such practice, what matters is not "cosmic powers," but embodying "virtues" and overcoming "the passions of the body" in cooperation with the Spirit.[35] Despite its divine origin, Miller sees that the human practice cannot

---

[29] Ibid., 172–203 (see especially 180).
[30] Ibid., 33–4.
[31] Ibid., 202.
[32] Ibid., 202–3 (emphasis original).
[33] Colin D. Miller, *The Practice of the Body of Christ: Human Agency in Pauline Theology after MacIntyre* (Cambridge: James Clarke & Co, 2014), 24; 29–30. See Alasdair MacIntyre, *After Virtue: A Study in Moral Theory*, Third Edition. (Notre Dame: University of Notre Dame Press, 2007).
[34] Miller, 61–2.
[35] Ibid., 102.

be attributed to anything other than human agency. The rest of the chapters (Romans 12–15) can also be viewed in the light of this programme. Thus, Miller concludes that "the church is a community of practice and to become skilful at such practice is to live what MacIntyre calls the life of virtue and what Paul in Romans calls the life of δικαιοσύνη, justice."[36]

The insight Miller borrows from MacIntyre helpfully illuminates the fact that to detach human beings from their practice is problematic, that the divine and human agencies are not in competition with each other. Nevertheless, several points of his exegetical work weaken an otherwise strong argument. For instance, it is still questionable whether δικαίωμα (Rom. 5:16) can strictly mean "just practice" given to believers as "gift," because the concept of gift is not as concrete in the context as much as Miller claims (cf. 5:17). Also, we can hardly dismiss the influence of the counterpart in 5:16 (i.e. κατάκριμα), which shows that δικαίωμα in 5:16 has a general meaning of righteousness.[37] The fact that the counterpart of κατάκριμα in 5:18 is δικαίωσιν ζωῆς,[38] and equivalent to δικαίωμα in 5:16, also makes it hard to see δικαίωμα in 5:16 as "just practice." Furthermore, although Miller's caution not to weaken the role of human agency is understandable, he seems to go too far when he "demythologises" personified Sin in Romans 6–8, where Sin clearly plays an antagonistic role against God and the Spirit. Therefore, Miller's extensively anthropologically-oriented understanding of the goal of the divine-human relationship reaches its limit in explaining the particularly cosmic and eschatological dimension of Romans 6–8.

1.2.2 Apocalyptic Paul

The issue of the divine-human relationship is also a crucial topic in another stream of Pauline scholarship, i.e. the "apocalyptic" interpretation of Paul,[39] which centres on the meaning of God's cosmic invasion to set humanity free from the grip of Sin and death, malicious cosmic powers. The works of J.L. Martyn, based on his interpretation of Galatians, have a formative influence on current scholars on the "apocalyptic" interpretation, which is also applied to Romans.[40] Martyn's point of view on the divine-human relationship is reflected well in his summary of the "apocalyptic" framework:

> Paul's view of wrong and right is thoroughly apocalyptic, in the sense that on the landscape of wrong and right there are, in addition to God and human beings,

---

[36] Ibid., 4.
[37] BDAG, 2006.3 points out the possibility that Paul intentionally used δικαίωμα in order to harmonize with the other words in the passage that end in –μα.
[38] Although Miller argues that δικαίωσιν can mean "the process of doing a just act," the modifier ζωῆς imposes a sense of status on δικαίωσιν (Miller, 71).
[39] Although J. Louis Martyn and others use the title "apocalyptic" to characterize their typical hermeneutic enterprise, the term itself is discussed in diverse contexts. Cf. Ben C. Blackwell, John K. Goodrich, and Jason Maston, eds., "Paul and the Apocalyptic Imagination: An Introduction," in *Paul and the Apocalyptic Imagination* (Minneapolis: Fortress, 2016), 3–21.
[40] It is known that Ernst Käsemann's emphasis on the cosmic dimension of Paul's gospel deeply influenced Martyn. See J. Louis Martyn, "A Personal Word about Ernst Käsemann," in *Apocalyptic and the Future of Theology: With and Beyond J. Louis Martyn*, ed. Joshua B. Davis and Douglas Harink (Eugene: Cascade, 2012), xiii–xv.

powerful actors that stand opposed to God and that enslave human beings ... And since humans are fundamentally slaves, the drama in which wrong is set right does not begin with action on their part. It begins with God's militant action against all the powers that hold human beings in bondage. Thus, that action of God, instead of consisting at its center of a call for the slaves to repent and seek forgiveness (!), proves to be the deed by which God frees human beings.[41]

In this framework, human beings are helpless and passive, and their destiny is totally dependent upon God's actions. Thus Martyn sets a robust contrast between "God's presupposition-less grace" and "human efforts," arguing that "a salvific circular exchange between human beings and God" can never happen.[42] In a similar vein, human faith cannot be seen as a genuine human response or decision to the message from God, but is elicited by the "proclamation" per se.[43]

Several scholars who sympathize with Martyn's reading also promote a similar scheme in their interpretation of Paul. Douglas Campbell argues that what is revealed in the Christ-event is the "benevolence" of God, which is "unconditional," in contrast to conventional readings grounded in "justification theory," which seem to mistakenly endorse human acts in salvation as fulfilling their "contract" with God.[44] In terms of ethics, Campbell also resists accepting any emphasis on human practice. Campbell insists that "the saving transformation of the human being through participation in Christ in the Spirit is simultaneously an ethical transformation," which makes human beings "ethical automatically."[45] Given this inclination, it appears reasonable that Campbell prefers a "Christocentric" reading when he discusses the meaning of faith (πίστις) in passages that are related to soteriological issues (e.g. Rom. 3:21–26).[46] Thus, in every way Campbell highlights humanity's unilateral dependence upon God and is sceptical about the possibility of "exchange" between God and human beings, which is not genuinely Pauline from his perspective.[47]

However, it is questionable whether Campbell's construal of "justification theory" can properly accommodate the traditional points of view that commonly stress the centrality of justification in Paul's theology.[48] In addition, even though Campbell tries to exclude human agency in his emphasis on "participation," it is still unclear how such participation becomes available to human beings. Is participation available merely through the Spirit, regardless of any human response? Given Campbell's statement

---

[41] J. Louis Martyn, *Theological Issues in the Letters of Paul* (Edinburgh: T&T Clark, 1997), 87–8.
[42] J. Louis Martyn, "The Apocalyptic Gospel in Galatians," *Int* 54.3 (2000): 250.
[43] Martyn, "Apocalyptic," 251–2. Thus, Martyn supports a subjective genitive reading of πίστις Χριστοῦ.
[44] See especially Chapter 3 of Campbell's book, where Campbell points out the "systematic" difficulties of "justification theory." Campbell puts forward his own "alternative theory," which he considers to be superior to the "justification theory" in terms of its logical consistency. Douglas A. Campbell, *The Deliverance of God: An Apocalyptic Rereading of Justification in Paul* (Grand Rapids: Eerdmans, 2009), 62–95.
[45] Ibid., 83.
[46] Ibid., 640–7.
[47] In Campbell's scheme, most of Romans 1–4, which highlights the notion of "justification," is seen as Paul's parody of his antagonist, whereas Romans 5–8 contains Paul's own theological outlook.
[48] For a similar critique, see Francis Watson, "Review of The Deliverance of God," *EC* 1.1 (2010): 179–85.

about God's anger that "it [anger] can be a response to a prior initiative and its repudiation"[49]—which seems to leave the possibility for human beings to reject God's benevolence—it is uncertain whether it could be the same in the opposing case.[50]

Similarly, holding on to the hermeneutic key that "the universal reign of sin and death has been defeated by God in Jesus Christ,"[51] Beverly Gaventa raises the question of the human capacity to respond to God's initiative. Gaventa, based on her reading of Rom. 5:12–21, argues that "in Jesus Christ, God is acting unilaterally to reclaim the world from the powers that have held it captive, most notably sin and death," and claims that since "both Adam's disobedience and Christ's obedience implicate the whole of humanity," the human response is not an "entry pass" or necessary condition to receive benefit from God's cosmic enterprise.[52] Furthermore, even if Paul seems to speak of the human response in some places (cf. Rom. 1:16–17; 3:21–22; 10:9, 13), what constitutes the response is not the human ability itself, but "the activity of the Spirit."[53] Whatever abilities human beings have, they are "purely and only gifts," and therefore, "the human response to the divine initiative is itself also an outworking of the divine initiative,"[54] as it is the same to faith, which is not "a human act or decision but a result of God's own gift."[55]

Although Gaventa's recognition of some exceptional cases in which the human response seems to be strongly restricted (e.g. dementia) may enlarge the scope of our understanding of the human response, her main contention regarding the receptivity of human beings invites several questions. Firstly, it is questionable whether the universal characteristic of God's work in Christ necessarily presupposes its absolute effectiveness over the whole of humanity. In fact, what Gaventa finds as textual evidence for her argument is also controversial (e.g. all Israel's salvation [Rom. 11:26; cf. 11:32]).[56] Also, as we found in Campbell's work, Gaventa appears to undermine the dynamic between the divine and human agents in understanding the empowerment of humanity. As we carefully look at Paul's description on this theme, for instance the work of the Spirit, we can find that it is not merely human receptivity that Paul underscores (cf. Rom. 8:1–13). Thus, it is insufficient to determine the nature of the divine outworking only with a certain moment of the divine initiative, and equally unhelpful to assign the views that allow human freedom to a certain degree in the interaction with God to "exchange theory."[57]

Despite Paul's particular emphasis on the decisiveness of God's action, it is difficult to eliminate the role of human beings in Paul's picture of the divine-human relationship. In fact, Martyn's later works reflect his concern over this aspect. Although still putting

---

[49] Campbell, *Deliverance*, 930.
[50] See also David Hilborn, "A Response to Campbell's 'Connecting the Dots,'" in *Beyond Old and New Perspectives on Paul*, ed. Chris Tilling (Cambridge: James Clarke & Co, 2014), 122.
[51] Beverly Roberts Gaventa, "Which Humans? What Response? A Reflection on Pauline Theology," *ExAud* 30 (2014): 53.
[52] Ibid., 56–7.
[53] Ibid., 56–8.
[54] Ibid., 59.
[55] Ibid.
[56] Cf. ibid., 56.
[57] Ibid., 57; 65.

an emphasis on the continuation of the divine agent's "causative activity,"⁵⁸ Martyn sees that through the Spirit "God creates *the corporate, newly competent and newly addressable agent.*"⁵⁹ Therefore, believers do not remain passive, but are placed "in the front trenches of his [God's] war of cosmic liberation *for all.*"⁶⁰ Although Martyn sees that the human "response" cannot be autonomous from the divine workings,⁶¹ within different contexts (e.g. eschatological restoration or ethical exhortation) Martyn appears rather accommodating in acknowledging the significance of the role of human agents.⁶² Similarly, when Martyn speaks of "dual agency," he admits that "love, joy, and living at peace" are human acts,⁶³ although they are not autonomous human works, just as faith is incited by the power of the gospel. These states are the works of a "dual agency," in which both God and human beings participate mutually.

However, we must ask whether speaking of the human decision for faith necessarily dismisses the divine influence on faith. The fact that for Paul faith is not static but can be variable (cf. Rom. 12:3; 14:1-2; cf. 15:1) makes Martyn's (and Campbell's) view debatable. Moreover, such a point of view is vulnerable to the critique that Paul does not ascribe sin as a human activity entirely to Sin as a cosmic power. If Martyn acknowledges the human role in committing sin as "active complicit,"⁶⁴ it would also be reasonable to admit a similar kind of operation in the opposite case. In addition, although the "apocalyptic" framework would make sense of a specific facet of Paul's picture of salvation, it does not overarch the whole picture, since some crucial soteriological concepts cannot be explained well with such a framework (e.g. reconciliation).

1.2.3 Χάρις in Paul

For several scholars, the way in which they comprehend the nature of the concept of χάρις (gift/grace) in Paul reflects how they understand the interaction between God (giver) and human beings (recipients). Such scholars commonly analyze the ancient notion of χάρις, a central leitmotiv of the Graeco-Roman reciprocity system, and how Paul's use of the term χάρις can be understood in the light of his contemporary social conventions.

James Harrison stresses the unilaterality of God's χάρις in Paul. What Harrison mainly argues through his comparative study is that Paul, unlike his contemporaries, redefines χάρις by its Christological foundation.⁶⁵ Christ's death in Rom. 5:6-11 is "the

---

⁵⁸ J. Louis Martyn, "Epilogue: An Essay in Pauline Meta-Ethics," in *Divine and Human Agency in Paul and His Cultural Environment*, ed. John M.G. Barclay and Simon J. Gathercole (London: T&T Clark, 2008), 182.
⁵⁹ Ibid., 180 (emphasis original).
⁶⁰ Ibid., 182 (emphasis original).
⁶¹ Ibid., 182 (n. 27).
⁶² Ibid., 181; idem, "Afterword: The Human Moral Drama," in *Apocalyptic Paul: Cosmos and Anthropos in Romans 5-8*, ed. Beverly Roberts Gaventa (Waco: Baylor University Press, 2013), 163-4.
⁶³ Martyn, "Afterword," 164.
⁶⁴ Ibid., 163.
⁶⁵ James R. Harrison, *Paul's Language of Grace in Its Graeco-Roman Context* (Tübingen: Mohr Siebeck, 2003), 311.

guarantee of God's beneficence,"⁶⁶ as it is "an unprecedented act of favour" of God as "cosmic and covenantal Benefactor."⁶⁷ Harrison also stresses Christ's initiative for reconciliation, contrasting it with the notion of grace in the Augustan period that had no consideration for those who were socially worthless.⁶⁸ In addition, what makes Paul distinguished from his contemporaries is the fact that the divine gift in Paul does not require reciprocation. Harrison is negative about applying the logic of reciprocity to the divine-human relationship, since God's love (ἀγάπη) and grace (χάρις) are evidently distinctive from Paul's contemporary conventions of reciprocity. Therefore, Harrison confirms that "only the grace of Christ—in sharp contrast to the beneficence of gods and human beings—is unilateral, not reciprocal."⁶⁹

However, despite this emphasis, Harrison displays a contradictory attitude in also accepting that it is equally important for Paul that human beings "respond worthily of the Benefactor."⁷⁰ Can a human response to God be considered as a certain form of reciprocation? In one place Harrison indicates the link between God's sacrificial act and believers' appropriate lifestyle toward it, stating that "loveless acts towards one's fellow believers, therefore, overlook the fact that Christ has died for them too."⁷¹ However, Harrison's articulation of the link between God's grace and human love mainly touches upon an ethical aspect, i.e. the relationships between believers, and he is not concerned about the dynamic between believers and God, a dynamic which would influence the aforementioned ethical behaviour.⁷² Are there any implications of the behaviour resulting from the love between fellow believers for the relationship with God? Can such behaviour be regarded as a sort of response toward God for his χάρις?⁷³

Although Harrison consistently argues that grace through the sacrifice of Christ is unilateral and "expected no requital,"⁷⁴ this cannot summarize the whole shape of the interactions in the divine-human relationship. Although Harrison is right in arguing that God's grace is superior to everything and that no human act can suffice to meet the measure of grace, such a character of grace is not incompatible with the necessity of human reaction toward God characterized by faithfulness (fidelity) and obedience, which naturally creates a mutual relational dynamic in the relationship with God. In this sense, it is also questionable that Harrison does not refer to mutuality while acknowledging that "God demands loyalty of the dependents" and that believers should offer gratitude and honour to the God who is their Benefactor.⁷⁵

---

⁶⁶ Ibid., 234.
⁶⁷ Ibid., 223.
⁶⁸ Ibid., 226-34. See also idem, "Paul, Eschatology and the Augustan Age of Grace," *TynB* 1.50 (1999): 79-91.
⁶⁹ Harrison, *Grace*, 288.
⁷⁰ Ibid., 247-9; 287.
⁷¹ Ibid., 268.
⁷² Cf. ibid.
⁷³ Similarly, see John M.G. Barclay, *Paul and the Gift* (Grand Rapids: Eerdmans, 2015), 181 ("[A]s he insists, whatever humans return to God is in no way commensurate with God's giving ... but this does not itself establish whether God's gifts are, or not, intended to elicit some return").
⁷⁴ Harrison, *Grace*, 266.
⁷⁵ In fact, in terms of gratitude and honour, Harrison points out that there are only a few passages that explicitly express thanksgiving to God (Rom. 6:17; 7:24-25a; 2 Cor. 2:14; Col. 1:12), and this restricts the scope of discussion, while Paul mentions diverse shapes of human response to God's grace. Cf. Harrison, *Grace*, 273; 284.

In contrast to the perspective that generally advocates unilaterality of χάρις in Paul, more than a few interpreters have attempted to expound the other facet of χάρις. Troels Engberg-Pedersen concentrates on the notion of χάρις with a strong critique against the misunderstanding chiefly propagated by the Kantian notion of gift, which does not admit the possibility of "self-regarding concern" (e.g. Derrida and Bourdieu).[76] Engberg-Pedersen argues that in ancient ethical theory "true other-regard does not necessary exclude some form of self-regarding concern," referring to Seneca's *De beneficiis*, which he deems to be an important work for grasping the background of Paul's articulation of χάρις in Romans 1–8.[77] Engberg-Pedersen summarizes Seneca's ethical instruction about gift-giving in three points: 1) gift-giving and returning gratitude, which are desirable in themselves, should be motivated by "other-regard concern"; 2) gift-giving creates a "personal involvement" in the form of friendship; and 3) the exchange of a gift is not "completely disinterested," since it results in some benefits to both the giver and the receiver.[78] In this way, Engberg-Pedersen argues that the pureness of gift and the interestedness of gift coexist in Seneca's thought.

Engberg-Pedersen also finds similar points with Seneca from Paul's articulation of the Christ-event as a gift of God. On the one hand, "God's concrete act with its ultimate purpose was 'desirable in itself,'"[79] as the Christ-event is "an expression of God's love," which demonstrates God's "personal investment" and, at the same time, justifies the future hope of salvation.[80] On the other hand, Engberg-Pedersen also observes that God's gracious act in Christ shows God's own interest in terms of proper recognition (e.g. honour) and of human beings' doing his will (8:3–4). These aims are fulfilled by human beings' response to the gift with faith, love and hope (8:17–30).[81] Particularly regarding 5:1–11, Engberg-Pedersen focuses on the meaning of receiving the Holy Spirit (5:5), which enables believers to develop a deeper relationship with God without fear, thereby making them respond to God's love with their love.[82]

The major contribution of Engberg-Pedersen's investigation can be found from his critique that utilizes Seneca against modern views on the practice of gift-giving. Also, by reclaiming the ancient notion of χάρις, Engberg-Pedersen shows that to speak of mutuality in the divine-human relationship with regard to χάρις is not theologically illegitimate but is a natural consequence of reading within a close cultural context. What distinguishes God's grace is not its unilaterality but its capability to include all sorts of people and to transform them in accordance with the original purpose of the relationship. Furthermore, Engberg-Pedersen aptly observes the fact that the divine-human relationship can be developed in the course of mutual interactions in order to fulfil the goal of grace (χάρις) underlying the relationship, i.e. "recognition and doing of God's will on the side of God; justification and eternal life on that of human beings."[83]

---

[76] Troels Engberg-Pedersen, "Gift-Giving and Friendship: Seneca and Paul in Romans 1–8 on the Logic of God's Χάρις and Its Human Response," *HTR* 101.1 (2008): 16.
[77] Ibid., 18.
[78] Ibid., 18–21.
[79] Ibid., 26.
[80] Ibid., 27–33.
[81] Ibid., 32–40.
[82] Ibid., 38.
[83] Ibid., 28.

However, there are still several points that raise additional questions. Firstly, it is unclear to what extent the gift-giving system is effective for providing a consistent overall picture of Romans 1–8, inasmuch as Engberg-Pedersen notes that the gift-giving system does not lie behind Rom. 1:16–3:20.[84] This demonstrates the restriction of the gift-giving system, which is unable to embrace the ongoing history of God's relationship with his people, including the past, present and future. In addition, Engberg-Pedersen does not focus enough on the eschatological and cosmic dimension of the goal of the divine-human relationship, a crucial theme of Romans 8. Without this aspect, it will be hard to fully explain how each partner's interest in the relationship is mutually related and reinforcing.

David deSilva also highlights mutuality as a crucial characteristic in his interpretation of χάρις in Paul. Firstly, God's grace is not only for "forgiveness of sins"; rather it is closely connected to the issue of "how to live the life that God gave."[85] Secondly, Paul implies that one ought to respond to God's favour with "actual obedience."[86] Failure to do so results in losing of the favour (cf. Rom. 8:13–14).[87] The response to God's favour in the present life also defines the shape of "eschatological favour," i.e. "the favor of life beyond or life in the resurrection."[88] Thirdly, deSilva tries to accentuate the dual aspects of forgiveness; forgiveness implies not only God's gracious forbearance but also the fact that one should repent and change one's own heart and life in response to God's favour as such.[89]

When it comes to Rom. 5:6–11, it is noteworthy that deSilva expounds the mutual aspect implied in Paul's thought. On the meaning of God's sacrifice, i.e. Christ's death, deSilva contends:

> God has taken a fresh and supremely generous step toward the recalcitrant in order to make the way back for them easier to traverse, to facilitate repentance and walking in newness of life (Rom. 5.6–11) ... God has nevertheless issued a fresh and winsome invitation to people in the person, and especially in the self-giving death, of his Son to turn from their response of dishonor and ingratitude, accept the new standing in favor that is being offered, and make a fittingly grateful response with their hearts and lives.[90]

In this way, deSilva interprets that Christ's death not only represents God's love or eschatological assurance but also anticipates a positive response from the recipients. deSilva justifies his argument on the grounds of ancient gift-giving conventions in which the giver's expectation of the recipient's response is inherent in the gift.[91] deSilva

---

[84] Enberg-Pedersen sees that the framework underlying 1:16–3:20 is "a covenantal one," which belongs to "a different conceptual system from that of gift-giving." See ibid., 24–5.
[85] David deSilva, "Grace, the Law, and Justification in 4 Ezra and the Pauline Letters: A Dialogue," *JSNT* 37.1 (2014): 41.
[86] Ibid., 41.
[87] Ibid., 45–6.
[88] Ibid., 41; 44–5.
[89] Ibid., 41.
[90] Ibid., 42.
[91] E.g. *Ben.* 1.3.2–5; 1.4.3; 2.25.3; 2.35.3–4; 3.1.1; 5.11.5; Aristotle, *Eth. nic.* 1163b12–15 (see ibid., 29 [n. 10]).

sees that "the gift of the Holy Spirit" is a solution to the problem of Sin, and the solution originates from Christ's sacrificial death.[92]

Although deSilva grasps the relational implication of Christ's death, one further point remains to be investigated. Although dealing with the eschatological favour for believers, deSilva does not explain the eschatological outcomes in detail that God would share with believers as a result of their transformation. As can be witnessed in Romans 8, the expected eschatological outcomes appear to be more various and specific than the experience of "the favor of life beyond death or life in the resurrection."[93]

John Barclay also takes the notion of gift in Paul as a central concept for identifying the nature of the Christ-event.[94] Barclay appears to agree with Enberg-Pedersen and deSilva that the ancient notion of gift that naturally entails "expectation and obligation" is meaningful for understanding the Pauline χάρις.[95] In this respect, his point of view also has a close connection with Käsemann, who attempts to extract obligation from the concept of gift in Paul.[96] According to Barclay, human obedience in Paul is not a sort of recompense for the gift of God (i.e. *quid pro quo*), but is meant to fulfil the original expectation inherent in the gift.[97] Also, Barclay understands the relationship between divine agency and human agency as "non-competitive," in contrast to a "divine monergism," arguing that what Paul signifies is an "energism" wherein human beings become fit for "the Christ-gift" through the work of the Spirit.[98] It is also significant that for Paul the gift can be "rejected or repudiated" (cf. Rom. 11:21–22),[99] and believers remain as "responsible agents who are required to present their bodies in one direction" lest they nullify the meaning of the gift.[100]

Barclay also notices that "the gift of God in Christ has a content and a purpose,"[101] i.e. to transform the originally unfit recipients to be in a shape that is congruent with the relationship with God and his gift.[102] As the beginning of a single act of gift, Christ's death demands a proper response from human beings. For this reason, believers become under obligation (ὑπὸ χάριν) to react properly to Christ's death.[103] Barclay also

---

[92] Ibid., 43.
[93] Ibid., 41.
[94] Barclay, *Gift*, 449–50.
[95] John M.G. Barclay, "Believers and the 'Last Judgment' in Paul: Rethinking Grace and Recompense," in *Eschatologie-Eschatology* (Tübingen: Mohr Siebeck, 2011), 201. See idem, *Gift*, 11–65 for a detailed treatment on the differences between the ancient and modern notions of gift.
[96] Barclay, "Last Judgment," 205 ("[T]he connection between *Gabe* and *Aufgabe* was self-evident in antiquity"). Cf. Ernst Käsemann, "'The Righteousness of God' in Paul," in *New Testament Questions of Today*, trans. W.J. Montague (London: SCM, 1969), 170.
[97] Barclay, "Last Judgment," 207.
[98] Ibid., 205–7. See also idem, "By the Grace of God I Am What I Am: Grace and Agency in Philo and Paul," in *Divine and Human Agency in Paul and His Cultural Environment*, ed. John M.G. Barclay and Simon J. Gathercole (London: T&T Clark, 2006), 153; 157.
[99] Thus, the "efficacy" of the gift is not a "central concern" in Romans. Cf. Barclay, "Last Judgment," 201; idem, *Gift*, 503; 518; 557–8; 569.
[100] Barclay, *Gift*, 518.
[101] Barclay, "Last Judgment," 204.
[102] Ibid.
[103] John M.G. Barclay, "Under Grace: The Christ-Gift and the Construction of a Christian Habitus," in *Apocalyptic Paul: Cosmos and Anthropos in Romans 5–8*, ed. Beverly Roberts Gaventa (Waco: Baylor University Press, 2013), 63–4.

indicates that Rom. 6:12–23 depicts the proper life of the recipient "under grace." This is because the gift of God is "unconditioned," not "unconditional."[104] What fundamentally distinguishes Paul's notion of gift from that of his other contemporaries is the "incongruity" of the gift, as God's gift is bestowed upon unworthy people, which runs counter to the general conception (e.g. Wisdom, Philo and 4 Ezra);[105] that is, "the Christ-gift does not match the worth of its recipients but is given precisely in their abject worthlessness."[106] As Barclay admits, this interpretation stands in contrast with those who marginalize the notion of judgement (i.e. "singularity") or obligation (i.e. "non-circularity") with respect to gift in Paul.[107]

Barclay also detects the cosmic and eschatological framework encircling Romans 5–8, in which the sphere of the flesh and the sphere of the Spirit are still in tension (in a "tug-of-war"),[108] discussing the connection between "the Christ-gift" and the "last judgment," the point when the degree to which the goal has been fulfilled will be appraised.[109] However, similar to others, Barclay does not develop his interpretation to spell out believers' roles at the eschaton, which cannot be dismissed when we consider the "purpose" of the Christ-event, especially in terms of the fulfilment of God's cosmic vision. As Paul alludes to in Rom. 8:18–30, the goal of the "Christ-gift" is not restricted only to the human realms, but also entails a cosmic significance, following the example of the role of the representative human figures (e.g. Abraham in Romans 4; Adam and Christ in Romans 5) in this epistle.

In summary, Barclay's interpretation reflects a strong sense of mutuality between God and human beings. Although he admits that Paul sees believers as entirely dependent on "the life of Another,"[110] this does not mean they are totally passive agents:

> God's grace does not exclude, deny, or displace believing agents; they are not reduced to passivity or pure receptivity. Rather, it generates and grounds an active, willed conformity to the Christ-life, in which believers become, like Christ, truly human—that is, obedient agents (5:19). Without this obedience grace is ineffective and unfulfilled.[111]

If the "Christ-gift" in Paul intends such mutuality, we must investigate how Paul encourages the recipients to fulfil the obligation implied in the gift. Certainly, the help of the Spirit remains the most essential element; however, Paul also endeavours to spur his hearers by referring to the ultimate outcomes they will receive in the eschaton through their faithful alliance with God.

---

[104] Barclay, *Gift*, 500.
[105] Barclay, "Under," 59. Cf. idem, "Pure Grace? Paul's Distinctive Jewish Theology of Gift," *ST* 68.1 (2014): 8–11; idem, "By the Grace of God," 141–8; idem, *Gift*, 194–328.
[106] Barclay, "Under," 59.
[107] For example, Douglas Campbell (cf. Barclay, *Gift*, 171–3; 465 [n. 41]).
[108] Barclay, "Under," 69.
[109] Barclay, "Last Judgment," 206–7.
[110] Barclay, "Under," 65.
[111] Ibid., 76.

1.2.4 Covenantal relationship (N.T. Wright)

When discussing the divine-human relationship, N.T. Wright takes a distinctive approach in his attempt to embrace the grand narrative of Israel, humanity and creation as well as their relationship with God.[112] Wright regards "the twin themes of creation and covenant" as arriving at a "spectacular fresh expression" in Romans 1–11,[113] and sees that what is underlying Romans is "the theological story of the creator's dealings with Israel and the world, now retold so as to focus on Christ and the Spirit."[114] By sketching the failure of the past (i.e. Adam/Israel)[115] and the purpose of God's promise to Abraham,[116] Wright finds the climactic moment of the covenantal relationship in the Christ-event, which attests the covenant faithfulness of God.[117] For Wright, therefore, the concept of "righteousness" (δικαιοσύνη) in Romans primarily points to "the covenantal faithfulness of God,"[118] and the Christ-event is the instance that "the creator/covenant God has brought his covenant purpose for Israel to fruition *in Israel's representative, the Messiah, Jesus.*"[119] Thus, what is important for both Jews and Gentiles is to be incorporated into the representative of the faithful Israel.[120]

Wright's covenantal framework has the advantage in explaining several different facets of the development of the divine-human relationship in Romans, an aspect which is underdeveloped in the "apocalyptic" school because of its strong emphasis on God's sudden invasion.[121] Wright is conscious of the goal of the divine-human relationship, which originates from the promise to Abraham and his family (cf.

---

[112] N.T. Wright, *Paul and the Faithfulness of God* (London: SPCK, 2013), 519–21.
[113] N.T. Wright, *Paul: Fresh Perspective* (Minneapolis: Fortress, 2005), 29. As Wright indicates, E.P. Sanders' bringing attention to the theme of covenant in Jewish literature is crucial. However, Sanders does not directly apply this interpretative framework to Paul, though he recognizes the possibility that there are parallels between Paul and his Jewish contemporaries. Cf. E.P. Sanders, *Paul and Palestinian Judaism: A Comparison of Patterns of Religion* (Philadelphia: Fortress, 1977), 511–15. Other scholars also agree on the similarity between Sanders' "covenantal nomism" and the covenantal pattern in Paul's thought, e.g. John M.G. Barclay, *Obeying the Truth: Paul's Ethics in Galatians* (Vancouver: Regent College Publishing, 2005); Morna D. Hooker, "Paul and 'Covenantal Nomism,'" in *From Adam to Christ: Essays on Paul* (Cambridge: Cambridge University Press, 1990), 155–64; Don B. Garlington, *The Obedience of Faith* (Tübingen: Mohr Siebeck, 1991), 263–5; Dunn, *Theology*, 631–3; Kent L. Yinger, *Paul, Judaism, and Judgment According to Deeds* (Cambridge: Cambridge University Press, 1999), 288–90; James D.G. Dunn, *The New Perspective on Paul* (Grand Rapids: Eerdmans, 2007), 178–9. However, Wright's emphasis on the covenant relationship is distinguishable from them because he promotes a meta-narrative that connects the past Israel with the Christ-event.
[114] N.T. Wright, "Romans and the Theology of Paul," in *Pauline Theology*, ed. David M. Hay and E. Elizabeth Johnson, Volume III (Minneapolis: Fortress, 1995), 34.
[115] Cf. Wright, *Faithfulness*, 783–95.
[116] Cf. ibid., 804–15.
[117] Cf. N.T. Wright, *The Climax of the Covenant: Christ and the Law in Pauline Theology* (Edinburgh: T&T Clark, 1991), 210; 241–6; 258–67; idem, *Faithfulness*, 889–91.
[118] Cf. Wright, *Faithfulness*, 799–801.
[119] Wright, "Theology," 34 (emphasis original).
[120] Wright, *Faithfulness*, 825–35.
[121] For recent attempts to connect the two different emphases, see David A. Shaw, "Apocalyptic and Covenant: Perspectives on Paul or Antinomies at War?," *JSNT* 36.2 (2013): 155–71, which insists on the continuity between Romans 1–4 and 5–8; and J.P. Davies, "What to Expect When You're Expecting: Maternity, Salvation History, and the 'Apocalyptic Paul,'" *JSNT* 38.3 (2016): 301–15, which investigates the way in which the "birth metaphor" used in 4 Ezra 4, 6, Revelation 12 and in Romans 8 shows that the metaphor denotes both continuity and discontinuity.

Romans 4), elaborated at a cosmic scale in Romans 8,[122] although his emphasis on an inaugurated eschatology (cf. Rom. 15:7–12) appears to make what would be done further in the future less discussed (cf. Rom. 8:18–39).[123] In addition, Wright's investigation is helpful in suggesting that a type of relational (i.e. covenantal) framework allows for discussion of different emphases of Paul's soteriology (i.e. forensic, participatory, apocalyptic, salvation history, anthropological, transformational) without playing one off against the other, which is also essential for maintaining the integrity of Paul's thought in Romans.[124]

However, apart from the question of whether Wright's construction of the meta-narrative faithfully represents Paul's own idea,[125] Wright's emphasis on the meta-narrative tends to undercut the role of the real participants who constitute one of the central pillars of the story. For instance, when dealing with the theme of reconciliation, Wright is keen on expounding the attribute of God revealed in his self-sacrificial action, but he does not pay sufficient attention to the direct message that God's act gives to the human partners.[126] In a similar vein, Wright's covenantal framework appears to operate at the expense of sensitivity to Paul's specific language of exhortation. Although Wright refers to the Spirit's role to "redefine" the identity of the people of God and to transform them, his explanation still lacks a detailed treatment of how the people communicate with the Spirit.[127] Even though Wright recognizes that "a confluence between the divine life and the human life is precisely what the gospel brings about,"[128] the focus of his view on the dynamic within the divine-human relationship appears to remain at the macroscopic level.

Wright might well be correct in seeing the story of Paul's ancestors exercising a critical influence on Paul's articulation of the gospel. Nevertheless, this cannot guarantee that every element in Paul's letters can be understood and explained in light of OT narratives. Given the various contexts that could be influential on Paul's thought-world (e.g. the Graeco-Roman influence), we would rather adopt an inclusive framework in which diverse backgrounds can coexist, than stringently cling to the nomenclature of "covenant."[129]

1.2.5 Summary and prospect

Through the survey of major strands of Pauline scholarship, several key points and questions have been raised with regard to the way in which they conceive of the

---

[122] Cf. Wright, *Faithfulness*, 1022–3.
[123] Cf. ibid., 962–4; 1024.
[124] Cf. ibid., 777–83; 1010–13; 1025.
[125] This question is raised by several scholars. See Martinus C. de Boer, "N.T. Wright's Great Story and Its Relationship to Paul's Gospel," *JSPHL* 4.1 (2014): 52 ("it is evident that the triple narrative has been constructed by Wright from his own careful study of the Scripture [and of Second Temple Judaism], and that it has not been derived from Paul's letters, except secondarily") and John M.G. Barclay, "Review: Paul and the Faithfulness of God," *STJ* 68.2 (2015): 238–40.
[126] Cf. Wright, *Faithfulness*, 885–91.
[127] Cf. ibid., 952–60.
[128] Ibid., 955–6.
[129] Cf. ibid., 928.

divine-human relationship in Romans 1–8. There are two main streams that will help shape the particular direction of our investigation. Firstly, we have observed that a number of scholars do not properly take into account the dynamic nature of the divine-human relationship. Although Paul describes various stages of the relationship, implying its development in a positive sense, the discussions tend to revolve around a certain stage (i.e. salvation in a narrow sense). This tendency goes with overlooking the function and significance of several relational concepts that constitute crucial points in the divine-human relationship, such as "forgiveness" or "reconciliation." If we aim to determine the characteristics of the divine-human relationship, we must grasp the whole picture, embracing the past, present and future of the relationship.[130] Therefore, in our treatment, we will trace the development of the divine-human relationship through our reading of Romans 1–8, identifying crucial junctures that characterize each relational situation. Secondly, it appears that some scholars do not display enough sensitivity to the fact that the relationship operates with a goal shared between the two partners. As depicted in Romans 8, Paul implies that there is a certain goal to be sought by the divine-human alliance, thus the various dynamics found in the course of its development need to be understood within this scheme. As several studies claim, Paul sees that human beings are responsible partners who ought to respond properly toward God by means of divine empowerment, and this offers a crucial background for discussing the "goal" or "purpose" of the relationship. These two points imply that the divine-human relationship cannot be characterized by a single word. Thus, keeping these two points in mind, our study will seek to map the lively terrain of the divine-human relationship reflected in Romans 1–8.

Furthermore, our aim calls for a consistent analytic framework. Given the two main observations from our survey, we will secure logical plausibility by diagnosing different relational situations throughout the text, utilizing consistent criteria and terms while also attending to the nature and purpose of the divine-human relationship. In some studies, the concept of "gift" functions as a framework to investigate the interactions between God and human beings. However, because we aim to cover various sequences throughout Romans 1–8, what we need is a more general and overarching framework that will provide an entry to each specific relational situation. Based on this necessity, we will borrow an analytic framework from the field of social psychology, viz. "interdependence theory," which scrutinizes the relational dynamics in a dyadic relationship with regard to the "relational structure" shaped by the expectations of "outcomes" for each partner in the relationship. The rationale of such an attempt will be discussed in depth in the following chapter, along with the details of the theory.

1.3 The procedure of the study

Our study will proceed according to the relational flow of Romans 1–8, from betrayal through forgiveness and reconciliation to the final achievement of the goal. Before

---

[130] Cf. Peter Oakes, *Reading Romans in Pompeii: Paul's Letter at Ground Level* (London: SPCK, 2009), 166–71.

delving into the primary text, we will firstly introduce "interdependence theory." We will estimate its cogency as an analytic framework for our particular aim and material and will explicate the way in which we will deploy it (Chapter 2). Several methodological issues that can influence the historical and ideological validity of our approach will be discussed in the light of conversations carried out in the field of "social-scientific criticism" of the Bible.

In Chapter 3, we will start from the situation of the brokenness of the divine-human relationship (1:18–3:20). For the first part of the chapter (1:18–32), with the interdependence theory perspective on "betrayal," we will discuss the relational meaning of human sinfulness, identifying the reason behind it. For the second part (2:1–3:8), with the concept of "social norms" in interdependence theory, we will explain another facet of human sinfulness, expounding the relational connotations of the law and circumcision.

In Chapters 4 and 5, we will look at how Paul portrays the moment of the restoration of the broken relationship. In Chapter 4 (3:21–26), referencing the process of forgiveness and reconciliation in interdependence theory that revolves around the concept of "amends," we will investigate the meaning of Christ's death as characteristically represented by the concept of ἱλαστήριον, and will see in what way it works for forgiveness and reconciliation. In Chapter 5 (5:1–11), we will refer to the communication process in interdependence theory that consists of the two phases—"self-presentation" and "attribution"—to understand how God works by means of his self-sacrificial act in Christ to elicit a transformative response (i.e. "faith" [πίστις]) from human beings for reconciliation. Our discussion will show how mutuality between God and human beings is established in the course of the restoration of the relationship.

Chapter 6 will assess a different type of relationship, one that is antithetical to the divine-human relationship, namely, the Sin-human relationship (5:12–8:11). Through the analysis of the situation of the Sin-human relationship with reference to "non-voluntary dependence" according to interdependence theory, we will expound the meaning of the Christ-event that brings about change to the dilemmatic situation of humanity, as represented by the "I" in Romans 7. The reason that the "I" cannot escape from the grip of Sin will also be discussed, along with the issue of the identity of the "I".

In Chapter 7, we will examine the meaning of suffering that believers experience by reading the passages where the cosmic scope of Paul's eschatological vision is elaborated (8:12–39). By referring to the "investment situation" in interdependence theory, we will look at the relational implications of the endurance throughout suffering for maintaining the relationship for the purpose of achieving the shared goal. In particular, we will focus on how Paul depicts the interactions between the divine and human partners to progress towards the ultimate goal. We will also see that several strategies are operating to sustain the alliance between God and believers. Chapter 7 will illustrate the most developed picture of the divine-human relationship, in which the mutuality established from the restoration of the relationship comes to fruition in a dramatic fashion.

Finally, we will summarize and synthesize the findings of each chapter, offering a conclusion. We will also discuss the implications of the present study for the field of Pauline studies as well as for approaching other relational issues in Paul's letters with interdependence theory.

2

Methodology

2.1 Introduction

In this chapter we will discuss our methodology with two broad aims. Firstly, we will introduce "interdependence theory" (henceforth IT), our primary analytic framework. We will present the key concepts and theoretical background of IT, showing what fresh contributions the theory can make in studying human behaviour in interpersonal relationships. Secondly, we will deal with several methodological issues with regard to deploying IT for the interpretation of Romans 1–8. We will interact with relevant discussions from the social-scientific approach to the Bible in order to estimate the possibility of IT as a framework for this study.[1] The result of this chapter will identify the specific manner in which we will use IT to analyze the divine-human relationship in Romans 1–8.

2.2 An outline of IT

IT is a conceptual framework that analyzes "the relations between people in terms of situation structure [i.e. interpersonal structure], describing structure using variables such as dependence, covariation of interests, and information certainty."[2] What IT means by the term "interdependence" is "the manner in which two individuals influence each other's outcomes in the course of their interaction."[3] Originally developed by Harold H. Kelley and John W. Thibaut,[4] IT was grounded in Kurt Lewin's

---

[1] In the present study, drawing upon David Horrell's clarification of research terminology in social-science, we will consider IT as a theoretical framework rather than a model, since what IT primarily provides is a "research framework," though we will also refer to some empirical studies conducted with the research framework of IT in order to sharpen the focus of our discussion about a specific relational situation in each chapter. See David G. Horrell, *The Social Ethos of the Corinthian Correspondence: Interests and Ideology from 1 Corinthians to 1 Clement* (Edinburgh: T&T Clark, 1996), 11–12.
[2] Caryl E. Rusbult and Paul A.M. Van Lange, "Why We Need Interdependence Theory," *SPPC* 2.5 (2008): 2050.
[3] Harold H. Kelley et al., *An Atlas of Interpersonal Situations* (Cambridge: Cambridge University Press, 2003), 3.
[4] John W. Thibaut and Harold H. Kelley, *The Social Psychology of Groups* (New York: Wiley, 1959); Harold H. Kelley and John W. Thibaut, *Interpersonal Relations: A Theory of Interdependence* (New York: Wiley, 1978).

emphasis on interdependence as the essence of group formation.[5] Kelley and Thibaut also adopted the payoff matrices from "game theory"[6] to conceptualize the relational dynamics in a dyadic relationship shaped by the outcomes that both partners expect to obtain.[7] IT can be considered as one ramification of "social exchange theory";[8] however, IT is also distinguished from social exchange theory, given its far more inclusive interest in the various problems of interdependence and its psychological focus.[9]

Unlike many other psychological theories that only attribute human behaviour to intrapersonal characteristics, such as biological makeup, personality and cognitive processes, IT attempts to explain human behaviour by referencing interpersonal structure,[10] which functions as a core situational factor. In this respect, IT belongs to the discipline of social psychology, as it deals with the subject of classical psychology (i.e. an individual's behaviour), focusing on the power of situational factors (i.e. interpersonal structures).[11] IT investigates the ways in which psychological factors (A and B) and situational factors (S) influence interactions (I) in a dyadic relationship between actors. The basic framework as such can be expressed in a shorthand formula of $I = f(S, A, B)$.[12] While A and B denote each actor's "needs, thoughts, and motives," what determines S, that is, "interdependence situation," is a relational structure shaped by "outcomes."[13]

2.2.1 Reward and cost

Outcomes from a relationship can be stated in terms of reward in relation to cost, and the two elements are usually combined into a single scale of goodness of outcome (outcome = reward − cost).[14] Reward is what causes benefits to a person,

---

[5] Cf. Kurt Lewin, *Resolving Social Conflicts: Selected Papers on Group Dynamics*, ed. Gertrud Weiss Lewin (New York: Harper & Row, 1948).
[6] Cf. Robert D. Luce and Howard Raiffa, *Games and Decisions: Introduction and Critical Survey* (New York: Wiley, 1957).
[7] Kelley et al., 17.
[8] Cf. Peter M. Blau, *Exchange and Power in Social Life* (New York: Wiley, 1964). Stephen Joubert occasionally refers to Blau's work, though he does not directly deploy "social exchange theory." Cf. Stephan Joubert, "Coming to Terms with a Neglected Aspect of Ancient Mediterranean Reciprocity: Seneca's Views on Benefit-Exchange in De Beneficiis as the Framework for a Model of Social Exchange," in *Social Scientific Models for Interpreting the Bible: Essays by the Context Group in Honor of Bruce J. Malina*, ed. John J. Pilch (Leiden: Brill, 2001), 55; 63.
[9] Cf. Kelley and Thibaut, *Interdependence*, v.
[10] Caryl E. Rusbult, "Interdependence Theory," in *Encyclopedia of Psychology*, ed. Alan E. Kazdin, Vol. 4 (Oxford: American Psychological Association; Oxford University Press, 2000), 330; Caryl E. Rusbult, Ximena B. Arriaga and Christopher R. Agnew, "Interdependence in Close Relationships," in *Blackwell Handbook of Social Psychology: Interpersonal Processes.*, ed. Garth J.O. Fletcher and Margaret S. Clark (Oxford: Blackwell, 2003), 360.
[11] "Social psychology is a science that studies the influences of our situations, with special attention to how we view and affect one another ... it is the scientific study of how people think about, influence, and relate to one another" (David G. Myers, *Social Psychology* [New York: McGraw-Hill, 2010], 4).
[12] Rusbult and Van Lange, "Why," 2050.
[13] Ibid.
[14] Kelley and Thibaut, *Interdependence*, 8.

which can be either material or non-material. Cost is a negative factor that brings inhibition of behaviour, for example, physical or mental effort, embarrassment, anxiety, etc.[15]

2.2.2 Comparison level and comparison level for alternatives

At its core, it is the actors' needs and values, skills and abilities, and congruency of behaviour that determine the degree of the rewards and costs in a dyadic relationship; but IT is also concerned with the criteria against which one evaluates the level of satisfaction in a relationship. The prospect of the relationship depends upon this evaluation of satisfaction. IT offers two standards of comparison: "comparison level" (henceforth CL) and "comparison level for alternatives" (henceforth CL-alt). CL is the standard against which one evaluates the satisfaction of interaction outcomes.[16] CL reflects the quality of outcomes that one believes they deserve.[17] If the realized outcomes exceed CL, one experiences satisfaction; on the contrary, if the outcomes are below CL, it causes dissatisfaction. CL is not immutable but varies according to the consequences of experience within a given relationship.[18] For instance, CL rises if one repeatedly experiences higher satisfaction, and as CL rises, the level of satisfaction may gradually become lower.[19]

CL-alt describes the quality of the best available alternative choice.[20] In other words, CL-alt is the lowest level of outcome acceptable for maintaining the current relationship.[21] Thus, the decision about remaining in or leaving the given relationship is made according to CL-alt. CL-alt influences the level of dependence.[22] If the outcomes exceed CL-alt, one becomes more dependent in the given relationship. However, if the outcomes are lower than CL-alt, one becomes more independent. If the costs for renouncing the given relationship and establishing a new one are lower than CL-alt, one may leave the given relationship.[23]

2.2.3 Outcome table

IT generally utilizes an outcome matrix to abstractly display the various patterns of interdependence in a dyadic relationship, and it can be reshaped into the form of a table (see Figure 2.1).[24]

---

[15] Ibid.
[16] Rusbult, Arriaga and Agnew, 360.
[17] Kelley and Thibaut, *Interdependence*, 8.
[18] Rusbult, Arriaga and Agnew, 360.
[19] Ibid., 360–1.
[20] Ibid., 361.
[21] Kelley and Thibaut, *Interdependence*, 9.
[22] Rusbult, Arriaga and Agnew, 361.
[23] Thibaut and Kelley, 100–1.
[24] For readers' convenience, a form of a table (reshaped and modified by the author) will be used throughout this book instead of an "outcome matrix."

	Options (2X2) (for A, for B)	Outcomes
1	(a1, b1)	(0, 2)
2	(a1, b2)	(4, 4)
3	(a2, b1)	(4, 4)
4	(a2, b2)	(4, 2)

Figure 2.1 Illustration of 2 X 2 table.[25]

According to the 2 X 2 table, both persons, A and B, have two mutually exclusive behaviour segments (A chooses between a1 and a2, while B chooses between b1 and b2). The four options represent the intersection or joint occurrence of behaviour of the two actors, and the numbers placed in the parentheses are the representation of the goodness of the outcomes. For instance, if A chooses a1 and B chooses b1, they will receive 0 and 2, respectively (a larger number stands for a better degree of outcomes). Thus, the higher the entry, the more one becomes dependent on the relationship. For example, either when A chooses a1 and B chooses b2, or when A selects a2 and B selects b1, the two persons' outcomes will be maximized (4 for both A and B), which means that the degree of their dependence on each other is highest. Also, each person's dependence constitutes the basis for their partner's power in the given relationship.[26] We will utilize the outcome table, although, in most cases, we will not be able to refer to exact numerical values of outcomes (quantity) because of the nature of our main source. But by focusing on the quality of outcomes, we will still be able to evaluate and compare various types of outcomes with the table.

2.2.4 Various powers in the relationship: Partner control, joint control and actor control[27]

IT defines three kinds of powers involved in a dyadic relationship: "partner control" (PC), "joint control" (JC) and "actor control" (AC).[28] PC describes the degree to which one can unilaterally influence their partner's outcome.[29] For example if A can affect B's outcome regardless of B's choice, A has PC over B. According to Figure 2.2, B always receives 1 if A chooses a1, while B always receives 4 regardless of their choice when A chooses a2. When PC is acquired by both persons, i.e. "mutual partner control" (MPC),

---

[25] Based on Figure 1.1 in Kelley and Thibaut, *Interdependence*, 10.
[26] Kelley and Thibaut, *Interdependence*, 10.
[27] These elements were originally called "fate control" (PC), "behavior control" (JC) and "reflexive control" (AC) respectively in Thibaut and Kelley, *Groups*. These terms were altered in order to increase simplicity and clarity in Kelley et al., 43. Thus, I will utilize the newer terminology for this study.
[28] Rusbult and Van Lange, "Why," 2051.
[29] Kelley and Thibaut, *Interdependence*, 10–11; Rusbult and Van Lange, "Why," 2051.

	Options (2X2) (for A, for B)	Outcomes
1	(a1, b1)	(–, 1)
2	(a1, b2)	(–, 1)
3	(a2, b1)	(–, 4)
4	(a2, b2)	(–, 4)

Figure 2.2 Illustration of A's partner control over B.[30]

the outcomes of both are maximized when the two actors behave benevolently for the sake of the other, whereas the outcomes are minimized if both of them act entirely against their partner's benefit.[31]

JC stands for the power by which one can change the partner's action by varying one's own behaviour.[32] For example, Figure 2.3 reflects A's JC over B. By altering a1 to a2, A can make B change their behaviour from b2 to b1, because B will receive 1 if they keep choosing b2, whereas they can receive 4 by moving to b1, following A's change. JC can also be MJC, in which case, if the outcomes are corresponding, it becomes crucial to coordinate one's own choice with the other's choice in order to maximize the outcomes for both partners.[33]

	Options (2X2) (for A, for B)	Outcomes
1	(a1, b1)	(–, 1)
2	(a1, b2)	(–, 4)
3	(a2, b1)	(–, 4)
4	(a2, b2)	(–, 1)

Figure 2.3 Illustration of A's joint control over B.[34]

---

[30] Based on Table 7–1 in Thibaut and Kelley, 102.
[31] Kelley and Thibaut, *Interdependence*, 11.
[32] Kelley and Thibaut, *Interdependence*, 11–12; Rusbult and Van Lange, "Why," 2051.
[33] Kelley and Thibaut, *Interdependence*, 11.
[34] Based on Table 7–2 in Thibaut and Kelley, 103.

Another basic component that underlies a dyadic relationship is AC. AC means the degree to which each person can bring benefit to themselves by their own behaviour.[35] AC does not directly affect the degree of interdependence.

2.2.5 Four features of interdependence

The outcomes from the 2 X 2 table cause various patterns of interdependence. Kelley and Thibaut summarize the principal properties of interdependent relationships in four categories: a) degree of dependence, b) mutuality of dependence, c) basis of dependence and d) correspondence of outcomes.[36]

2.2.5.1 *Degree of dependence*

"Degree of dependence" describes the level to which one relies on the partner.[37] The degree of dependence would increase if CL-alt is not high enough (i.e. when the alternative option is not promising).[38] Degree of dependence can affect the manner in which two individuals interact. If one's dependence on the other increases, this evokes one's attention and cognition about both the personal and the situational matters of the partner.[39] Also, one's high degree of dependence on the partner will usually yield persistence in the relationship because it is critical to continue the relationship in order to acquire the unique benefits from the partner.[40] Specific strategies, such as "maintenance acts,"[41] to enhance interactions are also exhibited. If these attempts are not effective, the relationship will face a problematic situation that often leads to distress, threats and jealousy because of the partner's alternative relations.[42]

2.2.5.2 *Mutuality of dependence*

"Mutuality of dependence" describes the degree to which the two people are equally dependent upon one another.[43] A dyadic relationship can be either unilaterally dependent (i.e. when only one person is dependent upon the other), or mutually dependent if both are dependent upon each other (i.e. interdependent).[44] If dependence is unilateral, that is, when only one person has either the ability to provide high outcomes or the power to provide poorer outcomes than the partner can provide, or has more attractive alternatives, the less dependent person will naturally exert stronger

---

[35] Rusbult and Van Lange, "Why," 2051.
[36] Kelley and Thibaut, *Interdependence*, 77.
[37] Kelley and Thibaut, *Interdependence*, 77; Caryl E. Rusbult and Paul A.M. Van Lange, "Interdependence, Interaction, and Relationships," *ARP* 54.1 (2003): 355.
[38] Rusbult, Arriaga and Agnew, 366.
[39] Rusbult and Van Lange, "Interdependence," 355.
[40] Ibid.
[41] For example, constructive conflict resolution (if conflict occurs), a willingness to commit sacrifice, cognitive adjustment, etc. See Rusbult, Arriaga and Agnew, 366.
[42] Ibid.
[43] Rusbult and Van Lange, "Why," 2053.
[44] Rusbult, Arriaga and Agnew, 367.

control over the partner. In contrast, a greater burden of cost will be imposed upon the other, who is more dependent and vulnerable.[45]

The disparity of control between partners becomes dramatically salient when the relationship encounters conflicting situations. The relationship will last without problems if a person who has stronger control exercises benevolence, whereas some problematic situations will occur, such as abuse and exploitation, if the stronger person misuses their control.[46] The situation is quite different if the relationship is mutually dependent. According to Rusbult and Van Lange, interactions with mutual dependence are likely to yield several positive results, including a more placid and positive emotional experience (e.g. less anxiety, guilt and comfort), reduced use of coercion, less reliance on contractual agreements and greater congeniality.[47]

2.2.5.3 Basis of dependence

"Basis of dependence" describes the way in which partners affect one another's outcomes, either by PC or JC.[48] If unilateral partner control dominates relationships, some strategies, such as promises, threats and the activation of morality norms (e.g. "this is how decent people behave") will be involved in the relationship.[49] If PC is mutual (MPC), then the interaction between the two will rest on exchange (e.g. *quid pro quo*), and reciprocal norms will be established to incur good outcomes for the future.[50] If a relationship is characterized by JC, it becomes important to utilize relevant strategies to coordinate interactions.[51] Furthermore, if MJC exists in the relationship, coordination between the two persons is even more crucial, since attaining good outcomes is more contingent upon the proper behaviour of one's partner.[52]

2.2.5.4 Covariation of interests (correspondence of outcomes)

The pattern of interdependence is also explained in terms of the degree of correspondence.[53] Covariation of interests describes the extent to which the outcomes correspond between the partners.[54] Covariation ranges from perfectly corresponding situations, to moderately corresponding situations (mixed motive situations), to situations with absolutely conflicting outcomes ("zero-sum").[55] For instance, within the pattern of a mutually benevolent relationship that exhibits MPC, positive covariation of interests can be observed. In contrast, covariation of interests will be rarely observed if one's behaviour reduces the partner's outcome (e.g. conflicting situation). Moreover, covariation cannot

---

[45] Ibid.
[46] Rusbult and Van Lange, "Interdependence," 355.
[47] Ibid.
[48] Rusbult, Arriaga and Agnew, 367–8.
[49] Rusbult and Van Lange, "Why," 2053.
[50] Ibid.
[51] Ibid.
[52] Rusbult, Arriaga and Agnew, 368.
[53] Kelley and Thibaut, *Interdependence*, 34.
[54] Rusbult and Van Lange, "Why," 2054.
[55] Ibid.

	Options (2X2) (for A, for B)	Outcomes
1	(a1, b1)	(0, 0)
2	(a1, b2)	(5, 5)
3	(a2, b1)	(5, 5)
4	(a2, b2)	(0, 0)

Corresponding Situation

	Options (2X2) (for A, for B)	Outcomes
1	(a1, b1)	(5, -5)
2	(a1, b2)	(0, 5)
3	(a2, b1)	(0, 5)
4	(a2, b2)	(5, -5)

Conflicting Situation

Figure 2.4 Outcome tables of corresponding situation vs conflicting situation.[56]

exist if mutuality is totally absent in the relationship (e.g. an entirely independent relationship). In Figure 2.4, the table on the left represents a corresponding situation, since whenever A obtains the best outcomes (5), B simultaneously receives the best (5) (a1-b2/a2-b1). Similarly, whenever A receives the worst outcomes (0), B also receives the worst outcomes (0) (a1-b1/a2-b2). In the table on the right, in contrast, we can observe a conflicting situation, since A's best outcome (5) is associated with B's worst (-5)[57] (a1-b1/a2-b2), and vice versa (0 for A and 5 for B in the combination of a2-b1/a1-b2).

Covariation of interests influences interactions in four respects.[58] Firstly, it identifies the possibilities for congenial or conflicting interactions.[59] Secondly, the correspondence of outcomes enables partners to become more comfortable with one another in decision making.[60] If the relationship is in a correspondent situation, it is easier for one to choose their behaviour since what is good for them is also beneficial for the other. Thirdly, correspondence stimulates each partner's motives. Cooperative motives are activated by correspondent outcomes, whereas competitive motives are provoked by non-corresponding situations. Moderately corresponding outcomes will arouse various motives, such as fear or greed.[61] Fourthly, correspondence is an important criterion to identify trustworthiness. If one cooperates despite the non-correspondent outcomes, such an act demonstrates trustworthiness to the partner.[62]

2.2.6 Transformation of motivation: From "given situation" to "effective situation"

According to IT, people tend to behave in line with their self-interests. However, IT also acknowledges that this simple principle does not always determine human

---

[56] Based on Table 2.1 in Kelley et al., 20.
[57] A symbol "-" stands for a negative value.
[58] Rusbult, Arriaga and Agnew, 368-9.
[59] Ibid., 368.
[60] Ibid.
[61] Rusbult and Van Lange, "Interdependence," 356.
[62] Rusbult, Arriaga and Agnew, 369.

behaviour. Indeed, some people choose to behave in altruistic ways, at the risk of their own interests. IT explains this particular phenomenon with "transformation process," which describes the transition from a "given situation" to an "effective situation."

> Psychologically, they [transformations processes] are the ways in which a person can re-evaluate or reconceptualize the given matrix. In doing so, he no longer responds to his own outcomes in each cell. Instead, he views these outcomes in the contexts provided by his partner's outcomes and by past and future actions and interactions within the relationship.[63]

In Figure 2.5, the "given situation" (sequence 1) describes an interpersonal structure based on direct and immediate self-interest.[64] In this situation, one ignores the partner's interest as well as "long-term interaction" or "relationship-relevant" concerns.[65] In contrast to this situation, which is managed by one's "gut level" interest, sometimes people behave differently, basing their actions on broader concerns, such as concern for the partner's well-being, long-term goals and other strategic considerations for future outcomes.[66] This particular situation is termed "effective situation" (sequence 5), which describes the preferences modified by the transformation process.[67]

The transformation of behaviour is the process by which the given situation is changed into the effective situation. It begins by the activation of relevant interpersonal orientations for the perceived situation,[68] which influence the cognition, emotion and habit, and stimulate the transformation of motivation. Mental activities, such as cognition and emotion, help identify the pattern and key properties of a situation, the

Sequence 1	Given situation: Direct self-interest
Sequence 2	Activation of relevant interpersonal orientations (e.g. interpersonal dispositions, relationship-specific motives, social norms)
Sequence 3	Influence of the interpersonal orientations on cognition, emotion and habit
Sequence 4	Transformation of motivation
Sequence 5	Effective situation: Broader considerations
Sequence 6	Behaviour

Figure 2.5 Transformation process.[69]

---

[63] Kelley and Thibaut, *Interdependence*, 139.
[64] Rusbult, Arriaga and Agnew, 370; Rusbult, "Interdependence Theory," 331.
[65] Rusbult and Van Lange, "Interdependence," 358.
[66] Rusbult, Arriaga and Agnew, 370.
[67] Ibid., 371.
[68] Rusbult, Arriaga and Agnew, 371–2.
[69] Based on Figure 14.4 in ibid., 372.

possible behaviour options for oneself, and the partner's needs and motives.[70] People also tend to develop specific habitual tendencies to cope with certain situations as a result of adapting to repeatedly experienced patterns.[71] IT points out three classes of interpersonal orientations that influence mental and habitual activities: 1) interpersonal dispositions, 2) relationship-specific motives and 3) social norms.

Firstly, interpersonal dispositions can be broadly defined as "actor specific inclinations" by which one responds to particular situations across diverse partners.[72] Such dispositions are formed over the course of development, by encountering different people, histories, problems and interactions. As the result of these experiences, one acquires certain dispositions, which emerge when one perceives patterns of interactions and attempts to transform them.[73]

Secondly, relationship-specific motives can be defined as partner-specific inclinations by which one responds to particular interdependence patterns.[74] For example, commitment, one of the crucial motives in close relationships, is strengthened when the outcomes are satisfactory, alternatives are not so promising and investments already inputted are high.[75] This particular type of relationship-specific motive influences one's psychological attachment to the partner (emotion) and thoughts for persistence in the relationship (cognition), as well as the benevolent feelings and thoughts that cultivate pro-relationship behaviour (habit).[76]

Thirdly, social norms are "rule based, socially transmitted inclinations" by which one responds to particular interdependence situations.[77] Social norms affect the way in which one feels, thinks and acts.[78] For example, most societies have rules that regulate the expression of anger, and direct the proper way to feel about a specific incident, providing the criteria for interpreting situations. These rules become embodied by repetition. As social norms have prosocial aspects, long-term partners tend to develop relation-specific norms to prevent or solve problems over the course of multiple interactions.[79] For example, couples may establish a certain norm that imposes a heavy cost on the party involved in an alternative relationship. In this case, the norm helps to minimize the negative impact of extra-relationship involvement.[80]

2.3 Why do we need IT?

IT proposes an analytic framework to assess from an interpersonal perspective psychological issues that used to be approached in an intrapersonal manner.[81] For

---

[70] Rusbult and Van Lange, "Interdependence," 360.
[71] Rusbult and Van Lange, "Why," 2056.
[72] Ibid.
[73] Ibid., 2058.
[74] Rusbult, Arriaga and Agnew, 375.
[75] Ibid.
[76] Ibid.
[77] Rusbult and Van Lange, "Interdependence," 369; Thibaut and Kelley, 129.
[78] Rusbult and Van Lange, "Why," 2058.
[79] Rusbult and Van Lange, "Interdependence," 369.
[80] Rusbult, Arriaga and Agnew, 377.
[81] Rusbult and Van Lange, "Why," 2059.

instance, although qualities such as goal pursuits, persistence and trust are generally comprehended in an introspective manner, these same issues can also be discussed from an interpersonal point of view. It has been widely accepted that success of achieving a goal is based on individual characteristics, such as traits, skills and motivation.[82] Also, persistence is traditionally understood as stemming from a positive attitude toward one's endeavour. But, since persistence in a negative situation cannot be fully explained with this idea, psychologists usually attribute this unreasonable persistence to one's low self-esteem. Trust has also been understood as a "trait-based phenomenon" that derives from a frozen expectation that others will act in a benevolent manner.[83] All these explanations are commonly based on an intrapersonal perspective as well as an "actor-centred" perspective. Although it is true that intrapersonal matters influence an individual's behaviour, interpersonal matters should not be overlooked. Obviously, people are not entirely subject to their environment. Nevertheless, it is not only intrapersonal matters that define one's decision. With the aforementioned examples, studies based on IT show that one's success is also affected by a partner's support and affirmation of goal pursuit.[84] A JC effect is another crucial factor for success.[85] Persistence in negative situations is also explicable by several features of interdependence structure, such as poor alternatives and the high cost of investment.[86] A partner's commitment can also be a crucial source for creating and maintaining trust.[87] All these examples shed light on understanding psychological subjects in a relational way.

The particular emphasis of IT suggests a fresh way to approach our main topic. Although qualities such as persistence or trust in a human's relationship with God are often understood from a theological point of view, by referencing the relational structure of the relationship we can discover another layer to these qualities. In fact, there are several issues throughout Romans 1–8 that can be approached relationally. However, before delving into these issues, we need to identify to what extent the theoretical features of IT can influence the study of our main topic and source.

2.4 Methodological considerations: Toward a use of IT for the interpretation of Romans 1–8

Having grasped the outline of IT, the next step is to identify how we will use it for our specific topic. Since the time when "social-scientific approaches"[88] began to be used in

---

[82] Ibid. For example, "regulatory focus theory" suggests that people are more likely to achieve goals when they approach a goal with regulatory orientation in their minds. Cf. E.T. Higgins, "Beyond Pleasure and Pain," *APsy* 52 (1997): 1280–1300.
[83] Rusbult and Van Lange, "Why," 2063.
[84] Cf. Caryl E. Rusbult et al., "Self Processes in Interdependent Relationships: Partner Affirmation and the Michelangelo Phenomenon," *IntS* 6.3 (2005): 375–91.
[85] Rusbult and Van Lange, "Why," 2060.
[86] Ibid.
[87] Ibid., 2064.
[88] It would be unhelpful to apply the nomenclature "social-scientific approach" in a rigid manner, as there are a diverse spectrum of approaches with regard to the way and depth of utilizing social-scientific insights. For a suggestion of an inclusive understanding of the nomenclature "social-scientific

biblical studies,[89] discussions about the methodological validity have also been underway. In particular, like in our case, if the time and space in which the theoretical framework was devised is different from the socio-historical background of the text, methodological validity often becomes suspect. In this section, therefore, we will navigate the way in which we will practically deploy IT, discussing a few relevant methodological issues in light of previous social-scientific approaches. The significance of this section also derives from the fact that our study is the first attempt of which we are aware that brings IT into the field of biblical studies.

Firstly, we will discuss the main focus of IT and the way in which IT explains human behaviour. These issues are also closely linked to the historical and cultural appropriateness of the theory. As pointed out by several scholars, concerns about anachronism and ethnocentrism are important issues in deploying a social-scientific framework for biblical interpretation.[90] Thus, we will ask 1) to what extent our central focus on the interaction between individuals can be relevant for application to an ancient context and 2) to what extent the concept of outcome as an explanatory factor for human behaviour is appropriate. The latter also partly touches the issue of determinism.

Secondly, we will find the way in which we can position the subjects of the divine-human relationship within the roles of a dyadic relationship. With reference to IT and our current text (Romans), we will discuss how human beings as a group can be seen as functioning collectively as one individual actor. Then, we will examine how relevant it is to comprehend God and his actions in the relationship with reference to what has become known about human relationships. This issue also relates to the question of how the theoretical framework devised in a so-called secular setting can be used to interpret theological issues. We will also discuss how the specific nature of our main source (text) is relevant for IT.

2.4.1 On historical-cultural validity: The issue of the individual and IT

For this part, we will examine how the central focus of IT corresponds to the historical and cultural backdrop of our primary text. Several scholars have warned about the dangers of anachronism and ethnocentrism in deploying a theory devised in the

---

criticism," see Horrell, *Ethos*, 9–18; idem, "Models and Methods in Social-Scientific Interpretation: A Response To Philip Esler," *JSNT* 22.78 (2000): 83–105; idem, "Wither Social-Scientific Approaches to New Testament Interpretation? Reflections on Contested Methodologies and the Future," in *After the First Urban Christians: The Social-Scientific Study of Pauline Christianity Twenty-Five Years Later*, ed. David G. Horrell and Todd D. Still (London: Continuum, 2010), 6–20. See also Philip F. Esler, "Models in New Testament Interpretation: A Reply To David Horrell," *JSNT* 22.78 (2000): 107–13, for Esler's response to Horrell, which tends to prefer a more specific definition to emphasize an importance of a "model." For diverse types of social-scientific approaches, see Susan R. Garrett, "Sociology of Early Christianity," in *The Anchor Bible Dictionary*, Vol. 6 (New York: Doubleday, 1996), 93–7.

[89] For several important moments in the beginning period of social-scientific interpretations, see David G. Horrell, "Social-Scientific Interpretation of the New Testament: Retrospect and Prospect," in *Social-Scientific Approaches to New Testament Interpretation*, ed. David G. Horrell (Edinburgh: T&T Clark, 1999), 3–19.

[90] Cf. E.A. Judge, "The Social Identity of the First Christians: A Question of Method in Religious History," *JRH* 11 (1980): 201–17.

modern Western world for biblical interpretation. For instance, E.A. Judge has expressed suspicion about the historical validity of a sociological approach derived from modern studies, arguing that such an approach would end up committing "sociological fallacy" if the adopted model is not attested in terms of the cultural settings of the targeted object.[91] Thus, Judge puts it, "I should have thought there was no hope of securing historically valid conclusions from sociological exercises except by first thoroughly testing the models themselves for historical validity."[92] Klaus Berger also noted similar limitations of modern psychological criticism. Berger is worried about using a psychological framework without "historical sensitivity."[93] Therefore, for Berger, to rely on the categories of interpretation that belong to "any modern science of human behaviour" risks losing the historical distinctiveness connoted in the text.[94]

The issue of historical validity is also pointed out by scholars actively involved in using cross-cultural models, such as those belonging to "the Context group." For instance, Bruce Malina draws attention to the differences between the values of the first-century Mediterranean world and those of the contemporary U.S. In particular, what is relevant for our research is the discrepancy between the two different worlds regarding the way of understanding personality. Malina finds that the personality in a first-century Mediterranean society, where honour was deemed as a core value, is strongly "group-oriented" in contrast to individualism.[95] Thus, Malina says, "[P]ersons always considered themselves in terms of group(s) in which they experienced themselves as inextricably embedded."[96] Similarly, Philip Esler also expresses his suspicion of a certain academic stance in the field of social psychology that prioritizes the interactions between individuals in order to explain a phenomenon.[97] Esler argues that such a view, the origin of which is the highly individualistic US culture, ignores the "social dimension" of human behaviour, which is how a group cultivates its values to affect an individual's mind and behaviour.[98] Therefore, for Esler, it is rational to focus on the influence of the group, rather than that of the individual, to investigate issues of the text that have a collective background, for instance, both OT and NT.[99]

The scholarly concerns above raise the question of to what extent IT's focus on the individual level of interactions is acceptable, especially in terms of the historical and

---

[91] Judge, 209–12. Here, Judge is criticizing Bengt Holmberg, *Paul and Power: The Structure of Authority in the Primitive Church as Reflected in the Pauline Epistles* (Lund: Gleerup, 1978), which deploys Marx Weber's sociology of authority. For a similar concern, see Andrew D. Clarke, *Secular and Christian Leadership in Corinth: A Socio-Historical and Exegetical Study of 1 Corinthians 1–6* (Leiden: Brill, 1993), 3–6.
[92] Judge, 212.
[93] Cf. Klaus Berger, *Identity and Experience in the New Testament*, trans. Charles Muenchow (Minneapolis: Fortress, 2003), 2–4.
[94] Berger, 3. Therefore, Berger tries to reconstruct some concepts to understand the ancient's experience from the text itself.
[95] Bruce J. Malina, *The New Testament World: Insights from Cultural Anthropology*, Third Edition. (Louisville: WJK, 2001), 58–67; Bruce J. Malina and Jerome H. Neyrey, *Portraits of Paul: An Archaeology of Ancient Personality* (Louisville: WJK, 1996); John J. Pilch and Bruce J. Malina, eds., *Handbook of Biblical Social Values* (Peabody: Hendrickson, 1998), xv–xl.
[96] Malina, 62.
[97] Philip F. Esler, *Galatians* (London: Routledge, 1998), 41.
[98] Ibid.
[99] Ibid., 45–9.

cultural features of our main text. We will answer this question by examining the place of the individual in ancient societies close to the context of our primary text. Our discussion on this broad topic (i.e. individual and group in the ancient world) will be limited, since the topic in itself requires great consideration and work. Nonetheless, we will refer to several significant scholarly works that provide helpful explanations of the ancient perspectives on the individual. Our survey will suggest that speaking of the individual is not a purely modern concept, even within a society estimated as group-oriented, such as that of Paul. The discussion on self-interest will also suggest that the way in which the individual's behaviour is explained by IT is also meaningful from Paul and his contemporaries' point of view.

2.4.1.1 Understanding the individual in antiquity

We can consider the significance of the individual in antiquity in two points: the importance of interiority and self-consciousness of the individual, on the one hand, and the individual as an active religious actor, on the other. Regarding the former, Gerald Downing finds that "interiority" was of importance in ancient society to a degree, similar to how it is viewed in the modern world.[100] Several ancient writers, such as Epictetus (*Diatr.* 3.4.10; 4.5.34), Cicero (*Parad.* 17), Seneca (*Ep.* 124.23) and Philo (*Det.* 97) were also interested in interiority, a concern which can also be witnessed in the NT (e.g. Mt. 5:28; Mk. 7:20–23; Lk. 12:34; Rom. 2:16; 7:7–25; 1 Cor. 4:5; 14:15).[101] Downing argues against Malina's notion of "dyadic personality," indicating that the people in the modern world also are deeply concerned with others' opinions of themselves.[102]

Ben Dunson's treatment of Epictetus reflects a point similar to Downing's observation.[103] Dunson shows that in terms of ethical logic, there is a strong sense of individuality in Epictetus.[104] Dunson argues that "Epictetus never takes individual self-concern out of his sight when laying out the contours of the moral life."[105] This appears clearly when Epictetus discusses moral progress (cf. *Diatr.* 1.4; 3.2). Epictetus is concerned about the mental state of the individual, such as inner desire (cf. *Diatr.* 1.4.1–12).[106] For him, what is essential for happiness is control over one's self (*Diatr.* 3.3.2).[107] Also, Epictetus sees volition as "the essence of the good (*Diatr.* 1.29; 3.2.13)" and as "the core of human identity (cf. *Diatr.* 3.1–40)."[108]

Burnett also indicates that even in antiquity "self-conscious awareness is a prerequisite for any sort of ethical reflection or thinking."[109] Since a first-person perspective

---

[100] F. Gerald Downing, "Person in Relation," in *Making Sense in (and of) the First Christian Century* (Sheffield: Sheffield Academic, 2000), 43–61.
[101] Ibid., 58–60.
[102] Ibid., 46. Cf. Malina, 60–7.
[103] Ben C. Dunson, *Individual and Community in Paul's Letter to the Romans* (Tübingen: Mohr Siebeck, 2012).
[104] Ibid., 64.
[105] Ibid., 70–1.
[106] Ibid., 90.
[107] Ibid.
[108] Ibid., 87.
[109] Gary W. Burnett, *Paul and the Salvation of the Individual* (Leiden: Brill, 2001), 35.

"does not necessarily imply individualism," Burnett sees that even in the collective society the individual still matters.[110] Even in an honour and shame culture, one finds mention of guilt, which is deemed an introspective and individualistic value.[111]

Concerning the latter, it was equally important in the ancient world to "enhance" individuality so that one could manage proper relationships with others,[112] in particular, the relationship with the divine. For instance, in the *Iliad*, a human agent is not merely subject to the acts of gods, but the individual human being can make "an independent decision."[113] Burnett argues that Ajax and Socrates were individuals who exerted their individuality by "undermining the expectations of the world in which they lived."[114]

Jörg Rüpke also insists on the role of the individual as a religious agent.[115] He maintains that not only in Christianity but "non-Christian antiquity also knew individual religious practices (e.g. domestic cult)."[116] Rüpke argues that the particular socio-historical context of the ancient Mediterranean society enabled an individuation process in terms of religious practices, for instance, "unstableness of families (e.g. the high rate of mortality in birth and childbed)" or "military conflict which resulted in the death or slavery of the individual."[117] Therefore, within this particular milieu, the individual agent was capable of performing their own religious activity (e.g. domestic rituals, divination and magic).[118]

Tessa Rajak also observes the active role of the individual in Philo and Josephus, examining the way in which the individual responds to scripture.[119] In Philo's description of the *therapeutai* (*Contempl*. 75-8), the role of each individual is shown to be crucial for teaching and learning scripture, and in that community the interaction between individuals also shapes "the communal experience" (cf. *Contempl*. 86).[120] Philo also writes that the individual's religious activity is important for the interpretation of the scripture (cf. *Migr*. 34-9). When it comes to Josephus, Rajak indicates that "communal and individual prayer alike have their place" in Josephus' account of the Jewish practice of prayer (*C. Ap*. 2.196-7).[121] Rajak insists that it is not the individual

---

[110] Ibid.
[111] Ibid., 40-2 ("Shame and honour may have been prominent in Homer's culture, but there was a constant interplay with the more introspective values of guilt and justice" [e.g. *Odyssey*]).
[112] For instance, Quintilian, *Inst*. Cf. Downing, "Person in Relation," 52.
[113] Cf. Homer, *Il*. 1.224-9 (the story of Achilles); 11.477-81 (the story of Odysseus). Cf. Burnett, 31-2.
[114] Ibid., 34.
[115] Jörg Rüpke, "Individualization and Individuation as Concepts for Historical Research," in *The Individual in the Religions of the Ancient Mediterranean*, ed. Jörg Rüpke (Oxford: Oxford University Press, 2013), 6.
[116] Ibid., 6-7.
[117] Ibid., 8. A similar point of view can be found in Justin Meggitt's work. Meggitt argues that it was hard for the vast numbers of people in the Empire cities, many of who were immigrant and poor, to depend upon family ties or friendships for their survival, since most of them were experiencing economic difficulties. Cf. Justin J. Meggitt, *Paul, Poverty and Survival* (Edinburgh: T&T Clark, 1998), 169-72. Burnett sees that this particular condition has also promoted individualization (see also Burnett, 54).
[118] Rüpke, 14-23.
[119] Tessa Rajak, "The Individual and the Word in Hellenistic Judaism: Cases in Philo and Josephus," in *The Individual in the Religions of the Ancient Mediterranean*, ed. Jörg Rüpke (Oxford: Oxford University Press, 2013), 298-314.
[120] Ibid., 303-5.
[121] Ibid., 308-9.

prayer per se, but rather the "egoism and selfishness" that Josephus criticizes.[122] Moreover, Josephus' own example shows how an individual agent actively engages in religious practice in relation to the community (cf. *J.W.* 3.350–4).[123] Those examples illustrate, to quote Rajak, how "the sacred writings conferred capacity on individuals, touching and transforming lives."[124]

2.4.1.2 *Paul's understanding of the individual*

Despite the anti-individualistic trend emerging from the late twentieth century in the field of Pauline studies,[125] it is hard to dismiss the fact that Paul has an interest in the individual. It might be true that so-called traditional individualistic interpretation (e.g. the Lutheran interpretation) has not done justice to the text by ignoring the distinctive historical context of the text and overly emphasizing personal aspects. However, this should not prevent us from speaking of the individual in Paul, as the Pauline emphasis on the communal aspect does not necessarily undermine the importance of each individual member.[126] Thus, Burnett argues for an interpretation that considers both aspects.

> We might find in Paul a more balanced theology of individual and the community, where there is a concern for an individual's relationship with God within an overarching community narrative and view of the purposes of God which concerned both the people of God and the individual members of that people.[127]

Burnett takes as examples several passages in Romans in order to draw attention to the significance of the individual and their salvation. For instance, he reads that faith in Rom. 1:16-17 speaks of the individual's "personal, cognitive response" to God's righteousness,[128] which reflects God's faithfulness in his relationship with humanity.[129] Although Burnett also agrees that faith can be regarded as a communal identity marker of the people of God,[130] Burnett does not weaken his emphasis on the meaning of faith at the individual level inasmuch as the actual subject of faith should be each individual.[131] In a similar vein, the "I" in Romans 7, can be understood as primarily indicating an individual, including Paul and his immediate readers,[132] and this reflects

---

[122] Ibid., 309.
[123] Ibid., 309 ("his private salvation became fused with that of the Jewish people. He was God's messenger").
[124] Ibid., 312.
[125] Cf. Ben C. Dunson, "The Individual and Community in Twentieth- and Twenty-First-Century Pauline Scholarship," *CBR* 9.1 (2010): 63–97.
[126] Cf. Douglas J. Moo, *The Epistle to the Romans* (Grand Rapids: Eerdmans, 1996), 27–30.
[127] Burnett, 106.
[128] Ibid., 147. "Faith clearly involves mental, cognitive and emotional activities, all of which operate on a personal, individual level" (ibid., 172).
[129] Ibid., 117–25.
[130] Ibid., 151. Cf. N.T. Wright, *Jesus and the Victory of God* (Minneapolis: Fortress, 1996), 259.
[131] Burnett, 165–6.
[132] Ibid., 226.

Paul's concern about each individual's salvation.[133] Although on some occasions Burnett appears to downplay the importance of the community,[134] he rightly questions how a community would be capable of operating without each individual member's behaviour or decision.

Dunson also demonstrates that the concern about the individual is also present in Paul's mind, by isolating several types of individuals from Paul's letter to the Romans. On the one hand, the categories of individuals, such as "characteristic" (cf. Rom. 2:15, 17–25; 3:1–9), "generic" (cf. Rom. 2:6–16, 26–29; 3:10–20), "binary" (cf. Rom. 1:13–14, 16; 2:14–19; 3:9, etc.), and "exemplary individual" (cf. Rom. 4:5–8, 11–12, 16, 23–25), show that one cannot easily grasp what Paul tries to say if the fact that it is the individual actor acting in the scene is neglected.[135] On the other hand, Dunson tries to see how the individual's position can be understood in relation to its community. Other categories, such as "representative" (cf. Rom. 5:12–21), "negative exemplary" (cf. Rom. 7:7–21), "somatic" (cf. Rom. 12) and "particular" (cf. Rom. 16), commonly show that the individual member can represent the idiosyncratic character of the community as well as its function to build up the whole community.[136] Thus, there cannot be an "isolated individual" per se in Paul.[137] Nonetheless, this is not without consideration of the individual. Paul's theology "never ceases to pertain in foundationally important ways to individuals and individual action within the life of the community."[138] Although Dunson's categories may not be definitive, as some of them share a common feature (i.e. representativeness), his approach is still helpful to show that the relationship between the individual and the community in Romans is not competitive.

In relation to the individual's relationship to the community, Paul exhibits a similar attitude in 1 Cor. 6:19 regarding the meaning of temple (ναός). As Gupta argues, each human body is the place where "the ownership and rule of God" should be manifested (cf. 1 Cor. 6:19–20).[139] Also, it is the communal temple that needs to be managed by everyone (cf. 1 Cor. 3:16–17).[140] The picture that Paul draws in 1 Corinthians becomes comprehensible when we accept the possibility that Paul is talking about both individual and communal dimensions when he makes use of body imagery. Gupta's suggestion that Paul's self-awareness is not to be ignored also deserves attention,[141] as several other scholars also admit the vital role of Paul's own experience in forming his theology.[142]

---

[133] Ibid., 228.
[134] For instance, it is curious whether his intention that seeks the balance between the individual and the community is achieved when he insists that "Paul had a primary focus on the individual," discussing Romans 7 (ibid., 209). For Burnett's aim of the study see ibid., 18–19; 114; 221; 228. It is regrettable that he appears not to offer detailed explanations on how concerns about both the individual and the community can coexist in the selected passages.
[135] Cf. Dunson, *Individual*, 143–5.
[136] Cf. ibid., 175–6.
[137] Ibid., 147–77.
[138] Ibid., 176–9.
[139] Nijay K. Gupta, "Which 'Body' Is a Temple (1 Corinthians 6:19)? Paul beyond the Individual/Communal Divide," *CBQ* 72 (2010): 527.
[140] Ibid., 536.
[141] Ibid., 533.
[142] For instance, Dunn, *Theology*, 179 (see Gupta, "Body," 533).

Paul often sees himself as a paradigmatic individual,[143] and rather freely shifts between "I" and "we."[144]

To summarize, we have identified that concern for the individual was also present in the ancient world. Some of Paul's contemporaries regarded the individual as an active religious agent. Therefore, in terms of the historical and cultural context, what IT primarily investigates can still be meaningful in dealing with the ancient materials. In particular, Romans, our main text, takes an interest in the individual, which it exhibits when dealing with the divine-human relationship. Therefore, our attempt to discuss the divine-human relationship in Romans by means of IT can secure methodological validity.

2.4.1.3 *The concept of "outcome" and self-interest*

We have shown that interest in the individual is not a feature exclusively found in modern Western society, but that it was also an important matter for ancient writers, including Paul. Thus, it is our next task to examine to what extent the manner in which IT explicates aspects of human behaviour in interpersonal relationships in terms of "outcome" is plausible historically and ideologically. We will investigate how self-interest, a concept equivalent for the IT concept of "outcome," is understood by Paul and his contemporaries in comparison to IT. The results of the discussion will also show how IT can be understood in terms of the issue of determinism. Although a growing number of scholars agree on the necessity of using a theoretical framework for social-scientific interpretation,[145] the danger of determinism is also pointed out by several scholars.[146] Therefore, bearing the concern about determinism in mind, we will also specify the manner in which we treat IT as an interpretive framework regarding its hermeneutic leverage.

According to IT, the goodness of "outcome" from the relationship is a crucial element for shaping a relational structure, which functions as a situational factor that influences an individual's behaviour. Therefore, IT utilizes the concept of "outcome" as a factor to explain and predict human behaviour. In this respect, IT admits that the pursuit of good "outcomes" is one of the natural motives that regulate human behaviour, though this does not mean that IT sees human beings always regulated by such an impulse.[147] Although emphasizing the concept of "outcome" might appear to reflect a hint of modern rationalism, self-interest itself is not a concept alien to the people of antiquity. Some helpful examples can be drawn from some of Paul's contemporary thinkers, such as Epictetus and Seneca, who are also interested in this issue. Both of

---

[143] Cf. Brian J. Dodd, *Paul's Paradigmatic "I": Personal Example as Literary Strategy* (Sheffield: Sheffield Academic, 1999).
[144] Cf. John M.G. Barclay, "Paul's Story: Theology as Testimony," in *Narrative Dynamics in Paul: A Critical Assessment*, ed. Bruce W. Longenecker (Louisville: WJK, 2002), 146 (see Gupta, "Body," 534).
[145] See Andrew D. Clarke and J. Brian Tucker, "Social History and Social Theory in the Study of Social Identity," in *T&T Clark Handbook to Social Identity in the New Testament*, ed. J. Brian Tucker and Coleman A. Baker (London: Bloomsbury, 2014), 41–58.
[146] See Garrett, "Sociology of Early Christianity," 92–3; Horrell, *Ethos*, 13; 22–6; Horrell, "Models," 84–94.
[147] Cf. section 2.2.6 of the present study ("the transformation of motivation").

them consider self-interest and give teachings about the proper attitude towards it; for Paul, the issue of self-interest is also a crucial topic in his moral exhortation.

Firstly, as Epictetus's teaching extensively stresses the importance of "self-preservation," the pursuit of self-interest is indispensable for him. As John Sellars rightly indicates, for Stoic thinkers such as Epictetus, it is crucial to "take seriously the primitive behaviour of animals and human beings," and the Stoics do not "try to pretend that selfish motivations are not at the heart of most people's actions"[148] (cf. *Diatr.* 1.19.11–12;[149] 2.22.15–16[150]), though it is not their intention to defend any "selfish concern."[151]

However, Epictetus's concern about the self is not restricted to the individual sphere. The relationship with others can also be a domain in which one can meditate on self-interest, as "the interests of others become integrally related to one's own self-preservation."[152] Epictetus argues that "it can no longer be regarded as unsocial for a man to do everything for his own sake," since contributing to the common interest can bring about good outcomes to the individual actor, and the reverse also holds true (cf. *Diatr.* 1.19.12–13 [Oldfather, LCL]).[153] William Stephens also recognizes this and explains that for Epictetus, "a human being contributes to the public good by filling her niche in the world as a whole," indicating that it is a natural impulse to try to obtain one's own private good.[154] By putting one's self-interest and common goods together on to "one scale," one can understand that their interest is not separate from the common good (cf. *Diatr.* 2.22.18–19).[155] The idea that "a man is a part of a state," just as the foot is for the whole body, corresponds to this sort of understanding. In such a state, everyone's outcomes are intertwined with one another, and one cannot be totally independent (cf. *Diatr.* 2.6.24–29).

Two things can be observed from this short survey. Firstly, from Epictetus's example we find that a concern about self-interest is present in the minds of some ancient thinkers. It is not a purely modern innovation to speak of self-interest. Rather, self-interest seems to be a natural human impulse. Secondly, Epictetus's idea on self-interest cannot be characterized by selfishness, because he also considers that the welfare of others is of importance, even in promoting one's own self-interest. Thus, it is reasonable for Epictetus to say that "the good of others is my own concern,"[156] as pursuing the good for one's self is not incompatible with pursuing the good for others.

---

[148] John Sellars, *Stoicism* (Berkeley: University of California Press, 2006), 108 (cited in Dunson, *Individual*, 68).
[149] "This is not mere self-love; such is the nature of the animal man; everything that he does is for himself" (Oldfather, LCL). All English translations of Epictetus and Seneca are from the Loeb Classical Library (LCL) edition unless otherwise noted.
[150] "It is a general rule—be not deceived—that every living thing is to nothing so devoted as to its own interest... For its nature is to love nothing so much as its own interest."
[151] Dunson, *Individual*, 70.
[152] Ibid., 94 (n. 122).
[153] Cf. ibid., 96 ("[T]he good of others becomes vital to one's own self-interest").
[154] Cf. William O. Stephens, *Stoic Ethics: Epictetus and Happiness as Freedom* (London: Continuum, 2007), 82.
[155] Ibid., 83.
[156] Ibid., 82.

Seneca's *De beneficiis* provides another example. The concept of reward and cost is also crucial in Seneca's thought on reciprocity (cf. *Ben.* 6.5.1–2). In fact, one can hardly think and talk about giving and receiving without implying these concepts. In other words, the estimation of outcomes is inherent in the gift-giving system according to Seneca. Of course, this is not to say that the calculation of benefits is the only standard by which one decides their own behaviour. For example, Seneca criticizes the act of giving for direct self-interest. Seneca writes "he who has given a benefit in order that he may get something back has really not given it," and claims that the behaviour as such is not so different from giving food to animals in order to get service or food from them (cf. *Ben.* 4.14.2–4 [Basore, LCL]). According to Seneca, "it is a contemptible act, without praise and without glory, to do anyone a service because it is to our own interest (*quia expedit*)" (*Ben.* 4.14.3 [Basore, LCL]). Rather, Seneca suggests a reversed point of view for calculating good outcomes.

> The true desire of giving a benefit summons us away from all these motives, and, laying hand upon us, forces us to put up with loss, and, forgoing self-interest (*utilitates relinquit*), finds its greatest joy in the mere act of doing good.
>
> *Ben.* 4.14.4 [Basore, LCL]

Thus, the act of giving without directly pursuing reciprocation can be a good outcome in itself (cf. *Ben.* 1.6.1; 2.2.2; 4.1.3; 4.12.3),[157] and this is a striking reversal of the conventional idea. For Seneca, it is to resemble gods to give or act "without any reward, without attaining any advantage" (*Ben.* 4.25.3 [Basore, LCL]).

Seneca expounds a similar understanding of reward for the giver in *Ben.* 4.22.2–3.

> It is evident that the great reward (*merces*) for an action lies in the deed itself … "But there are many advantages (*commoda*)," you say, "that spring from it; good men live in greater security, and have the love and respect of good men, and existence is less troubled when accompanied by innocence and gratitude."
>
> Basore, LCL

The reward from the act of giving and the additional advantages that Seneca accepts are very different from the notion of self-interest in general. The reward is neither immediate nor direct. Also, the quality of the advantage mainly looks immaterial. However, Seneca still admits self-interest by identifying the acceptable type of self-interest for a giver. David Briones characterizes the self-interest acceptable to Seneca as "other-oriented self-interest."[158] Seneca sees that although one does not pursue direct self-interest, when the person seeks to give some benefits to the other, one could naturally be granted some sort of interest as a reward for such behaviour (cf. *Ben.*

---

[157] Cf. John M.G. Barclay, "Benefiting Others and Benefit to Oneself: Seneca and Paul on 'Altruism,'" in *Paul and Seneca in Dialogue*, ed. Joseph R. Dodson and David E. Briones (Leiden: Brill, 2017), 113; 115.

[158] David E. Briones, *Paul's Financial Policy: A Socio-Theological Approach* (London: Bloomsbury, 2013), 50–1.

6.13.1–2).¹⁵⁹ Thus, Seneca affirms this kind of self-interest, whereas what he actually rejects is the "exploitative" self-interest that benefits only one party.¹⁶⁰

From these short examples—but ones that are crucial for understanding Seneca's idea on self-interest—we can observe two things. On the one hand, Seneca assumes that self-interest can be an influential factor on human behaviour in interpersonal relationships. In Seneca's exhortation, it is a natural human tendency to follow self-interest without the guidance of ethical teachings. On the other hand, like Epictetus, Seneca takes into consideration other people's good when he thinks about self-interest. Pursuing the good of others is not only a condition for promoting self-interest, but a factor that grants multiple benefits to the giver.

How does Paul view this issue? Paul recognizes that pursuing only self-interest is one of the typical characteristics of corrupted humanity. Paul warns that there will be God's "wrath and fury" upon those who are self-seeking (τοῖς ἐξ ἐριθείας [Rom. 2:8]). Also, Paul exhorts his recipients not to have an attitude of ἐριθεία (2 Cor. 12:20), epitomizing ἐριθεία as the work of the flesh (Gal. 5:20). Thus, we see that self-interest exists in a negative form in Paul's thought. For Paul, it seems natural to seek one's own self-interest unless one follows an alternative lifestyle.

Paul teaches that it is a praiseworthy lifestyle for believers to take care of others' circumstances (or "interests"¹⁶¹), not adhering only to one's own self-interest (ἐριθεία) (cf. Phil. 2:3–4). For instance, in Phil. 1:21–25, Paul abandons his own self-interest (i.e. to depart and be with Christ) because of the Philippian believers' necessity.¹⁶² Nevertheless, Paul's decision is not only for the sake of the Philippians, but also results in "fruitful labour" (καρπὸς ἔργου) for Paul.¹⁶³ What is striking is that in this case, "self- and other-interest leads to mutual gain."¹⁶⁴ Paul does not merely force his recipient into relinquishing all kinds of self-interests,¹⁶⁵ but what he tries to do is to establish mutually beneficial relationships throughout the community.¹⁶⁶ Of course, it is one of the crucial conditions to forsake immediate self-interest for such a relationship (cf. Phil. 4:17). Thus, in Paul, self-interest is not pursued in and of itself, but it can exist in a modified way.¹⁶⁷

Even though IT does not pass an ethical judgement on the self-centred lifestyle, IT notes that in many cases people do not simply pursue self-interests in their relationships.

---

¹⁵⁹ Cf. Barclay, "Altruism," 117 ("Seneca combines what might seem to us, at first glance, two incompatible positions: that the individual should pursue the virtue of benevolence for its own sake, and without regard to her own *utilitas*, but that she thereby cements and secures a tie of friendship whose purpose is a mutual flourishing, without zero-sum calculation by which a benefit to one offsets a benefit to the others").

¹⁶⁰ "For Seneca, gleaning some form of profit (*utilitas*) from granting a gift is acceptable, as long as the receiver also obtains a share in the profit (*si modo me in consortium admisit*) and the giver, at the moment of giving, acknowledges the interests of both parties (*si duos cogitavit*)" (Briones, *Financial*, 51).

¹⁶¹ Cf. NRSV.

¹⁶² Briones, *Financial*, 121.

¹⁶³ Ibid.

¹⁶⁴ Ibid.

¹⁶⁵ In particular, it becomes more evident when we take καί in Phil. 2:4 as "also."

¹⁶⁶ Barclay, "Altruism," 119–21.

¹⁶⁷ Cf. ibid., 126.

Kelley et al. acknowledge that interpersonal relationships often motivate parties to give up their self-interests:

> We cannot emphasize too strongly that this [IT] is not an economically grounded theory of self-interest, that is, of the sort that begins (and ends) with the premise that people seek to "maximize rewards and minimize costs." Instead, our analysis follows Kelley and Thibaut (1985) in rejecting that narrow assumption. Self-interest is but one of a number of motives applicable to the analysis of interpersonal situations. Although we rely on terms familiar to self-interested economic models – for example, "reward," "cost," and "investment" – we use them to describe objective properties of situations or their corresponding patterns of interaction in abstract but readily accessible language. In fact, as readers will see, in many instances our analysis begins with the observation that people often forsake immediate self-interest in favor of other interpersonal motives – altruism, justice, loyalty, accommodation, heroism, self-destruction, and the willingness to sacrifice, to name but a few.[168]

Seeing that "the tendency to take one's social partners into account is an essential condition of social life,"[169] IT does not consider self-interest as the only principle for maintaining a relationship with others. According to Kelley et al., "a major advantage" of the situational analysis of IT is "the ability to consider, within a single theoretical model, the varieties of behavior displayed when self-interest and other social motives conflict."[170]

Moreover, similar to the aforementioned ancient perspectives, IT also admits that there are some occasions in which benefit for one does not necessarily exclude the other's benefit. Kelley and Thibaut argue against the viewpoint that insists on the incompatibility between altruism and "any logic or sign of self-interest."[171]

> Genuinely altruistic impulses can coexist with thoughts of ultimate gain and reciprocity. To discount the first by the presence of the second may simplify one's

---

[168] Kelley et al., 15. See also Harold H. Kelley and John W. Thibaut, "Self-Interest, Science, and Cynicism," *JSCP* 3.1 (1985): 26–32.

[169] Kelley et al., 15.

[170] Kelley et al., 15. For a further treatment for the benefits of abstract functional analysis, see John G. Holmes, "The Benefits of Abstract Functional Analysis in Theory Construction: The Case of Interdependence Theory," *PSPR* 8.2 (2004): 146–55.

[171] Here, Kelley and Thibaut, "Self-Interest," 31 is responding to Wallach and Wallach's critique of IT— "what ultimately guides your social acts, however concerned for another they may, are the outcomes to yourself. To be sure, you may set aside your own outcomes and act out of purely moral considerations, such as commitment to honesty or justice as an ideal, or out of concern for the welfare of others. At some level, however, you keep an accounting of the consequences that these actions produce in benefits to yourself" (Michael A. Wallach and Lise Wallach, *Psychology's Sanction for Selfishness: The Error of Egoism in Theory and Therapy* [San Francisco: W.H. Freeman, 1983], 176). It is striking that what Wallach and Wallach argue appears to correspond to the modern concept of gift (or "the impossibility of gift" by Derrida), whose inappropriateness to comprehend the ancient notion of gift is indicated by several scholars (see our discussion about Seneca above and the review of scholarship on χάρις in Chapter 1).

attributional work, but is inconsistent with a sophisticated understanding of altruism.[172]

Several studies based on IT show that sometimes self-sacrificial behaviour in a dyadic relationship can result in better outcomes for both partners. Rusbult, Arriaga and Agnew find that "although sacrificial behavior necessitates forgoing direct self-interest, the willingness of committed individuals to sacrifice ... yields clear benefits in ongoing relationships."[173] Therefore, suggesting "the transformation process" through which one rejects immediate self-interest,[174] IT takes into account various factors that can be influential on the formation of such altruistic behaviour. However, IT does not see that such "altruism" can only exist if there is some form not explainable in any way by "self-interest."[175]

To summarize, the writers of antiquity were conscious of the concept of self-interest. However, some of them, including Paul, do not think that a proper lifestyle merely pursues immediate self-interest; but at the same time, they did not totally abandon such a pursuit. Rather, as their ethical concerns reflect, they tried to propose a way in which everyone could benefit one another in their respective ways. In a manner similar to the ancient thinkers, IT does not regard self-interest as the only impulse that governs human behaviour, while using the concept of "outcome" as a primary element for understanding human behaviour. Moreover, IT, as we will see further on, provides several cases in which forgoing immediate self-interest brings about better outcomes for both partners in the long run, particularly in the case of a long-term relationship. Thus, the common perception on self-interest that IT shares with Paul and his contemporaries can provide the groundwork upon which we will explore some relevant relational issues that appear in the ancient texts (e.g. Romans) from the perspective of IT.

The manner in which IT handles the concept of outcome/self-interest also represents how it perceives the issue of determinism, another important issue in the field of social-sciences.[176] In explicating human behaviour, IT primarily focuses on the influence from the external factor, namely, the relational structure shaped by "outcome" or self-interest; nevertheless, IT does not understand "outcome" as an absolute power. Rather, IT understands that a human actor has the ability to make a different choice that defies any immediate influence from the situational factor, though such a case might be considered unusual. Thus, our discussion of "outcome" remains still meaningful. It is also a matter of concern to explain why and how such a deviation happens. Likewise, in deploying IT, our research will initially revolve around the significance of "outcome," but we will also be sensitive to considerations of exceptional motives that can influence one's attitude in a relationship.

---

[172] Kelley and Thibaut, "Self-Interest," 32.
[173] Rusbult, Arriaga and Agnew, 379.
[174] Rusbult and Van Lange, "Interdependence," 359.
[175] Kelley and Thibaut, "Self-Interest," 31; Kelley et al., 379.
[176] Cf. Horrell, "Models," 91–2; Louise J. Lawrence, *An Ethnography of the Gospel of Matthew* (Tübingen: Mohr Siebeck, 2002), 129–39.

2.4.2 Placing the divine-human relationship into the framework of a dyadic relationship

If the primary interest and element of IT can also be regarded as pertinent from the ancient perspective, we need to navigate the way in which we can deploy the framework of IT for our main topic, i.e. the divine-human relationship. We will discuss this by considering the clarifications required for the peculiar natures of the subjects (God and human beings).

2.4.2.1 *Human beings: As group and as single entity*

Discussing the divine-human relationship with IT, we will locate God and human beings in the two positions of a dyadic relationship. In so doing, we will take human beings to be a single subject. We find ground for this from both the theoretical position of IT and Paul's way of treating human beings in Romans. Firstly, although IT primarily deals with the relationship between individuals, it can also be used to understand other types of relationships constituted by various types of subjects. Rusbult and Van Lange indicate that "intergroup relations" is one of the examples for which IT can be used to analyze interactions made between groups governed by "a mind of its own."[177] Rusbult and Van Lange's positive prospect is based on the fact that if a group upholds homogeneity, its actions and decisions can be understood as if those of an individual. In fact, it is rather common in micro-economics to understand a firm's action as if it were an individual's behaviour.[178] In the same vein, Thibaut and Kelley treat a group as one of the individual agents when discussing how a group induces its individual members to conform to the group's norms.[179] In this case, the group is considered as a single subject since it operates with a single aim and purpose.

What is more, although there are several different types of groups in Romans, such as Jews and Gentiles, each of them is often viewed as a single entity because of their homogenous and collective characters. For instance, in 1:18–32 the wickedness of human beings is depicted as if it were the evil of one individual, even though the evil behaviour mentioned in the passage is that of a group of people.[180] They are not simply the sum of many persons, but each group possesses a single, shared mind (cf. 1:28).[181] In addition, in 3:9–18, Paul is also free to describe the universal human wickedness in terms of the individual. The OT catena portrays the epitome of the wicked individual. According to Dunson, it is "the generic individual" that Paul is depicting here.[182] The same thing can be observed in another scene. In 5:1–11, when Paul employs the first-person plural (we), this indicates that he is referring to a sort of group (believers). However, at the same time, the members of the group are seen as having an identical

---

[177] Rusbult and Van Lange, "Why," 2066.
[178] Cf. Christian List and Kai Spiekermann, "Methodological Individualism and Holism in Political Science: A Reconciliation," *APSR* 107.04 (2013): 639.
[179] Thibaut and Kelley, 242; 245.
[180] See in particular 1:28–32 and the plural form of the words.
[181] Cf. Burnett, 115–47 (at 137–46).
[182] Dunson, *Individual*, 121–3.

character to one another (e.g. "the weak," "ungodly," "sinners," etc.). Accordingly, the whole group can be treated as one individual agent in the relationship with God.

Romans 7:7–25 provides a concrete example, which shows that Paul actually represents the situation of a group through the voice of an individual (ἐγώ). Similarly, in 1:16–17, although Paul points out the individual and the importance of their decision, "the righteous" (ὁ δίκαιος) can also connote a group of people simultaneously. 2:17–25 shows that when Paul addresses the individual interlocutor as "you a Jew" (σὺ Ἰουδαῖος), this individual can symbolize the hypocritical Jewish people in general who do not obey the law.[183] The "man" (ὦ ἄνθρωπε cf. 2:1; 3) in 2:1–5 can be the same type of individual, who has a representative quality.[184] Therefore, the manner in which both IT and Romans view a group with a homogenous character enables us to treat human beings in Romans 1–8 as a single actor in a dyadic relationship, since the group is constituted by a single feature (i.e. universality).

2.4.2.2 Can God be like a human actor?

In deploying IT, we also need to be sensitive to the ideological difference between our main topic (theological) and the specific developmental background of the method (social psychological). How does this difference affect our approach? It has been argued that one of the weaknesses of social-scientific approaches is the tendency to reduce theological practice to a purely sociological one.[185] Therefore, John Milbank has objected to the use of social theories in biblical interpretation because they possess a different "genesis."[186] The main focus of Milbank's discussion can be different from our case, since our issue is about the different modes, not about the different levels of explanations of a single phenomenon (sociological or theological). However, this issue reminds us that we ought to find a link that connects different modes of perceptions when we attempt to put God in the position of being humanity's partner in a dyadic relationship.

God is not a human actor, as is clear from the fact that his divinity makes him very distinguished from human beings (cf. Rom. 1:20; 11:33–36). Thus, our attempt does not intend to diminish or deny the ontological gap between God and humanity. Rather, we want to pay attention to the specific way in which Paul articulates the divine-human relationship. When Paul spells out certain aspects of the divine-human relationship, he frequently utilizes concepts familiar to interpersonal relations. One of the striking examples can be found in Rom. 5:6–11, where Paul explains the meaning of Christ's self-sacrificial death. In that passage, Paul's standpoint is the human perspective. The

---

[183] Dunson terms this individual "characteristic individual." See Dunson, *Individual*, 111–15.
[184] If this figure is identical to a Jew in 2:17–25, then the representative characteristic can be highlighted even more. Cf. Dunson, *Individual*, 112.
[185] See Gerd Theissen, *Psychological Aspects of Pauline Theology* (Philadelphia: Fortress, 1987), 1. Cf. Horrell, "Social-Scientific," 11–12.
[186] John Milbank, *Theology and Social Theory: Beyond Secular Reason*, Second Edition. (Oxford: Blackwell, 2006), 101–43. For discussions about Milbank's claim see Stephen C. Barton, "Social-Scientific Criticism," in *Handbook to the Exegesis of the New Testament*, ed. Stanley E. Porter (Leiden: Brill, 1997), 280–1; Horrell, "Social-Scientific," 11–12; 25–6.

meaning of Christ's death becomes more vivid when it is viewed as an event that happened between human beings (cf. 5:7). Of course, Paul's case does not denigrate the theological meaning of Christ's death at all. On the contrary, by understanding it from the human perspective, Paul can express more profoundly how much the love of God revealed in Christ's death is extraordinary.

Several scholars recognize this point.[187] For instance, Simon Gathercole draws attention to examples of vicarious deaths well-known in Paul's contemporary society, such as those based on "conjugal love" (e.g. Euripides' *Alcestis*), "friendship" (e.g. Seneca and Epictetus) and "family ties" (e.g. Philonides). Gathercole argues that these cases provide the background of Rom. 5:6–11.[188] Most importantly, Gathercole views Paul as placing Christ's death among those human cases.

> Paul sees that there is common ground between these pagan instances and the death of Christ, otherwise the analogy simply would not work. The common ground is that there is a death of one person for others … The most obvious indication that Paul is talking about substitutionary deaths of Jesus and of other heroic figures in Romans 5 is that they employ the same language of X "dying for" Y. Paul also acknowledges the bravery involved in the heroic deaths of these pagans … and again that same terminology appears in the classical writers. Paul is apparently comparing one substitutionary death with other substitutionary deaths.[189]

The similarity found in the comparison between the heroic deaths and Christ's death is mainly about "vicariousness," and the comparison is rendered meaningless if it is between a transcendent, supernatural incident and a human occasion. As Gathercole insists, "without dissimilarity a comparison is meaningless, but without similarity a comparison is simply impossible."[190]

In addition, Paul utilizes several motifs related to human relationships to explain about the divine-human relationship. "Reconciliation" is one of the examples of this (cf. Rom. 5:1–11; 2 Cor. 5:11–21). In a Greek marriage record, the word καταλλάσσω refers to the relationship between a husband and a wife (P.Oxy. 104). We find a similar use in Paul (1 Cor. 7:11).[191] Although καταλλάσσω is sometimes used in a religious context (cf. 2 Macc. 1:5; 7:33; 8:29; Jos. *Ant.* 6.143), the religious usage is also grounded in the general meaning, which reflects a concrete aspect of human lives. Other instances, such as the slave-master relationship (Rom. 6–7) and the father-child relationship (Rom. 8:14–19; 2 Cor. 6:18; Gal 3:26–4:7; Phil. 2:14–15) contain the same feature. By adopting such concepts of interpersonal relationships, Paul points to a specific nature of the

---

[187] Cf. Cilliers Breytenbach, "The 'For Us' Phrases in Pauline Soteriology: Considering Their Background and Use," in *Grace, Reconciliation, Concord: The Death of Christ in Graeco-Roman Metaphors* (Leiden: Brill, 2010), 59–81.
[188] Cf. Simon J. Gathercole, *Defending Substitution: An Essay on Atonement in Paul* (Grand Rapids: Baker Academic, 2015), 90–103.
[189] Ibid., 104.
[190] Ibid., 103.
[191] Friedrich Buechsel, *TDNT*, "καταλλάσσω", 1.254–57.

relationship. The slave-master relationship denotes believers' obligation to obey their master. The notion of adoption (υἱοθεσία) emphasizes intimacy as well as the privileges and obligations that believers have in their relationship with God who is their Father.

In fact, it is not a strange practice for other ancient authors to liken the divine-human relationship to human relationships. For instance, the OT frequently depicts the divine-human relationship as an intimate human relationship. The father-child relationship[192] or mother-child relationship[193] are the ones after which the divine-human relationship is repeatedly modelled. In these cases, it is the general characteristics of the parental relationship, for instance, love and obedience, that frame each specific context of the divine-human relationship.[194] In some places, the relationship is also described as a marital relationship.[195] The core of the analogy is the emphasis on faithfulness in the relationship. It is also noteworthy that in these cases, God—like a husband betrayed by his wife—is described as experiencing negative emotions, such as fury, jealousy and wrath.[196]

Philo is also familiar with this practice of using human analogies. Philo recognizes that the divine-human relationship being represented as a father-child relationship is already present in the Torah (cf. *Leg.* 3.27).[197] In many cases, the appellation "father" denotes God's position as "creator" or "originator" (cf. *Opif.* 7).[198] Also, the paternal language points toward the fact that God takes care of his people as a human father does (cf. *Mut.* 29, 129).[199] Philo, although acknowledging God's transcendence over human beings, thinks that God's act of caring for human beings shares a similarity with that of the care displayed by human beings (cf. *Somn.* 1.237). This is not to mention the fact that by this point in antiquity, terms such as "begetting" and "fatherhood" were much favoured metaphors for depicting the divine-human relationship.[200]

Given this particular tendency of articulating the character of God and the relationship with him, several scholars have attempted to understand the divine-human relationship by focusing on a specific framework of interpersonal relationships that underlies it.[201] For instance, Jerome Neyrey tries to understand the divine-human

---

[192] Cf. Deut. 32:5–6; 2 Sam. 7:14–15; Ps. 68:5; 89:26; 103:13; Isa. 1:2, 4; 64:8; Jer. 3:4, 19, 22; 31:20, 22 ("faithless daughter" [MT]).
[193] Isa. 49:15; 66:13 (MT).
[194] See also Heb.12:9.
[195] Cf. Isa. 50:1; 54:5–8; 62:5; Jer. 3:1, 8, 20; Ezek. 16:32, 35–43.
[196] Cf. section 3.2.1 of this study (on effects of betrayal in IT).
[197] Philo quotes Gen. 18:17 in *Leg.* 3.27.
[198] E.g. "Father of the universe (τὸν πατέρα τῶν ὅλων)" (*Opif.* 72, cf. 75, 77). See also *Her.* 62, 98, 110, 200, 205, 236; *Leg.* 1.18; *Deus.* 31; *Ebr.* 74; *Conf.* 144, 170, 175; *Migr.* 46, 135, 195; *Fug.* 84, 177, 197; *Mut.* 45, 127.
[199] Orrey McFarland notes that there exists "a strong doctrine of providence" in this passage as well as an acknowledgement of God's creative activity (Orrey McFarland, *God and Grace in Philo and Paul* [Leiden: Brill, 2016], 32).
[200] Folker Siegert, "Philo and the New Testament," in *The Cambridge Companion to Philo*, ed. Adam Kamesar (Cambridge: Cambridge University Press, 2009), 192.
[201] Jerome H. Neyrey, "Prayer, in Other Words: New Testament Prayers in Social Science Perspective," in *Social Scientific Models for Interpreting the Bible: Essays by the Context Group in Honor of Bruce J. Malina*, ed. John J. Pilch (Leiden: Brill, 2001), 369–73. See also Zeba A. Crook, *Reconceptualising Conversion: Patronage, Loyalty, and Conversion in the Religions of the Ancient Mediterranean* (Berlin: de Gruyter, 2004), 76–89.

relationship in the NT with the "patron-client" model.²⁰² Neyrey's approach is based on the idea that the original recipients of the texts would classify the descriptions of the divine-human relationship "immediately in the patterns of social relations (i.e. patronage model)."²⁰³ In a similar vein, Malina indicates that many biblical writings explain God with reference to "the makeup of human beings."²⁰⁴ Even though Malina recognizes the difference between God and human beings, noting that "everything about God is simply beyond human beings, including God's concern for his own,"²⁰⁵ he finds a number of occasions that describe the nature of God and his actions with "analogies based on human behaviour" performed by eyes (cf. 1 Sam. 16:7), mouth (cf. Ps. 33:9), ears (cf. Ps. 94:9) and hands (cf. 1 Kgs 8:42).²⁰⁶

To summarize, the descriptions comparing the divine-human relationship to human relationships are observed in a number of ancient texts. This practice is based on some central similarities that the two kinds of relationships share. Paul, among other ancient writers, employs various types of interpersonal relationships to explain different dimensions of the divine-human relationship (e.g. father-son, master-servant, friendship, etc.). In adopting such points of view, Paul and others do not restrict the possibility of interaction between the divine and human agents, nor do they simply stress the otherness of God by upholding the existential discrepancy between the two parties. Rather, they focus on the interaction between the two agents; this is especially obvious in Paul's writings. In this respect, it is possible for us to discuss the divine-human relationship with the framework of IT. Also, inasmuch as the divine-human relationship in Romans 1–8 is articulated with several characteristic relational stages, we will not only use the basic concepts of the theory to conceptualize these situations, but also bring some relevant case studies conducted with IT into our discussion, comparing them to parallel ancient examples, if necessary, in order to grasp a clearer picture of each relational situation.

Our discussion also offers an insight into understanding the relationship between biblical interpretation (or theology) and a social-scientific approach. Although there may be some territories where the two perspectives cannot meet, from our case we have found that social knowledge is a crucial means through which theological or religious knowledge is expressed and comprehended. If knowledge about general human society is used to explain certain theological facts, then it is essential to comprehend the real social world, and it is this process to which the studies with a particular interest in social world can contribute. Our position also concurs with other scholars who find room for social-scientific criticism in biblical

---

²⁰² Jerome H. Neyrey, *Render to God: New Testament Understandings of the Divine* (Minneapolis: Fortress, 2004). Although the validity of the cross-cultural model is still in question, as there may be cultural variations according to different regions and time periods, the question does not affect our point, for it is still a common phenomenon that the divine-human relationship is framed within human relational terms (regardless of how differently the actual relational dynamics are perceived). For concern on cultural peculiarities, see Zeba A. Crook, "Critical Notes: Reflections on Culture and Social-Scientific Models," *JBL* 124.3 (2005): 515–20.
²⁰³ Neyrey, *Render*, 195–6.
²⁰⁴ Malina, 68.
²⁰⁵ Ibid., 72.
²⁰⁶ Ibid., 71–5.

interpretation.²⁰⁷ Therefore, in this respect, it is our quest to find a creative way in which social-scientific perspectives can interact with theological facts, and not to entirely rule out the potential of social science.

2.4.3 Using text as source

It is also important to verify the nature of the source for our investigation. For our research, we will use data from texts as primary materials. Since in many cases, social psychological theories are developed and used in conditioned experiments,²⁰⁸ it can be unusual to utilize the data from texts for such an investigation, though we already have a number of examples that adopt a social psychological theory for biblical interpretation using primary texts.²⁰⁹ Thus, we will consider two points to see to what extent it is viable to use an ancient text as a primary source for our investigation with IT: 1) the specific developmental background of IT and 2) the nature of our main text as a reflection of human life and relationships.

Regarding the first point, we see that in the very early stages of the development of IT, the theorists exemplified a text, *Family Happiness* by Tolstoy,²¹⁰ as a test case to explain and testify to some major concepts of the theory.²¹¹ We see that the major concepts of IT are presented and explained with the stories of Marya and Sergey's marital life. The author's description and the monologues of each character form clues through which one can understand and estimate the state of their relationship. We note that the outcomes for each partner are mainly non-material, and this can easily be observed from the descriptions of the characters' emotions and behaviour. For example, in Marya's case, the theorists observe that her CL keeps increasing as she faces new aspects of life.

> The intense and novel joys of courtship, falling in love, and the honeymoon weeks established a high CL that the ensuing routines of a country household could not equal ... The sheer excitement she felt about her life in society gradually subsided partly because satiation set in and partly because her CL rose as it incorporated her recent experiences.²¹²

However, Marya had to come back to her family because of her estimation of CL-alt. When it comes to CL-alt, it is noteworthy that various situations—both cultural and emotional—and experience are intertwined with one another:

> "I was constantly in society where I did not need him." We may guess that, in some degree at least, Marya remained with Sergey because of the high cost of exit

---

²⁰⁷ Cf. Horrell, "Social-Scientific," 25–6; Barton, "Social-Scientific Criticism," 281–6.
²⁰⁸ Myers, 4.
²⁰⁹ For example, Esler, *Galatians*; idem, *Conflict and Identity in Romans: The Social Setting of Paul's Letter* (Minneapolis: Fortress, 2003).
²¹⁰ Leo Tolstoy, *Family Happiness*, trans. D. Bondar (London: Bath, Sir Isaac Pitman & Sons, 1945).
²¹¹ See Kelley and Thibaut, *Interdependence*, 5–13.
²¹² Ibid., 9.

(disapproval from kinfolk, friends, church, and the wider society, feelings of guilt about broken obligations, and hurt to Sergey). These exit costs would serve to depress CL-alt . . . she understood or remembered how much her future happiness depended on them.[213]

As the illustrations show, the situations that the character faced and the choices that she made are analyzed through the lens of IT. The reasons that make this approach valid are, first of all, the text narrates interpersonal relationships, as the whole story revolves around the relationship between two or more people; secondly, the text provides enough descriptions about the relationship from general human viewpoints that it becomes possible to understand the qualities of several core concepts of IT (e.g. outcomes, CL, CL-alt). Of course, the possibility of using a text also originates from the nature of the theory. The major concepts of IT are not only observable from experimental settings but are also often discernible in our ordinary lives.

Such a theoretical characteristic becomes more evident when we look up an extensive application of IT in *An Atlas of Interpersonal Situations*.[214] This work deploys the theoretical framework of IT to give explanations of twenty-one occasions that embed particular relational issues. The occasions are categorized by a few characteristics, such as the number of people involved in each case, informational situation, etc.[215] What is notable is that the situations discussed from the IT perspective are summarized in ordinary terms, which shows that the abstractness of the framework of IT promotes its applicability. For example, the situations titled "I scratch your back, you scratch mine (that highlights mutual partner control),"[216] "the prisoner's dilemma"[217] and "you are the boss (about asymmetric dependence)"[218] capture the variety of interpersonal situations that happen in our lives. A short illustration offered in the chapter about "conflicting mutual joint control,"[219] despite the simplicity of the story, presents the essential interpersonal structure in which the main topic of the chapter is engaged.

> A younger brother wants to "hang out" with his older brother and be at the same place as the older one, but the older brother finds that the younger one "cramps his style" and prefers not to have the younger one around. So the situation is one of "hide and seek," with the older brother doing the hiding and the younger, the seeking.[220]

The illustration shows that the use of IT is not limited to controlled experiments, but that it can be deployed to expound the relational dynamics in other types of

---

[213] Ibid. 9–10.
[214] Kelley et al., *Atlas*.
[215] For the content for such subcategories, see Kelley et al., vii–viii.
[216] Ibid., 142–9.
[217] Ibid., 171–91.
[218] Ibid., 149–70.
[219] Cf. ibid., 162–76.
[220] Ibid., 162.

materials, for instance, texts. It is still possible to define the relational structure of the relationship without the numerical data compiled in experimental settings. As stressed above, the abstractness of the core concepts of IT enables us to perceive the core elements more easily within a variety of settings. Unquestionably, the specific criteria and expressions of outcomes vary by cultures and societies—wherein one culture may value a specific behaviour highly, whereas another culture not[221]—we have found that it is a general human phenomenon to consider the outcomes from relationships.[222]

When it comes to our primary text, even though it is a written source, it can still provide adequate information to be discussed under IT, because Paul's articulation of the divine-human relationship often portrays key stages of interpersonal relationships, either explicitly or implicitly: betrayal (Rom. 1:18–3:20), forgiveness and reconciliation (3:21–26; 5:1–11), an exploitive relationship (non-voluntary dependence) (5:12–8:11) and persistence in the relationship (8:12–39) are key stages of the divine-human relationship expressed from an interpersonal point of view, and in these cases what forms the core of each relational situation is often associated with the matter of "outcomes." Although it might not be possible to reconstitute the whole shape of a certain cultural atmosphere simply by investigating a text,[223] it is hard to exclude the fact that a text reflects its original context in various ways, and thus we are able to detect some features of reality from it.[224] If we admit that a text is an artefact of its society, it should contain discernible characteristics of the real human lives of that society.[225]

Our discussion also offers an answer to some questions about the efficacy of a social psychological approach to the Bible with regard to the difference between controlled experiments and real human lives.[226] Although controlled experiments might be seen as distant from real human lives, as long as the data under consideration in the experimental situation are also observable in our daily lives, the theories can still illuminate some aspects of real human lives. Also, given that social psychological experiments generally aim to re-create circumstances to mimic real lives by controlling any side effects that might blur the effect of a manipulated variable, what is observed from the experiment can still be meaningful for the comprehension of human behaviour in real lives, including those reflected in a text. In this respect, such a research method of social psychology can be regarded as a strong point, not as a weak point, as it can reveal the correlation between human behaviour and a certain situational factor more clearly.

---

[221] Kelley and Thibaut, *Interdependence*, 15.
[222] See Section 2.4.2. For a short instance, MPC can be observed in the ordinary interpersonal relationships of both the ancient people and the modern people as a form of *quid pro quo* or tit-for-tat (cf. *Ben*.2.22).
[223] Cf. Esler, "Models," 107–8.
[224] Cf. Horrell, "Reflections," 17–18.
[225] Cf. Horrell, *Ethos*, 52–3 ("texts will be viewed as a form of social action in which the rules and resources which comprise a symbolic order are produced and reproduced").
[226] Cf. John M.G. Barclay, *Pauline Churches and Diaspora Jews* (Tübingen: Mohr Siebeck, 2011), 6–7 (n. 10).

2.5 Conclusion

In this chapter we have navigated the actual ways in which we will deploy IT, discussing several methodological issues that derive from either the nature of IT or the nature of our primary topic and material. The survey elucidates the point where IT and our topic can come together. In regard to the issue of historical and cultural validity, although IT was developed in the Western world in the twentieth-century CE, the fact that concerns for the individual and the relationship between individuals were present in the consciousness of late antiquity shows that our attempt can avoid the pitfalls of anachronism and ethnocentrism. It is also important that IT treats the power of "outcome" in a way similar to the manner in which Paul and several of his contemporary thinkers regarded self-interest. Based on prior discussions, we have identified the way in which we can understand the divine-human relationship within the framework of a dyadic relationship. Despite the complications presented by plurality, we have shown that "human beings" in Romans 1–8 can be treated as a single agent insofar as it is a homogeneous entity. In addition, although our topic is a theological one, the fact that the divine-human relationship (particularly, God and his acts) is often construed in human terms by Paul and other ancient authors, opens the door for our approach. Also, we have identified that we can still use Romans as a primary source as long as it can provide basic information about a dyadic relationship in terms of "outcomes." The general applicability of the core concepts of IT also enables IT to delineate various interpersonal relationships in real human lives according to its own terms. In the following chapters, we will investigate several key stages of the divine-human relationship seen in Romans 1–8 from the IT perspective, in conversation with relevant cases from Paul's contemporaneous context, if necessary, and will ask what kind of information the relational structure of each situation in the relationship can yield for understanding the gestures of both partners made over the course of ongoing interactions.

3

Diagnosing Human Corruption: Human Sinfulness as Betrayal (Rom. 1:18–3:20)

3.1 Introduction

Paul's statement about the gospel is twofold: it is about the saving activity of God that gives life for those who place their trust in it (1:17), and it simultaneously reveals God's wrath upon the ungodliness and wickedness of human beings (1:18).[1] These two opposite aspects of the gospel unsurprisingly imply two different types of relationship, i.e. the right and wrong relationships with God.[2] Although it is the former, the positive case, that Paul mainly highlights throughout his letter, this necessarily brings attention to the latter, the negative case, which functions as the background of the former.[3] In particular, it is this negative side that Paul highlights throughout Rom. 1:18–3:20, portraying the brokenness of the human relationship with God. Paul exemplifies a number of characteristics of corrupted human beings, both Gentiles and Jews, and these characteristics, which represent the universal sinfulness of humanity, converge into the state of their relationship with God. Paul affirms that all humanity, regardless of their ethnic origins, has broken its relationship with God, turning away from God and becoming subject to the power of Sin

---

[1] Regarding the twofold aspect of the gospel, Jonathan Linebaugh notes that "the dual revelations are tied to a single entity," pointing out the grammatical connections between 1:16, 1:17 and 1:18 formed by γάρ in each verse. Jonathan A. Linebaugh, *God, Grace, and Righteousness in Wisdom of Solomon and Paul's Letter to the Romans: Texts in Conversation* (Leiden: Brill, 2013), 107. A chiastic structure of 1:17–18 reflects the parallel between righteousness and wrath. Cf. Robert Jewett, *Romans: A Commentary* (Minneapolis: Fortress, 2007), 148–9.

[2] The importance of relationality in Romans is seen from the theme of peace identified by Michael Gorman. According to Gorman's analysis based on the usage of the concepts related to peace, our section is concerned with the reality of humanity as contrary to the divine intention of peace. See Michael J. Gorman, *Becoming the Gospel: Paul, Participation, and Mission* (Grand Rapids: Eerdmans, 2015), 169–80. Klaus Haacker also suggests that "the theology of Romans begins with an instruction on the basis of peace *with* God, goes on to develop strategies of peace in human interactions, and ends up with the promise of final peace *from* God in his final victory" (Haacker, 53). Similarly, Ralph Martin concentrates on the topic of peace and reconciliation in Paul. See Ralph P. Martin, *Reconciliation: A Study of Paul's Theology* (Atlanta: John Knox, 1981). Gorman, Haacker and Martin are helpful for recognizing peace as a prominent relational concept in Romans; nevertheless, a broader and inclusive framework is needed in order to conceptualize various phases of the divine-human relationship.

[3] In this regard, we can follow Sanders's proposal that Paul's understanding of the universal human plight originates from the illumination of the solution (i.e. the gospel). Cf. Sanders, 474–511.

(ὑφ' ἁμαρτίαν εἶναι [3:9]). In other words, the broken relationship with God is the epitome of the universal state of corruption in human beings.

In this chapter, we will propose that the problem Paul details with the extensive descriptions about human sinfulness is mainly a relational one. The extensive depictions of the human sinfulness in Rom. 1:18–3:20 ultimately bring attention to the brokenness of the divine-human relationship. We will also enquire into the original expectations for the relationship and the reason for the severance of the relationship. For this purpose, we will situate Paul's portrayal of the divine-human relationship in 1:18–3:20 within the framework of IT. We will firstly look at 1:18–32, which focuses on the Gentiles, verifying the nature of their evils and the reason which promotes it. We will examine this issue with the concept of betrayal in IT, and will explain the fundamental reason for the betrayal in terms of "outcomes," expounding the different modes of calculation reflected in the text. For the subsequent part (2:1–3:8), we will examine another aspect of human sinfulness, here with a focus on the Jewish people, looking at the meaning of the law and circumcision with reference to the notion of "social norms" in IT. As will be shown, what both cases of human sinfulness jointly demonstrate are the acts or decisions that resulted in the brokenness of the divine-human relationship.

3.2 The broken relationship between God and humanity (1): Betrayal by the wrong calculation (Gentiles) (Rom. 1:18–32)

In Rom. 1:18–3:20, Paul's ultimate focus is on humanity in general, not only in terms of the issue of corruption, but also regarding the universal scope of the eschatological divine activity (cf. 1:16–17; 2:1–16). In 1:18–32 it appears to be the condition of Gentiles at which Paul primarily aims, but Paul's universal focus is not lost throughout 1:18–3:20.[4] Paul presumes that human beings should have maintained the right relationship with God because it was clearly revealed to them who God is (cf. 1:19–23). Therefore, their ignorance of God is inexcusable (ἀναπολογήτος). Their current reality is a result of their refusal to follow what was originally expected of them. Referring to this background knowledge, we will ask 1) what human sinfulness means in terms of the relationship with God and 2) what the reason behind it is. Also, we will see 3) if there is another influential actor in the situation of 1:18–32. We will refer to the concept of "betrayal" from the IT perspective as an explanatory framework.

3.2.1 Betrayal in IT

Betrayal basically points to an attempt "to be unfaithful or disloyal," "to reveal something meant to be hidden," or "to seduce and desert."[5] When it comes to the context of close

---

[4] Cf. Leon Morris, *The Epistle to the Romans* (Grand Rapids: Eerdmans, 1988), 74. Ernst Käsemann, *Commentary on Romans*, trans. Geoffrey W. Bromiley (Grand Rapids: Eerdmans, 1980), 33. See also Morna D. Hooker, "Adam in Romans 1," in *From Adam to Christ: Essays on Paul* (Cambridge: Cambridge University Press, 1990), 75.

[5] Eli J. Finkel et al., "Dealing with Betrayal in Close Relationships: Does Commitment Promote Forgiveness?," *JPSP* 82.6 (2002): 957.

relationships, betrayal can be defined in relation to the norms set up between the partners. Thus, Eli Finkel et al. treat betrayal as "the perceived violation by a partner of an implicit or explicit relationship-relevant norm," and point out that it often inflicts harm to the offended party.[6]

Betrayal can be one of the most serious threats to a relationship, and it is difficult to resolve betrayal incidents.[7] Betrayal often produces interpersonal debts, causing "a signature constellation of negative feelings, thoughts, and behavioral tendencies" to manifest within the victimized person, which will then engender impulses such as "react[ing] with anger, confusion, and demands for atonement."[8] Although those who commit betrayal might also experience negative feelings (e.g. guilt or shame) and develop a willingness to apologize, they might also change their attitude and become self-defensive if the victims keep a hostile attitude.[9] Betrayal can also be regarded as proof of one's lack of commitment; since, if one is strongly committed to the relationship, they are likely to sustain the relationship even when the situation is not so favourable.[10] Thus, Finkel et al. indicate that betrayal has a "destabilising force," since such an act implies "a lack of commitment, undermine[s] trust, and upset[s] the balance of power."[11]

Betrayal can be seen as a failure to maintain an ongoing relationship, an occasion in which a calculation of outcomes is involved. The calculation of outcomes from the current relationship and an alternative choice can affect one's commitment level to the current partner, according to which different types of maintenance mechanisms are activated.[12] There are three elements that define one's commitment level to the partner and are important for the calculating process: the level of satisfaction, the quality of alternatives and the size of the investment.[13]

If one's outcome from the current relationship is higher than CL, then it will increase the level of satisfaction, whereas a poor level of satisfaction caused by outcomes lower than CL will have a negative effect on one's commitment to the partner. For instance, "rising expectations," "declining outcomes," "satiation," "the greater salience and potency of the negative outcomes in relationship to positive outcomes" and "ambivalence" toward the future can decrease satisfaction levels.[14] The quality of alternatives (CL-alt) is also a crucial factor for maintaining or disturbing an ongoing relationship. It is easy for one to maintain commitment to a partner if CL-alt is inferior to what one can obtain from the present relationship. However, if CL-alt is estimated to be higher than the acquired outcomes, it will lessen one's commitment level to the current partner,[15] and "to the extent that CL-alt exceeds obtained outcomes... partners may decide to end their relationship in order to pursue alternative involvements."[16]

[6] Ibid.
[7] Ibid., 956.
[8] Ibid., 958; Rusbult, Arriaga and Agnew, 379.
[9] Rusbult, Arriaga and Agnew, 379.
[10] Kelley et al., 295.
[11] Finkel et al., 972.
[12] Cf. Rusbult, Arriaga and Agnew, 377–81.
[13] Ibid., 381–3.
[14] Ibid., 382.
[15] Ibid.
[16] Ibid., 382–3.

Limited investment into the current relationship may also make it easy for one to abandon that relationship.[17]

3.2.2 The relational characteristic of human sin: Subversion and animosity (Rom. 1:21–32)

The problem of sin brought a destructive effect to the divine-human relationship. In particular, when we look at the specific nature of human sin described in 1:21–27, we can recognize that human sin is directed against God and results in betrayal. As in 1:21–23, the sinfulness of the Gentiles brings about a destructive effect on their relationship with God by subverting the original relational orders. It is interesting that the lists of evils here can be seen generally against Israel's duty to God in the Decalogue.[18] Specifically, the verb ματαιόω (1:21) is frequently employed in the context that refers to Israel's unfaithfulness to the relationship with God (1 Sam. 13:13; 2 Kgs 17:15; 1 Chron. 2:18; Jer. 2:5 [LXX]).[19] As Rom. 1:21 shows, the originally expected response for those who know God is to honour God (δοξάζω) and give thanks to him (εὐχαριστέω). Yet, the actual response from humanity is quite contrary. They exchanged (ἀλλάσσω/μεταλλάσσω) the original order for an unnatural and unsuitable one (1:23). The term "exchange" (or "change"), which appears three times in this context (cf. 1:23, 25, 26), characterizes the subversion of the original value intended for the relationship. It describes the exchange of the glory of the immortal God (τὴν δόξαν τοῦ ἀφθάρτου θεοῦ) for the form of an image of mortal human beings, birds, quadrupeds and reptiles. There are three sets of comparison that form corresponding pairs: glory–image, immortality–mortality and creator–creation.

The subversion of the original order is closely linked with the change of partnership. Romans 1:23 presumably implies the idolatry of Gentiles, but its connotation is broader than that.[20] It does not simply indicate the making of idols, but sketches the formation of the relationship with the idols. The place originally reserved for God is given instead to idols. Romans 1:25 elaborates upon the picture of 1:23. Romans 1:25 depicts the exchange that happened in 1:23 as the exchange of the truth of God (τὴν ἀλήθειαν τοῦ θεοῦ) for a falsehood (ἐν τῷ ψεύδει). Not only is the falsehood about the nature of the idols, but it also defines the nature of the human practice directed toward creation (τῇ κτίσει). Instead of glorifying and giving thanks to God, human beings worship and serve (ἐσεβάσθησαν καὶ ἐλάτρευσαν) the idols that were made according to the images of creatures. Their practice of worshipping and serving was originally supposed to be directed toward God; however, it is offered to another object made as a result of human beings' attempts to play the creator. Therefore, the relationship formed

---

[17] Ibid., 383.
[18] Cf. Moo, *Romans*, 102.
[19] Thus, ματαιόω anticipates the human abandonment of the relationship with God.
[20] Note that the Israelites had also practised idolatry (cf. Exodus 32). But in this context, Paul appears to evoke the idolatry of pagan culture since he does not explicitly mention the ancient history of Israel. Also, it is to be remembered that the broader context of the letter focuses on the Gentiles.

between human beings and idols is the other facet of the rejection of the relationship with God.

The subversive nature of human sin in the relationship with God is also reflected in human-to-human relationships. Another type of exchange happened between human beings in the realm of sexual relationships. Paul speaks of the exchange of a natural function for an unnatural one (μετήλλαξαν τὴν φυσικὴν χρῆσιν εἰς τὴν παρὰ φύσιν), one that overturns the originally designed order. The consequences are ironic, because by refusing to honour God (cf. 1:21), humanity ended up dishonouring itself (ἀτιμάζεσθαι τὰ σώματα αὐτῶν ἐν αὐτοῖς).

Another aspect of human sinfulness can be characterized by animosity toward God, which can also be one of the symptoms of "betrayal," reflecting a lack of commitment and affection to the original partner. The evil deeds listed in 1:28–31 also represent relational qualities. A few of them appear to represent human beings' attitude toward God, while the rest apply to human relationships.[21] For instance, θεοστυγής ("hating God [God-hater]")[22] is the most unconcealed expression that reveals humanity's negative attitude toward God. In a number of occasions in the LXX and in the NT, ὑπερήφανος ("arrogant") is frequently described as one of the typical characteristics of those who are in an antagonistic relationship with God.[23] The same can also be said for the instances of ὑβριστής ("an insolent person") (cf. Prov. 15:25; Isa. 2:12; Sir. 35:21) and ἀλαζών ("a boaster") (cf. Hab. 2:5). It is also notable that ἀσύνθετος ("faithless") is used in the LXX to indicate Judah's faithless attitude toward God (cf. Jer. 3:7–8, 10–11). Other characteristics, such as γονεῦσιν ἀπειθής ("disobedient to parents"), generally portray dysfunctional human relationships, which resemble the way in which human beings have mistreated God. Such attitudes can also be observed when one believes that the outcomes they can earn from a relationship are not satisfactory or are not proportionate to the input cost, in which situation the relationship often becomes fragile.[24]

Even though the corrupted humanity resists acknowledging God (οὐκ ἐδοκίμασαν τὸν θεὸν ἔχειν ἐν ἐπιγνώσει [cf. 1:28]), they already know what God's regulations are (οἵτινες τὸ δικαίωμα τοῦ θεοῦ ἐπιγνόντες), regulations which pronounce death to those who commit such acts of vice. This implies that their rejecting the relationship with God is not accidental or arbitrary, but deliberate and volitional (cf. 1:32). Thus, in this respect, humanity is culpable for those evil acts.

As shown above, Paul does not merely highlight the problem of immorality. Rather, a close reading of the human sins points to the actions of turning away from the original partner followed by the formation of another type of association. In this sense,

---

[21] Here, we can observe a certain pattern in 1:21–27: A (the destruction of the human relationship with God [1:21–23]) → B (the destruction of the relationship between human beings [1:24–27]) is similarly repeated in 1:28–32 (A': [1:28] → B': [1:29–32]).

[22] The meaning of θεοστυγής fits best within its context when it is taken in an active sense. Ps.-Clem., Hom. 1.12 also demonstrates θεοστυγής in an active sense. See also 1 Clem. 35.5 (θεοστυγία); EDNT, "θεοστυγής", 2.142.

[23] Cf. Ps. 17:28; 88:11; 93:2; 100:5; 119:21; Prov. 3:34; Pss. Sol. 2:31; Zeph. 3:6; Isa. 2:12; 13:11; Lk. 1:51; Jas 4:6; 1 Pet. 1:5.

[24] "Relationships characterized by noncorrespondence are stormy, with partners developing suspicious, distrustful or even hostile attitudes toward one another" (Rusbult, Arriaga and Agnew, 368).

human sinfulness can be seen as "betrayal." Both the subversion of the original order in the relationship and the development of animosity against the original partner are observed when the relationship is broken by one of the partners' betrayal.

3.2.3 The reason for betrayal: Different calculations of "outcomes" (humanity's perspective vs. Paul's perspective)

So, if the human sin in 1:18–32 correlates to aspects of betrayal, what is the main reason behind such a decision? To put this question in another way using IT terms, what are the presupposed CL and CL-alt for humanity? As shown above, humanity's rejection and exchange of the relationship is not arbitrary, but rather is done on the basis of a deliberate calculation, which they deem to be wise (σοφός [1:22]).[25] However, since their reasoning is vain and their senseless minds are also darkened (ἐματαιώθησαν ἐν τοῖς διαλογισμοῖς αὐτῶν καὶ ἐσκοτίσθη ἡ ἀσύνετος αὐτῶν καρδία), they are incapable of correct "reasoning," and eventually made the worst choice. What kinds of expected outcomes are implied in this calculation?

3.2.3.1 The calculation by humanity: The reason for leaving

IT suggests that betrayal can happen when one thinks that the outcomes from the current relationship are not good as the outcomes obtainable from an alternative relationship (i.e. CL-alt).[26] The quality of CL-alt looks more appealing if the current outcomes are lower than one's CL. When it comes to our text, although it is difficult to measure the exact quality of CL, the standard against which one evaluates "the attractiveness of the relationship,"[27] given the negative attitudes toward God that are present in the text, it seems that human beings have evaluated the outcomes from the relationship with God to be inferior to their CL. The gap between CL and the outcomes from the relationship with God in Figure 3.1 indicates humanity's dissatisfaction. Also, given that CL can change according to the series of relationships,[28] human beings' CL may have increased as they came to feel that there were no stimulating outcomes from a relationship with God but only demanding obligations (e.g. to honour and give thanks [1:21]). The attempt to be independent from God implies the possibility that humans had perceived their responsibilities as too demanding, which means that the cost for the relationship with God had become overbearing. Consequently, God is no longer a partner important to them (cf. 3:11), so much so that they do not even show proper respect to God (cf. 3:18). This makes them do whatever they wish, which represents an extreme version of human autonomy. Romans 2:4, although mainly aimed at Jews, hints at a similar point. Paul's accusation against his Jewish interlocutor's ignorance of "the riches of his kindness and forbearance and patience" mirrors the misunderstanding of what they are receiving from a relationship with God, which may have resulted in a boost of CL.

[25] Dunn, *Romans 1–8*, 76.
[26] Rusbult, Arriaga and Agnew, 361.
[27] Kelley and Thibaut, *Interdependence*, 8–9.
[28] Cf. ibid.; Rusbult, Arriaga and Agnew, 360–1.

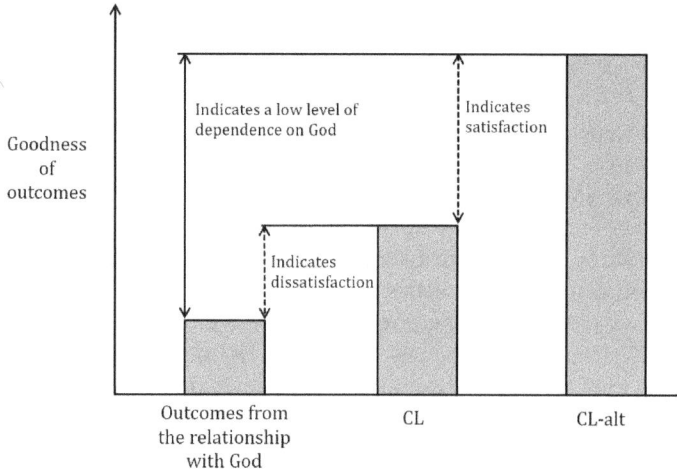

Figure 3.1 Humanity's calculation.

With regard to CL-alt, the expectation of "the quality of the best available alternative to a relationship,"[29] there is the possibility that the outcomes from the relationship with God are deemed as poorer than the quality of CL-alt, although it is difficult to measure the exact discrepancy (cf. Figure 3.1 [see the gap between CL-alt and the outcomes from the relationship with God]). Seen from the human perspective, CL-alt can be viewed as positive, since the pleasure of independence (reward) can offset any following costs, even death, a cost which was already known to them (1:32). Of course, humans might not comprehend exactly what the true nature of the cost for their alternative choice is because of their foolishness (1:21–22). Various descriptions about malice and immorality (1:24, 26–27, 29–31) are what humans have pursued as pleasure in their new position of being independent from God.

Similarly, ἐριθεία in 2:8, which characterizes those who commit evils, also deserves our attention (cf. 2:9).[30] The word can mean either "strife" or "selfish ambition," and the latter appears to be more relevant in this context.[31] Although selfishness can be primarily comprehended in terms of human relationships,[32] given that selfishness ignores anyone but the self, an attempt to exclude God from consideration for the sake of self-interest is a possible result. Thus, as Dunn puts it:

> This is an important insight into one aspect of human sinfulness—its character of rebellion against what is known to be right (or best), its act of defiance in the face of known and perilous consequences of the act, its seemingly heroic "I/we will do what I/we will do and damn the outcome!" The miserable list of antisocial

---

[29] Rusbult, Arriaga and Agnew, 361.
[30] The passages refer to both Jews and Gentiles.
[31] Cf. BDAG, 3123. Cf. "self-seeking" (NRSV; ESV; NIV) or "selfishly ambitious" (NASB).
[32] ἐριθεία in 2 Cor. 12:20, Gal. 5:20, Phil. 1:17; 2:3 can be translated in a similar manner. See also Jas 3:14, 16.

behaviour (vv. 29–31) illustrates just what human wisdom in its vaunted independence from God ends up justifying to itself.[33]

As noted earlier, an attempt to be independent from God involves the formation of an alternative relationship. In 1:18–32, there are several indications that the additional actor antithetical to God acts as an alternative partner, whose position is similar to that of Sin specified in the following passages (cf. 5:12–21). Firstly, it is notable that the corrupted humanity makes a relationship with an idol. In 1:23 and 1:25, Paul describes the practice of change (ἀλλάσσω/μεταλλάσσω), by which the likeness of the image (ὁμοιώματι εἰκόνος) of creatures (i.e. an idol) replaces God the Creator. What is supposed to be performed in the context of the relationship with God (e.g. worshipping and serving) is now reserved for the relationship with idols. The fact that the nature of an idol opposes God's characteristics (e.g. φθαρτός–ἄφθαρτος; ψεῦδος–ἀλήθεια) reflects the nature of this alternative relationship.

Also, an allusion to Adam's story in 1:18–32 suggests that Paul implies an additional actor who—being antithetical to God—plays the role of Adam's alternative partner in the Genesis story. Some scholars, such as Fitzmyer, undermine the importance of Adam's narrative in 1:18–32, arguing that "the alleged echoes of the Adam stories in Genesis are simply non-existent."[34] Nonetheless, there are several clues that inform us that Adam's fall story is influential on Paul's delineation of the human sinfulness in Romans 1. Dunn argues that "Paul's attempt to explain this dark side of humanity focuses on the figure of Adam and the account of 'man's first disobedience' in Genesis 2–3."[35] Hooker also indicates that Paul deliberately adopts "the terminology of the creation story" when he characterizes human sinfulness in relation to idolatry. The use of εἰκών and ὁμοίωμα (cf. Gen. 1:26–27), the allusion to the Creation (κτίσεως κόσμου [Rom. 1:20]) as well as some terms related to the Creation (e.g. κτίσις), the descriptions of creatures (Rom. 1:23; cf. Gen. 1:20–25) and the incorporation of parallels of languages (e.g., ἀόρατα [Rom. 1:20] – ἀόρατος [Gen. 1:2]; ἐσκοτίσθη [Rom. 1:21] – σκότος [Gen. 1:2]) reflect a close connection between the two texts.[36] Hooker also observes a parallel between Romans 1 and Genesis 1–3 in terms of "the sequence of events."[37] In particular, as Adam "obeyed" and "gave his allegiance to a creation rather than to the creator" in listening to the serpent's lie (Gen. 3:4),[38] Paul's depiction of human sinfulness describes a similar type of turning away, which takes the form of idolatry (Rom. 1:23, 25).[39] Therefore, if Paul had the story of Adam's fall in mind when writing Rom. 1:18–32, the existence of an alternative

---

[33] Dunn, *Romans 1–8*, 76.
[34] Joseph A. Fitzmyer, *Romans: A New Translation with Introduction and Commentary* (New Haven: Yale University Press, 2008), 274.
[35] Dunn, *Theology*, 81.
[36] Hooker, "Adam," 76–7.
[37] Ibid., 77.
[38] Ibid., 77–8.
[39] Ibid., 78; 80.

partner for humanity would have been an indispensable element, since Adam's story is not simply a story of guilt but a story of betrayal in which a counterpart to the original partner is essential.[40]

In addition, a close parallel exists between Rom. 1:18–32 and 5:12–21, where Adam's story surfaces. In both 1:18–32 and 5:12–21, an association formed outside the relationship with God is an important issue for Paul. Although such an association takes a form of idolatry in 1:18–32, in 5:12–14 the association between Adam as a representative of humanity and Sin as a personified cosmic entity is important for accounting for the origin of human sin.[41] Also, as the human sinfulness in 1:18–32 is characterized by subversion and animosity to God, Adam's transgression opposes God (cf. 5:17). In this respect, 1:18–32 and 5:12–21 focus on a similar theme despite different emphases, and we believe it to be likely that Adam's story has an important function already in Romans 1. Given this close connection between 1:18–32 and 5:12–21, the identity of the alternative partner who plays an antagonistic role is consistent throughout Romans 1–5, though it is from 5:12–21 where Paul begins to spell out the alternative partner's identity in earnest.

3.2.3.2 The calculation by Paul: The reason for remaining

On the other hand, the calculation made by Paul for the divine-human relationship is opposite to that of corrupted human beings. Paul views the human calculation as erroneous because it is driven by a futile reasoning possessed by darkened, senseless minds (cf. 1:21). From Paul's standpoint, the prospective value of outcomes from an alternative relationship (CL-alt) is markedly inferior to that of the outcomes from the relationship with God. The reward (i.e. the pleasure of independence from God and obligation) from the alternative relationship will be accompanied by a considerable amount of cost both in the present (cf. 1:27) and also in the future (i.e. death [1:32]; wrath and fury [ὀργὴ καὶ θυμός]; distress and anguish [θλῖψις καὶ στενοχωρία] [2:8–9]).[42] Thus, in Paul's estimation, CL-alt cannot exceed CL (see the gap between CL and CL-alt in Figure 3.2).

In contrast, the outcomes for those who manage the right relationship with God are clearly positive according to Paul. Although it might be indispensable to fulfil

---

[40] In addition, it is hard to rule out the allusion of Genesis 2–3 if one accepts the allusion to Genesis 1 in our text. Paul shows his interest in both Creation (cf. Genesis 1) and the story of human corruption against God (cf. Genesis 2–3) in Rom. 1:20. Even Genesis 1 is only the start of a narrative that reaches its preliminary conclusion in Genesis 3. Fitzmyer, *Pace*, 274 ("what allusions are alleged to be there are to Genesis 1, not to Genesis 2–3").

[41] Joseph Dodson also recognizes the significance of personified Sin and Death in Paul's explanation of the origin of sin, focusing on various aspects of the relationships between humanity and these personified subjects. See Joseph R. Dodson, *The "Powers" of Personification: Rhetorical Purpose in the "Book of Wisdom" and the Letter to the Romans* (Berlin: de Gruyter, 2008), 123–39.

[42] See especially Paul's use of ἀντιμισθία ("reward/recompense") in 1:27. It appears only twice in the NT (Rom. 1:27 [the relationship with God]; 2 Cor. 6:13 [the relationship between human beings]). Also, ἀντιμισθία appears several times in 2 Clement (1.3; 9.7; 11.6; 15.2), emphasizing the importance of the human response to God. In this sense 2 Clement follows Romans in seeing that one of the central axes that constitute the divine-human relationship is the offer of reward.

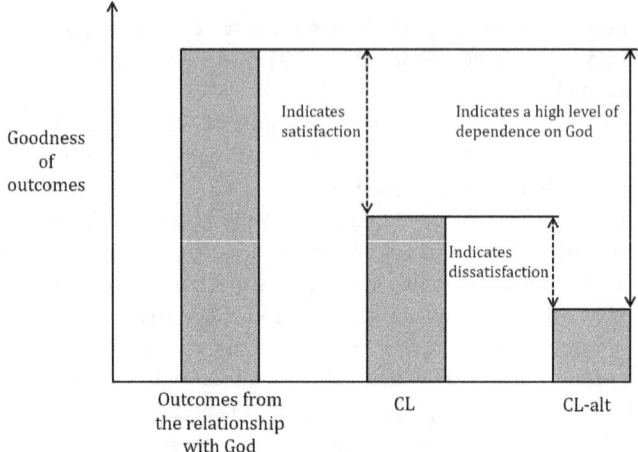

Figure 3.2 Paul's calculation.

some requirements (e.g. to honour and give thanks [cf. 1:21]; doing good, seeking glory and honour, and immortality by patience [cf. 2:7, 10]), the rewards from the relationship—such as eternal life (ζωή αἰώνιος [2:7]), glory, honour, and peace (δόξα, τιμή, εἰρήνη [2:10])—are seen as enough for offsetting the cost. Thus, we can consider that the outcomes from the relationship with God can exceed both CL (see the gap between outcomes from the relationship with God and CL) and CL-alt, which means that there is no reason to leave the current relationship (see the gap between outcomes from the relationship with God and CL-alt in Figure 3.2).

3.2.4 Summary

In Rom. 1:18-32, Paul, speaking with a particular focus on the Gentiles, claims that all humanity has turned away from God. The various kinds of evil practices in the text ultimately point to aspects of humanity's betrayal of God, reflecting their subversive and hostile nature against God. Nevertheless, that betrayal does not bring about the intended independence from God. It is because their calculation of outcomes from the alternative relationships is misguided by their futile reasoning and foolish hearts. Therefore, the association with the alternative partner (i.e. an idol) only worsens the situation. Both the allusion to Adam's story in Genesis and the close connection between Romans 1 and 5 reflect the hostile nature of the alternative partner, especially against God. Our reading suggests that there is a strong relational dimension in Paul's understanding of the sinfulness of humanity in 1:18-32. It is the relationship with a partner—either God or the alternative partner—that determines human beings' mode of existence. In this respect, Käsemann's exposition is illuminating: "A Person's reality is decided by what lord he has."[43] Although it is humanity's decision to leave the relationship with God, once they belong to an alternative relationship they are subject

---

[43] Käsemann, *Romans*, 179.

to the "lordship" of the new partner.⁴⁴ In the following passages, Paul attempts to enlarge the scope of his criticism to include other people, in order to put all human beings in the same boat—regardless of their ethnicity—concerning their broken relationship with God.

3.3 The broken relationship between God and humanity (2): Breaking "social norms" (Jews) (Rom. 2:1–3:8)

In Rom. 2:1–3:8, Paul draws attention to another aspect of human sinfulness, this time paying particular attention to the Jews. Here, the law and circumcision, the elements that render Jewish identity as distinct, play central roles in Paul's critique. In this section, with reference to the concept of "social norms" in IT, we will verify the relational implications of the law and circumcision in the divine-human relationship, and identify the nature of the Jewish people's sinfulness in terms of the relational implications.

3.3.1 The function of "social norms" in IT

In IT, "social norms"⁴⁵ are defined as "rule based, socially transmitted inclinations to respond to particular interdependence in a specific manner."⁴⁶ By keeping "social norms," partners can enhance the quality of outcomes—for such purpose, self-sacrificial choices may be required at some stage.⁴⁷ "Social norms" are particularly

---

⁴⁴ David Way's summary is helpful for clarifying Käsemann's point of view: "Human beings are not free agents who can determine their own destinies by the exercise of choice; rather, they are under the influence of the powers, and their actions merely ratify or reject the lordship under which they live" (David Way, *The Lordship of Christ: Ernst Käsemann's Interpretation of Paul's Theology* [Oxford: Clarendon, 1991], 112).

⁴⁵ Esler also adopts a similar sort of concept (i.e. "group norms") when he approaches the issue of the Mosaic law with "social identity theory." In social identity theory, "group norms" are a means to "install the group's distinctive identity on individual members" (Esler, *Romans*, 20). Esler understands that the Mosaic law can be an "identity descriptor" for "the Israelite outgroup" as it enhances the group identity by regulating the members' behaviour in a specific manner, seeing it as a counterpart of the group identity of the Christ-followers, an identity which has a distinct origin (cf. ibid., 335). However, Esler's deployment of "group norms" seems to lead him to miss the main purpose of the law in Paul, that is, to manage the right relationship with God (emic). The function of "group norms" as "identity descriptors" is rather derivative (etic), which follows the fulfilment of the primary purpose. Without prioritizing the "emic" dimension, it would be difficult to understand the manner in which Paul deals with the question of Mosaic law, as he does not totally negate the meaning of the law although acknowledging its clear limitations (cf. Romans 7). In this respect, Esler imposes too strict a distinction between "the Christ-movement" and the law, which appears to partly depend upon his reading of Galatians (cf. ibid., 334). As long as the concern for the right relationship with God is still central to Romans, the meaning of law, from which the emic dimension derives, cannot be regarded as purely negative. Yet again, although it would be natural for Esler to focus on aspects of group identity, given the location of "social identity theory" throughout his work, it appears that the notion of "social norms" and the main focus of IT has a stronger explanatory power for tackling Paul's immediate concerns in Romans regarding the meaning and function of the law.

⁴⁶ Cf. Rusbult and Van Lange, "Interdependence," 369.

⁴⁷ Rusbult, Arriaga and Agnew, 377.

crucial for long-term relationships, because it is essential to coordinate the outcomes between partners to prevent extra-relationship affairs,[48] for which goal they designate particular actions and manners to be promoted or forbidden over the course of multiple interactions. For instance, by setting up a high cost on leaving the relationship, the norms can act as a check against any temptation to form an alternative relationship and minimize the negative impact of extra-relationship involvements.[49] Although "social norms" may be established "as a simple matter of convenience," they tend to "take on the characteristics of a moral obligation" over the course of the relationship.[50]

"Social norms" are not restricted only to governing behaviour, but they can also "shape cognitive experiences."[51] The cognitive influence of "social norms" can be explained in terms of the "transformation process."[52] The set of accepted norms is one of the chief elements that promote the transformation process and thus can affect human cognition, eliciting a certain type of response in accordance with specific criteria of the norms.

Social norms are manifested in "(1) regularity of behavior, (2) attempts to regain control by appealing to the norm in situations where regularity is interrupted, and (3) feelings of indignation or guilt occasioned by violations of the norm."[53] It is also to be noted that betrayal usually involves the violation of "an implicit or explicit relationship-specific norm" (i.e. "social norms").[54] In this sense, the violation of "social norms" can be understood as one of the key factors that disrupt a dyadic relationship. As will be discussed, the three factors that reveal the nature of "social norms" are particularly important for comprehending the way in which Paul indicates the sinfulness of humanity in the case of the Jewish people.

3.3.2 Aspects of brokenness: Unfaithfulness to the law and circumcision as "social norms" (Rom. 2:1–5; 2:17–3:8)

With the introduction of a Jewish imaginary interlocutor in 2:1–5 (ὦ ἄνθρωπε),[55] one who holds a representative status, Paul focuses on aspects of human sinfulness in

---

[48] Ibid.
[49] Ibid.
[50] Finkel et al., 957. Cf. Thibaut and Kelley, 128.
[51] Rusbult and Van Lange, "Why," 2058.
[52] Cf. section 2.2.6 of the present study.
[53] Rusbult, Arriaga and Agnew, 377.
[54] Ibid., 379. Cf. Finkel et al., 957.
[55] Regarding Paul's polemic in 2:1ff, several suggestions have been made by scholars. Some view the previous section as primarily concentrating on human sinfulness, but with a particular interest in Gentiles—thus, the second person singular is also one of the Gentile believers who are in fact subject to the same sin. Cf. Ben Witherington III, *Paul's Letter to the Romans: A Socio-Rhetorical Commentary* (Grand Rapids: Eerdmans, 2004), 78; Stanley K. Stowers, *A Rereading of Romans: Justice, Jews, and Gentiles* (New Haven: Yale University Press, 1994), 12. See also Runar Thorsteinsson, *Paul's Interlocutor in Romans 2: Function and Identity in the Context of Ancient Epistolography* (Eugene: Wipf & Stock, 2015), 165–88; Matthew Thiessen, *Paul and the Gentile Problem* (Oxford: Oxford University Press, 2016), 52–4. However, 2:1–5 and 2:17–29 describe a similar sort of people who are hypocritical, and the second person singular, which appears again in 2:17, suggests that Paul has kept the same focus from 2:1 to the end of Romans 2. The repeated phrase Ἰουδαίῳ τε πρῶτον καὶ Ἕλληνι

2:17-3:8 that primarily apply to the Jewish people.[56] What is notable here is the sense of superiority of the interlocutor (e.g. a guide [2:19]; an instructor, a teacher, and the embodiment of knowledge and truth [2:20]), and it is the possession of law by means of which this Jew can assert such a special identity. The parallel between 2:17 and 2:23 (boasting in God [καυχᾶσαι ἐν θεῷ][57] and in the law [ἐν νόμῳ καυχᾶσαι]) especially shows that the law is also a crucial means that connects him to God. In this context, we can observe the characterization of the law as "social norm" in two main points.

Firstly, Romans 2:18 hints at the feature of the law that corresponds to "social norms" in terms of its regulatory force. This is because it is the law through which Jews are able to know God's will (τὸ θέλημα) and distinguish what is excellent (τὰ διαφέροντα). Therefore, for Jews, it is necessary to be guided by the law in order to maintain the right relationship with God. Although the law in this section deals with diverse matters, including moral commands, keeping the law can be regarded as an obligation of the Jewish people for the sake of the covenantal partner's honour (cf. 2:23-24). In particular, the quotation from Isa. 52:5 (LXX) reflects that in explaining the meaning of having the law Paul is also interested in the framework of covenantal relationship, of which Israel's obligations are significant elements.

Secondly, just as "social norms" aim to promote prosocial behaviour so that the relationship is perpetuated, the law also intends to facilitate prosocial behaviour for the partner (God) in order to maintain a faithful relationship with ideal outcomes.[58] Because of the law, Jews are obliged to behave in a certain manner for God's sake, which may restrict their autonomy (cf. 2:7, 21-22). But the following results are apparently positive: numerous blessings are promised to those who faithfully keep the law in the original OT context,[59] and Paul himself also mentions the positive eschatological rewards that will be given to doers of the law (οἱ ποιηταὶ νόμου) (cf. 2:6-16). The prosocial act promoted by the law is also crucial on the divine side since God's honour can be affected by the acts of his people (cf. 2:23-24). Although it is a negative case, Romans 2:24 (τὸ γὰρ ὄνομα τοῦ θεοῦ δι' ὑμᾶς βλασφημεῖται ἐν τοῖς ἔθνεσιν) shows that keeping the law by his people affects God's fame. The quotation of Isa. 52:5 (LXX) shows that the name of God, which generally stands in for his honour, is partly

---

reveals that Paul's targets are Jews along with Gentiles, whose case he already mentioned in Rom. 1:18-32. For more evidence, see C.E.B. Cranfield, *A Critical and Exegetical Commentary on the Epistle to the Romans* (Edinburgh: T&T Clark, 1975), 137. See also Colin G. Kruse, *Paul's Letter to the Romans* (Nottingham: Apollos, 2012), 118-19. Jewett, *Romans*, 196 more actively supports the view that Paul is dealing with all humanity.

[56] It would weaken the general conclusion of Rom. 1:18-3:8 (cf. 3:9) to view the interlocutor in 2:17 as "a Gentile who wants to call himself a Jew" (Runar Thorsteinsson, *Roman Christianity & Roman Stoicism: A Comparative Study of Ancient Morality* [Oxford: Oxford University Press, 2010], 197). For a detailed treatment of this issue and counter arguments see Lionel J. Windsor, *Paul and the Vocation of Israel: How Paul's Jewish Identity Informs his Apostolic Ministry, with Special Reference to Romans* (Berlin: de Gruyter, 2014), 147-51.

[57] Cf. NRSV ("boast your relation to God" [2:17]).

[58] Although Paul does not explicitly refer to the Decalogue in this context, it is interesting that the Decalogue concentrates on relational aspects, for instance, the relationship between God and humans (the first through fourth commands) and the relationship between human beings (fifth through tenth). Cf. Exod. 20:3-17; Deut. 5:7-21.

[59] Cf. Deuteronomy 28.

contingent upon his partner, i.e. Israel.⁶⁰ Also, the original context of the quotation denotes that Israel is responsible for its own exile, and God is harmed by their unfaithfulness. A similar picture is conveyed in Paul's critique of the Jewish interlocutor, who dishonoured God by rejecting the prosocial requirement of the law (διὰ τῆς παραβάσεως τοῦ νόμου τὸν θεὸν ἀτιμάζεις [2:23]).

Given the relational connotations of the law according to the concept of "social norms," what Paul tries to point out with his Jewish interlocutor's unfaithfulness to the law is not merely a matter of morality, but a matter of the relationship with God. In his criticism, Paul appeals to the original purpose of the law, and in doing so, manifests the characteristic of the law as "social norms" (cf. 2:21–23). We can also see that the violation of the law arouses God's indignation (cf. 2:5, 8).⁶¹ Therefore, what Paul aims to expose is the fact that the Jewish interlocutor has violated established "social norms," which resulted in the brokenness of the relationship with God. In this sense, the Jewish interlocutor's unfaithfulness to the law points to an aspect of betrayal.

In a manner similar to the law, the function of circumcision in this context can also be understood in terms of "social norms." Circumcision, as a marker of one's relationship with God,⁶² can have a regulatory force by imposing upon the bearer a responsibility to act in a proper way in the context of the relationship with God (cf. 2:25–26; 3:1–2). Nevertheless, it cannot guarantee the superiority of those who have it, because circumcision in and of itself does not point to a faithful or complete fulfilment of what is originally expected; rather, its usefulness can only be asserted when its regulatory force is successfully realized (cf. 2:26–27). Thus, the benefits from circumcision are conditional.

In Rom. 2:25–29, Paul expounds the fundamental meaning of circumcision by presenting an uncircumcised man (ἡ ἀκροβυστία) who keeps and fulfils the requirements of the law (τὰ δικαιώματα τοῦ νόμου), as in the case of the Gentile Christians in 2:14–15.⁶³ Paul asserts that a person's physical and superficial condition cannot be a true

---

⁶⁰ Unlike the MT (Isa. 52:5), which says that the dishonouring of God's name is because of Israel's being taken away without cause, the LXX explicitly stresses that the dishonouring occurs because of Israel.

⁶¹ Cf. Rom. 5:9. See Ralph P. Martin, "Reconciliation: Romans 5:1–11," in *Romans and the People of God*, ed. Sven K. Soderlund and N.T. Wright (Grand Rapids: Eerdmans, 1999), 38 ("God's ὀργή is real in terms of his moral resistance to evil and his juridical indignation it its presence").

⁶² Timothy W. Berkley, *From a Broken Covenant to Circumcision of the Heart: Pauline Intertextual Exegesis in Romans 2:17–29* (Atlanta: SBL, 2000), 114. Cf. Rom. 4:11.

⁶³ The different outlooks on the identity of the unique Gentiles in 2:14–15 can be summarized into three main categories: 1) Gentiles who follow the requirement of the law instinctively (Dunn, *Romans 1–8*, 104; C.K. Barrett, *The Epistle to the Romans* [London: A&C Black, 1991], 42–52); 2) hypothetical figures (Thorsteinsson, *Interlocutor*, 195; Richard H. Bell, *No One Seeks for God: An Exegetical and Theological Study of Romans 1.18–3.20* [Tübingen: Mohr Siebeck, 1998], 253); and 3) Christian Gentiles (Cranfield, 155–6; N.T. Wright, "The Law in Romans 2," in *Paul and the Mosaic Law*, ed. James D.G. Dunn [Tübingen: Mohr Siebeck, 1996], 131–50; Simon J. Gathercole, "A Law unto Themselves: The Gentiles in Romans 2.14–15 Revisited," *JSNT* 85 [2002]: 27–49; Jewett, *Romans*, 212–17). Given the expression in 2:15 (τὸ ἔργον τοῦ νόμου γραπτὸν ἐν ταῖς καρδίαις αὐτῶν), which alludes to "the new covenant" in Jer. 31:33 (38:33 [LXX]) (cf. Ezek. 36:26–27), option 3) appears to be the most persuasive. The allusion to Jeremiah suggests that the fulfilment of the law by Gentiles is an eschatological event inaugurated by the gospel event (cf. 1:16–18). Moreover, just as

marker of identity. Rather, he seeks to illuminate the original meaning of circumcision as an identity marker for God's people who stay faithful to the obligations in their relationship with God. In this respect, Paul's perspective on circumcision focuses on the inward condition (cf. 2:28-29). The physical marker can only find its fundamental meaning through inward genuineness.

The emphasis on the inwardness of circumcision also represents the function of "social norms" of promoting a "transformation process" by exerting cognitive influence on one's mind.[64] The expression περιτομὴ καρδίας (2:29) shows that the targeted area of circumcision is one's inner side, the place where the genuine practice of keeping the law originates. Paul elaborates on the character of this particular type of circumcision by connecting it with πνεῦμα, which represents inwardness, in contrast to γράμμα, an epitome of outwardness (cf. 2 Cor. 3:6). Although the heart-circumcision might be seen as symbolic, it indicates the true intent of circumcision, namely, directing a person to fulfil the law. The OT allusions in Rom. 2:29 also point to the importance of the heart-circumcision in order to follow what God commands (cf. Deut. 10:16; 30:6; Jer. 4:4),[65] being closely related to the theme of the transformation of heart (cf. Jer. 31:33 [38:33, LXX]; Ezek. 36:25-26).[66] In this respect, both Rom. 2:29 (and its OT background) and IT appear to agree that one can keep prosocial attitudes toward the partner as a result of the transformation of mind, and the notion of "social norms" explains the function of circumcision for carrying out such a process. Also, the fact that the inward Jew who is circumcised in the heart receives praise from God can point to the fundamental function of "social norms" to promote benefits in the relationship. Thus, regarding the relational attitude transformed by circumcision, Peter Stuhlmacher argues that "the true Jew ... is that Jew who has received from God the Spirit and circumcision of the heart so that he no longer turns away from his creator."[67] In this respect, the fact

---

in 2:14-15, the allusion to Ezek. 36:24-28 in 2:25-29 also implies that the fulfilment of the law by Gentiles has an eschatological significance (Wright, "Law," 135-6; Berkley, 154-5). Romans 13:8-10 informs us of how the fulfilment of the law is possible for the Gentile Christians (cf. Esler, *Romans*, 333-5). In the practical teachings throughout Romans 12-15, love as the fulfilment of the law (πλήρωμα νόμου) is neither merely abstract nor symbolic. For Kyle Wells, in Rom. 13:8, it is the allusion to Deut. 30:1-10 that provides Paul a link to "the center of Deuteronomy – love" (Kyle B. Wells, *Grace and Agency in Paul and Second Temple Judaism: Interpreting the Transformation of the Heart* [Leiden: Brill, 2015], 176-7). On the contrary, seeing ἡ ἀκροβυστία in 2:26-27 as "a Gentile synagogue adherent," Windsor treats 2:17-29 as "a coherent argument in its own right" (i.e. Paul's argument about "the meaning of Jewish identity itself") separate from 2:1-16 (about "a global world-setting") (Windsor, 145-7). Although Windsor argues that his distinction does not ignore the wider argument of 1:18-3.20, his approach does not fully reflect the broader flow of Paul's thought, which wants to confirm the universal sinfulness of humanity (one of the central topics in 1:18-3:20), by overemphasizing the difference between 2:1-16 and 2:17-29. Also, Windsor's reading partly originates from his failure to notice the metaphorical sense of Ἰουδαῖος in 2:28-29 (Windsor, 145-7; 181-4). Cf. John M.G. Barclay, "Paul And Philo on Circumcision: Romans 2.25-9 in Social and Cultural Context," *NTS* 4.44 (1998): 552 ("Paul radicalizes its [circumcision] import ... prioritizing the metaphorical sense over the literal and expanding its field of reference to include heart-circumcised Gentiles"). For a similar case, see Phil. 3:3, where Paul expresses metaphorically the concept of circumcision (περιτομή) in order to identify circumcision's genuine meaning.

[64] See Section 2.2.6. of the present study.
[65] Cf. Jewett, *Romans*, 236. See Lev. 26:41; Jer. 9:25; Ezek. 44:7, 9 for negative cases.
[66] Berkley, 154.
[67] Peter Stuhlmacher, *Paul's Letter to the Romans: A Commentary* (Louisville: WJK, 1994), 50.

that the Jewish interlocutor's attitude does not correspond with the original purpose of circumcision reveals his unfaithfulness in his relationship with God and simultaneously his unfaithfulness to the law. Therefore, by perverting the meaning of circumcision, this Jew is violating the "social norms" set up in the relationship with God, which will invoke the partner's wrath (ὀργή).

In summary, we can observe another type of brokenness in the divine-human relationship with particular reference to the Jewish people as represented by Paul's interlocutor. Looking at the meaning of the law and circumcision in Rom. 2:1-3:8 in the light of IT, we have identified the fact that the law and circumcision in the text work as "social norms," and that the Jewish interlocutor's unfaithfulness to the law and circumcision can be considered as betrayal as it breaks the "social norms" set up in the relationship with God. Therefore, Romans 2:1-3:8 confirms the fact that the Jewish people possess the same status with Gentiles in terms of their relationship with God. Although aspects of their sinfulness take a different shape, what Paul signifies is the fact that they have violated "social norms" in their relationship with God, thereby committing betrayal.

3.4 The universality of brokenness (Rom. 3:9-20)

Paul's argument throughout 2:1-3:8 is summarized and emphasized again in 3:9-20: there is no one who is righteous, not even one (3:10). Paul confirms that Jews are by no means superior to others (e.g. Greeks), since both Jews and Gentiles are under sin (ὑφ' ἁμαρτίαν[68] [3:9]). The statements about the relational status of all humanity reflect what Paul targets with his claims throughout Rom. 1:18-3:8. The fact that the focus of the OT catena in 3:10-18 is on all humanity is also clear.[69] Because Paul, in contrast to the original OT contexts that mainly indict specific unrighteous people, aims to accuse all humanity, both Jews and Gentiles, the Jews who already know the original context of the quotations would be astounded to hear that they themselves belong to the category of the unrighteous.[70] Although it will be discussed in more detail in the following chapter,[71] the phrase under sin (ὑφ' ἁμαρτίαν) pictures the universal human condition of being cut off from God by their betrayal and being associated with an alternative partner.

---

[68] Also rendered as under "the power of sin" (NRSV).
[69] Gathercole appears to miss the connection between 3:9 and 3:10 when he argues that the OT catena is primarily directed toward "Israel under the power of sin" (Simon J. Gathercole, *Where Is Boasting?: Early Jewish Soteriology and Paul's Response in Romans 1-5* [Grand Rapids: Eerdmans, 2002], 213). 3:10 supports its preceding statement (3:9) by providing some proofs. We can see a number of cases in Romans in which the characteristic expression καθὼς γέγραπται is used for a similar purpose (Rom. 1:17; 2:24; 3:4, 10; 4:17; 8:36; 9:13, 33; 10:15; 11:8, 26; 15:3, 9, 21. See also 1 Cor. 1:31; 2:9; 2 Cor. 8:15; 9:9). Therefore, Gathercole's assertion that "the traditional view that a universal depravity is the primary focus in 3:10-19a needs correction" should be revised (see ibid.). Paul's use of several inclusive expressions in 3:19b (e.g. πᾶν στόμα, ὁ κόσμος, πᾶσα σάρξ) appears intentional in drawing a general conclusion. Cf. Cranfield, 196; Dunn, *Romans 1-8*, 152.
[70] Dunn, *Romans 1-8*, 146-7; Kruse, 168-9.
[71] See Chapter 6 of the present study.

The OT catena also epitomizes the brokenness of the divine-human relationship, describing human beings' total ignorance of their relationship with God.[72] In particular, Romans 3:11 and 3:18 straightforwardly show that human beings, both Jews and Greeks, do not possess the right attitude to their partner, God, and therefore do not give proper attention to him. The accusation that "all have turned aside" (πάντες ἐξέκλιναν [3:12]) also indicates that the nature of human sinfulness is betrayal.[73]

3.5 Conclusion

In this chapter we have attempted to understand the relational nature of human sinfulness in Rom. 1:18–3:20 from the IT perspective. By referring to the notion of betrayal in IT, we have recognized that what Paul describes in 1:18–32 with regard to human sinfulness (mainly in the case of the Gentiles) can be seen as aspects of betrayal because Paul characterizes sinfulness by its subversiveness and animosity against the partner (God) and the resulting formation of an alternative relationship. Although the alternative partner's identity does not surface much in the context, the allusion to Adam's story in Genesis gives us some clues to see Sin (as a personified cosmic force) as the prime suspect. Moreover, by giving the estimations from humanity's calculation behind the betrayal in terms of CL and CL-alt (CL-alt higher than CL and the current outcomes), we have seen that such calculation is proven to be erroneous from Paul's view (CL-alt lower than CL and the current outcomes). The situation of the Jewish people (2:1–3:8) represented by Paul's interlocutor is not fundamentally different from 1:18–32. We have attempted to understand the relational status of the Jewish people in their relationship with God, by looking at the relational implications of the law and circumcision with reference to the concept of "social norms" in IT. Both the law and circumcision can work as "social norms" in the relationship with God because they have a regulatory force that promotes prosocial behaviour toward the partner in order to sustain the relationship for better outcomes. Thus, the violation of the "social norms" stands for the Jewish people's unfaithfulness to their covenantal partner, which can also be defined as betrayal. Our reading of 1:18–3:20 not only expounds the meaning of human sinfulness relationally, but also hints at the solution for solving the problem of sinfulness, proposing an overarching framework through which the subsequent parts of the letter are to be read.

---

[72] For the totality of the human sinfulness, see Neyrey, *Render*, 119.
[73] In Rom. 16:17, Paul uses the verb ἐκκλίνω with the preposition ἀπό in a relational sense. Cf. BDAG, 2372.1B.

4

The Relational Significance of Jesus' Death (1)—"Making Amends for Sins": Jesus as ἱλαστήριον and the Process of Forgiveness (Rom. 3:21–26)

4.1 Introduction

From Rom. 3:21, which marks a great moment of transition from the previous situation,[1] Paul starts spelling out the significance of Jesus' death for the salvation of humanity. Paul utilizes several relational concepts and images in explicating his soteriological vision. In particular, two passages that speak of the meaning of Jesus' death deserve our attention—Romans 3:21-26 and 5:1-11. Therefore, throughout Chapters 4 and 5, we will focus on the relational significance of Jesus' death found in these two passages. That is, the significance of Jesus' death for the restoration of the divine-human relationship as well as its effect for laying the foundation of mutuality in the relationship.

In Rom. 3:21-26, forgiveness is a main issue, and Jesus as ἱλαστήριον plays a core function in the process of forgiveness. We will bring the framework of forgiveness based on IT into our discussion in order to better understand how the process of forgiveness operates in the text and what implications Jesus' death has for the process in relation to Jesus' characterization as ἱλαστήριον. The studies of forgiveness based on IT indicate that the process of forgiveness involves mutual communication, not merely an expression of unilateral benevolence, by drawing attention to the meaning of amends. In addition, we will compare some ancient perspectives on forgiveness with our IT framework to gauge to what extent the framework of IT is historically and culturally relevant. Examining the function of ἱλαστήριον on the basis of the IT framework, we will also propose an alternative way to solve an exegetical problem of the meaning of ἱλαστήριον.

---

[1] Νυνὶ δὲ in 3:21 signifies this transition. Cf. Kruse, 178; Moo, *Romans*, 221.

4.2 The process of forgiveness in IT

Unlike "victim-centered" approaches to the process of forgiveness that extensively focus on the effect of the victim's personality traits and personal values,[2] the studies based on IT draw attention to the importance of mutual endeavour for a successful restoration of the relationship.[3] Hannon et al. explain that "interdependence theory proposes that to understand the resolution of interdependence dilemmas, interaction is the name of the game; that is, both partners' actions matter."[4] In this regard, IT focuses not only on the effect of a victim's gesture of accepting an apology but also a perpetrator's role of making amends. Hannon et al. indicate that mutual interactions for forgiveness can bring about positive effects to both partners.

> We propose that both perpetrator amends and victim forgiveness play key roles in the successful resolution of betrayal incidents and that betrayal resolution is beneficial to relationships from the perspective of both victims and perpetrators.[5]

Such an understanding of the process of forgiveness can be explicated in terms of "transformation of motivation" in IT. In the "given situation," it is more natural for victims to react in a negative manner to perpetrators (i.e. "gut-level reactions"), for instance, attempting vengeance or seeking retribution.[6] Nevertheless, through the transformation process, victims can experience a change of attitude by "tak[ing] into account considerations extending beyond direct self-interest, including long-term goals," transferring to the "effective situation."[7]

The acts of betrayal, forgiveness and making amends are core concepts that constitute the whole process of forgiveness. Each element explicates a specific part or moment of the process. Hannon et al. define betrayal as "the perceived violation of an implicit or explicit relationship-relevant norm."[8] Regarding the effect of betrayal on victims, Hannon et al. put it as follows,

> Given that betrayals are harmful to victims and violate morality-based expectations, victims typically experience righteous indignation, believe that the perpetrator has incurred an interpersonal debt, and perceive that such incidents bode poorly for the relationships.[9]

---

[2] For instance, Everett L. Worthington, *Handbook of Forgiveness* (New York: Routledge, 2005). Cf. Peggy A. Hannon et al., "In the Wake of Betrayal: Amends, Forgiveness, and the Resolution of Betrayal," *PR* 17.2 (2010): 253.
[3] Hannon et al., 253.
[4] Ibid., 255.
[5] Ibid., 254.
[6] Ibid.
[7] Ibid. For the process of transformation, see Chapter 2 (2.2.6).
[8] Cf. Finkel et al., "Betrayal."
[9] Hannon et al., 254. Cf. Mark R. Leary et al., "The Causes, Phenomenology, and Consequences of Hurt Feelings," *JPSP* 74.5 (1998): 1225–37.

Hence, it is vital to resolve the problem of betrayal in order to make the relationship persist.[10]

Concerning forgiveness, Hannon et al. regard forgiveness as "both psychological *and* behavioral event."[11] Accordingly, forgiveness can be defined as "the victim's willingness to (a) forgo vengeance and demands for retribution and [psychological] (b) react to the betrayal in a constructive, less judgemental manner [behavioural]."[12]

The concept of making amends also reflects both dimensions. Hannon et al. define making amends as "accepting responsibility for an act of betrayal [psychological], offering genuine atonement for one's action [behavioural]."[13] Amends can be either explicit or not so explicit, but it should be sincere in order to function properly, otherwise it might "backfire."[14] Hannon et al. explain that amends can work as "a form of situation selection,"[15] offering a chance to both partners "to move toward interaction opportunities with superior behavioral options and outcomes."[16] The illustration below shows how amends work for forgiveness and reconciliation.

> When John communicates that he feels betrayed, Mary may calmly discuss the incident with him. Recognizing that her actions hurt him, she may offer amends, apologizing for her actions or making things right by atoning for the harm she has caused. In turn, John may find it easier to let go of his hurt and anger. John's gradual movement toward forgiveness may also make it easier for Mary to offer further amends, continuing to respond in a loving and benevolent manner. Thus, perpetrator amends and victim forgiveness may be mutually reinforcing over the course of extended interaction.[17]

---

[10] Hannon et al., 254.

[11] Ibid (emphasis original). Hannon et al. indicate that it is the psychological aspect of forgiveness (e.g. "the set of motivational changes") that has been mostly emphasized by previous studies (see ibid.). Cf. Michael E. McCullough, Everett L. Worthington, and Kenneth C. Rachal, "Interpersonal Forgiving in Close Relationships," *JPSP* 73.2 (1997): 321–2.

[12] Hannon et al., 254. This definition draws on Finkel et al., "Betrayal."

[13] Hannon et al., 255. Unlike the theological usage of atonement, here the word "atonement" is used in a more general sense (e.g. "propitiation of an offended or injured person, by reparation of wrong or injury"). See Oxford English Dictionary 4.a. (www.oed.com/view/Entry/12599?redirectedFrom=atonement#eid).

[14] Hannon et al., 255.

[15] What Hannon et al. mean by "situational selection" is that by choosing to offer amends, the relationship can move toward the situation favourable for forgiveness and reconciliation. In suggesting such a transitional stage, Hannon et al. signify that the process of forgiveness is not a one-off event (i.e. from betrayal directly to forgiveness) but offering and accepting amends is a mediating stage on the way to reaching forgiveness and reconciliation (i.e. from betrayal through [offering and accepting] amends to forgiveness). Regarding the concept of "situation selection," Kelley suggests a method termed "transition lists" to "make possible a delineation of the sequential and temporal constraints under which interdependent persons interact" (e.g. from one outcome matrix to another one). Cf. Harold H. Kelley, "The Theoretical Description of Interdependence by Means of Transition Lists," *JPSP* 47.5 (1984): 956. Kelley argues that "transition lists" can represent the fact that "people are interdependent not only in how they control their own and each other's immediate outcomes, but also in their movement through a network of interdependence situations" (ibid., 960).

[16] Hannon et al., 255.

[17] Ibid. Although a directly parallel example of "gradual movement toward forgiveness" and "further amends" is not readily apparent in Romans, Romans 5:1–5 alludes to a gradual development of the intimacy of the divine-human relationship as a post-forgiveness and post-reconciliation event.

Given that the process of forgiveness and reconciliation can be mutual and can affect the quality of an ongoing relationship, the victim's attitude is also important for the perpetrator to offer amends appropriately, since the perpetrator may attempt to activate a "defence mechanism" to justify their misbehaviour if the victim exhibits a reproachful attitude toward them.[18] It is possible that the perpetrator can suffer from "sadness, shame or guilt."[19] Therefore, it may also be difficult for perpetrators to find a proper way to make amends.[20]

Unlike conventional perspectives that see forgiveness as "the endpoint," Hannon et al. attempt to examine "what transpires following victim forgiveness."[21] Based on IT, Hannon et al. try to take account of the lively nature of interpersonal relationships (e.g. ongoingness). They adopt "a broadened time frame, examining not only amends and forgiveness but also reconciliation,"[22] identifying that successful betrayal resolution, in turn, affects "relationship quality" of the ongoing relationship.[23] According to Hannon et al., for a successful betrayal resolution, it is crucial that the betrayal event "no longer colors interaction."[24]

4.3 Recompense and forgiveness (and reconciliation) according to ancient perspectives

Several ancient materials also note the significant role of perpetrators for the process of forgiveness. As John Fitzgerald finds, in a number of occasions the ancient writers exhibit what is regarded as "the standard paradigm of reconciliation," in which the perpetrator's willingness to offer recompense is vital for eliciting forgiveness from the victim, leading to reconciliation.[25] Polybius 21.16.9 shows a case in which the one (Antiochus) negotiates peace by offering some reparation to the other (Rome).[26] Fitzgerald indicates that a plea or appeal made to the offended party is a non-material form of reparation, though it is not always effective (e.g. Gen. 50:15–21 [Joseph's brothers' plea]; Plutarch, *Pel.* 26.2 [Alexander, tyrant of Pherae, to Pelopidas]; *P.Mich.* VIII.502, 7–8 [Valerius Gemellus to his brother]; *Il.* 9.496f [Pseudo-Demetrius's plea to his friend]).[27]

---

[18] Cf. R.F. Baumeister, A. Stillwell and S.R. Wotman, "Victim and Perpetrator Accounts of Interpersonal Conflict: Autobiographical Narratives about Anger," *JPSP* 59.5 (1990): 994–1005.
[19] Cf. R.F. Baumeister, A. Stillwell and T.F. Heatherton, "Personal Narratives About Guilt: Role in Action Control and Interpersonal Relationships," *BASP* 17.1–2 (1995): 173–98.
[20] Hannon et al., 255.
[21] Ibid., 256.
[22] Ibid. Cf. Suzanne Freedman, "Forgiveness and Reconciliation: The Importance of Understanding How They Differ," *CV* 42.3 (1998): 203. Although, unlike IT, Freedman appears not to focus on the importance of a perpetrator's role in forgiveness, her distinction between forgiveness and reconciliation helps us to recognize that the two processes are not to be conflated, despite the fact that the latter frequently follows the former in a continuous manner.
[23] Hannon et al., 256.
[24] Ibid.
[25] John T. Fitzgerald, "Paul and Paradigm Shifts: Reconciliation and Its Linkage Group," in *Paul Beyond the Judaism/Hellenism Divide*, ed. Troels Engberg-Pedersen (Louisville: WJK, 2001), 251.
[26] Fitzgerald, 322 (n. 58).
[27] See also *BGU* III.846; *P.Giss.* 17. These examples are from Fitzgerald, 248–52.

Other scholars point out a similar pattern of forgiveness/reconciliation in ancient texts. Upon examining the usage of the vocabularies related to reconciliation (διαλλάσσω/καταλλάσσω) in the ancient Greek sources, Howard Marshall observes that a certain means can be involved in the process of reconciliation in the case of "X gives up his own anger against Y."[28] For instance, 2 Maccabees shows that although Israel's sin evoked God's wrath upon them and consequently sufferings as the divine punishment (cf. 2 Macc. 7:18), the punishment can also be recognized as "a means of inducing God to forgive" the national sin.[29] 2 Maccabees 7:37-38 shows such recognition:

> I, like my brothers, give up body and life for the laws of our ancestors, appealing to God to show mercy soon to our nation and by trials and plagues to make you confess that he alone is God, and through me and my brothers to bring to an end the wrath of the Almighty that has justly fallen on our whole nation.
>
> 2 Macc. 7:37-38 [NRSV]

Although the distinction between forgiveness and reconciliation is not so clearcut here, since reconciliation seems to presuppose forgiveness, we can still observe that a certain type of amends is also in effect for the restoration of the divine-human relationship.[30]

Stanley Porter also observes a similar pattern in various ancient Greek writings (up to the sixth-century CE) that utilize the verb καταλλάσσω. Although Porter concedes that the means of reconciliation is often unclear when καταλλάσσω is used in the passive voice,[31] nevertheless, there are some meaningful cases from Porter's examples that illuminate the means through which reconciliation is possible. For instance, several examples of the case when "the subject effects reconciliation by giving up its own anger against another party (passive voice form),"[32] which is similar to Marshall's aforementioned category, imply that a certain form of means of reconciliation operates between the two parties (e.g. Euripides, *Iph. aul.* 1157-58;[33] *Resp.* 8.566E;[34] *Vita Aesopi* 2.100[35]).[36]

---

[28] I. Howard Marshall, *Jesus the Saviour: Studies in New Testament Theology* (London: SPCK, 1990), 269. In this case ("the category D"), διαλλάσσω/καταλλάσσω is used in the passive voice (ibid). Marshall's three other categories are "A. X persuades Y and Z to give up their mutual anger (active); B. X persuades Y to give up Y's anger against X (active); C. X persuades Y to give up Y's anger against X (passive/deponent)."

[29] Ibid., 261; Stanley E. Porter, Καταλλάσσω *in Ancient Greek Literature, with Reference to the Pauline Writings* (Cordoba: Ediciones el Almendro, 1994), 62. Cf. 2 Macc. 7:33 ("he will again be reconciled [καταλλαγήσεται] with his own servants").

[30] Apart from *Ajax* 743-74, 2 Maccabees contains the first religious usages of καταλλάσσω (1:5; 7:33; 8:29). Cf. Porter, Καταλλάσσω, 16.

[31] Ibid., 17. For instance, P.Oxy. I 104.25-27 (cf. ibid., 67).

[32] Cf. Ibid., 17.

[33] Ibid., 25.

[34] Ibid., 34 (though it is rather implicit).

[35] Ibid., 46 (the examples are at least before the first century CE).

[36] Including 2 Maccabees.

Although Paul does not simply accept "the standard paradigm" of his day without any modification, it still plays a crucial role as the basis of a "paradigm shift" observable in his writings (e.g. Rom. 5:10-11; 2 Cor. 5:18-20).[37] What makes Paul's paradigm distinguishable is the reversal of roles for offering "reparation": it is God, the offended party, who offers "reparation" payment through Jesus' death.[38] Fitzgerald also observes a similar paradigm shift in Rom. 3:25, in which Paul designates God as "the one who offers the sacrifice," overturning the OT paradigm of sacrificial ritual.[39] However, along with the radical paradigm shift in Paul, we should remember that Paul's modification is not *ex nihilo*. It is still based on the standard paradigm because it accepts the necessity of "reparations."[40] Marshall and Porter's linguistic analyses reflect a similar point. What distinguishes Paul from others is the fact that, despite the result that is similar to "X gives up his own anger against Y," Paul signifies that God, the victim, takes the initiative in the programme of forgiveness and reconciliation.[41] Therefore, every element of the standard paradigm is still operative in Paul's case, but is used differently from his contemporaries.[42]

To summarize, we find a crucial similarity between "the standard paradigm" in the ancient world and our IT framework concerning the importance of the perpetrator's role, since it is the perpetrator who makes reparation or amends in order to restore a broken relationship. Moreover, given that "the standard paradigm" is still a meaningful seedbed for Paul's innovative thinking, it is equally beneficial to analyze to what extent Paul's understanding of forgiveness and reconciliation is distinctive in the light of IT.

4.4 Forgiveness in Rom. 3:21-26: From an interpersonal perspective

Scholars have noted the rarity of the concept of forgiveness in Paul.[43] The only reference to forgiveness in Romans (ἀφέθησαν [4:7]) is quoted from Ps. 31:1 (LXX).[44] Nevertheless, keeping our focus on the relational dynamics described in the text, we

---

[37] Cf. Fitzgerald, 252-7.
[38] Ibid., 254-5.
[39] Ibid., 247.
[40] Ibid., 256-7.
[41] Marshall, *Saviour*, 263; Stanley E. Porter, "Paul's Concept of Reconciliation, Twice More," in *Paul and His Theology*, ed. Stanley E. Porter (Leiden: Brill, 2006), 132-3.
[42] Porter, "Reconciliation," 133. See also Porter, Καταλλάσσω, 159-60; Marshall, *Saviour*, 269.
[43] Ernst Käsemann, "The Saving Significance of the Death of Jesus in Paul," in *Perspectives on Paul*, trans. Margaret Kohl (London: SCM, 1971), 44; Dunn, *Theology*, 327-8.
[44] Cf. Krister Stendahl, "The Apostle Paul and the Introspective Conscience of the West," in *Paul among Jews and Gentiles* (Philadelphia: Fortress, 1976), 82. See also ibid., 23-5. Stendahl's main target is the individualistic Western introspective tendency in interpreting Paul (e.g. Rudolf Bultmann). Some scholars tend to limit the importance of forgiveness in a different way, arguing that the concepts of forgiveness are not originally Pauline, but depend upon the early Christian tradition. Cf. Cilliers Breytenbach, "Forgiveness in Early Christian Tradition," in *Grace, Reconciliation, Concord: The Death of Christ in Graeco-Roman Metaphors* (Leiden: Brill, 2010), 291-2. A similar point is stressed in Cilliers Breytenbach, "'Christus Starb Für Uns.' Zur Tradition Und Paulinischen Rezeption Der Sogenannten 'Sterbeformeln,'" *NTS* 49.4 (2003): 447-75.

find that the issue of forgiveness is a central theme in Rom. 3:21–26. Moreover, given that reconciliation, for which forgiveness is a prerequisite, is a distinctive Pauline soteriological concept, forgiveness is an indispensable element for understanding the saving significance of Jesus' death in Paul.[45]

Of course, the Jewish cultic background of 3:21–26 has been a source of discussion about forgiveness in this passage.[46] However, it cannot be the only background against which Paul explains the meaning of Jesus' death. Even in 3:21–26, there are several different words from distinctive backgrounds besides the sacrificial-cultic context (e.g. ἀπολύτρωσις/χάρις).[47] Also, as several scholars maintain that the cultic background cannot be a proper source for the concept of reconciliation in Paul,[48] adhering to a specific background does not aid in understanding the positive change brought by the Christ-event as a whole. Rather, by focusing on relational structure from an interpersonal perspective, we will show how forgiveness and reconciliation in Romans relate to one another.

Therefore, our aim is to verify the fundamental features of the relational structure reflected in the text by examining several distinctive metaphors. Our approach is primarily distinguished by the manner in which we view the theme of forgiveness. By understanding forgiveness from an interpersonal viewpoint, we are not confined to the lexical realms of the notions of forgiveness and reconciliation; instead, we will treat them as concepts that encompass the lexical dimension. Therefore, we will speak of forgiveness/reconciliation without directly referencing a specific lexical term (e.g. ἄφεσις/καταλλαγή), though such terms do provide help when the issue of forgiveness or reconciliation is present in the text. Our aim is not to simplify the variegated backgrounds of the text; rather, we will see how such backgrounds commonly point to the central relational situation described in the text.

In fact, we do not go against the flow of the text in seeing that forgiveness and reconciliation are linked to one another. Although we believe there to be a meaningful connection between the two concepts from the text, some scholars have

---

[45] Similarly, Buchanan argues that in Paul justification and forgiveness are "synonyms and metaphors dealing with the same reality." See George Wesley Buchanan, "The Day of Atonement and Paul's Doctrine of Redemption," *NovT* 32.3 (1990): 238.

[46] Cf. C.H. Dodd, "Ἱλάσκεσθαι, Its Cognates, Derivatives and Synonyms in the Septuagint," *JTS* 32 (1931): 352–60.

[47] There are different outlooks on the Jewish cultic background in 3:21–26. A number of scholars support a non-sacrificial reading of this passage, e.g. Sam K. Williams, *Jesus' Death as Saving Event: The Background and Origin of a Concept* (Missoula: Scholars, 1975); David Seeley, *The Noble Death: Graeco-Roman Martyrology and Paul's Concept of Salvation* (Sheffield: JSOT Press, 1989); Douglas A. Campbell, *The Rhetoric of Righteousness in Romans 3.21-26* (Sheffield: Sheffield Academic, 1992); Stowers, *Rereading*; B. Hudson McLean, *The Cursed Christ: Mediterranean Expulsion Rituals and Pauline Soteriology* (Sheffield: Sheffield Academic, 1996); Daniel G. Powers, *Salvation through Participation* (Leuven: Peeters, 2001). For a detailed review of these scholars, see Jarvis Williams, *Christ Died for Our Sins: Representation and Substitution in Romans and Their Jewish Martyrological Background* (Cambridge: James Clarke & Co, 2015), 14–16.

[48] Cf. Joseph A. Fitzmyer, "Reconciliation in Pauline Theology," in *To Advance the Gospel: New Testament Studies*, Second Edition. (Grand Rapids: Eerdmans, 1998), 171; Cilliers Breytenbach, "Salvation of the Reconciled (with a Note on the Background of Paul's Metaphor of Reconciliation)," in *Grace, Reconciliation, Concord: The Death of Christ in Graeco-Roman Metaphors* (Leiden: Brill, 2010), 175–6.

stressed the distinction between the two concepts in Romans. Fitzmyer negatively speaks of reconciliation in Rom. 3:21–26, arguing that the passage has "nothing to do with reconciliation,"[49] because Paul does not use a sacrificial image when he speaks of reconciliation.[50] For that reason, Fitzmyer disagrees with Käsemann's interpretation, which accepts the close connection between καταλλάσσειν and ἱλάσκεσθαι.[51] Fitzmyer contends that "in associating καταλλάσσειν and ἱλάσκεσθαι, he [Käsemann] does what Paul has never done, and this enables him to attribute to the figure of reconciliation a cultic nuance and a liturgical background which it does not have."[52] However, the continuity between forgiveness and reconciliation is as crucial as the distinction. As Breytenbach correctly points out, in Paul's system the two distinctive semantic fields merge into one.[53] Although Fitzmyer might be correct in arguing that the two concepts have different origins, they are closely tied to each other in Paul's portrayal of the restoration of the divine-human relationship.

In particular, there are several similarities between 3:21–26 and 5:1–11 that reflect the continuity between forgiveness and reconciliation. Above all, the Christ-event is the common denominator. Barclay suggests that it is the theme of the Christ-gift that closely joins the two passages. According to Barclay, Paul deals with "the justice of the Christ-gift" in 3:21–26, while it is the "costly significance" of the gift that is highlighted in 5:1–11.[54] Also, in both passages, Paul explains the meaning of Jesus' death, and its effect on the divine-human relationship. Even though Paul is using distinctive relational terms in 5:1–11 that cannot be found in 3:21–26 (εἰρήνη [5:1]; καταλλάσσω [5:10]; καταλλαγή [5:11]), what both 3:21–26 and 5:1–11 point to is fundamentally the same—namely, the restoration of the broken relationship. The elements that constitute the situation in 3:21–26 are also present in 5:1–11, and the past status of humanity as the weak, ungodly, sinners and enemies (cf. 5:6–10) necessitates forgiveness in order to accomplish complete reconciliation.[55] There are also key words held in common: blood (αἷμα) appears in both 3:25 and 5:9, symbolizing Jesus' death; and the character of humanity that enters the reconciled relationship is regarded as righteous (δίκαιος) (cf. 3:24, 26; 5:9). These parallels between 3:21–26 and 5:1–11 offer helpful clues for recognizing that both passages focus on a similar relational issue, and 3:21–26 is also significant for comprehending aspects of the reconciliation between God and humanity.

---

[49] Fitzmyer, "Reconciliation," 170.
[50] Ibid., 182–3.
[51] Cf. Ernst Käsemann, "Some Thoughts on the Theme 'The Doctrine of Reconciliation in the New Testament,'" in *The Future of Our Religious Past: Essays in Honour of Rudolf Bultmann*, ed. James M. Robinson, trans. Charles E. Carlston and Robert. P. Scharlemann (London: SCM, 1971), 50.
[52] Fitzmyer, "Reconciliation," 171–2. According to Fitzmyer, the concept of reconciliation derives from "social or political associations of interpersonal, intergroup relationships quite independently of cult." There is a consensus among scholars to find the origin of the concept of reconciliation from the Graeco-Roman background of interpersonal (or intergroup) relationships. See also Section 4.3 of the present study.
[53] Cilliers Breytenbach, *Versöhnung: Eine Studie zur paulinischen Soteriologie* (Neukirchen-Vluyn: Neukirchener Verlag, 1989), 221.
[54] Barclay, *Gift*, 475.
[55] See also ἀσέβεια (1:18) – ἀσεβῶν (5:6).

4.5 Situating Rom. 3:21–26 within the process of forgiveness in IT: God as "victim," humanity as "perpetrators," sin as "betrayal" and ἱλαστήριον as "amends"

Building on our discussion thus far, we will situate Rom. 3:21–26 within the process of forgiveness in IT. Using IT, we can locate the moment of forgiveness depicted in 3:21–26. Here, Paul deals with the problem generated by human sin that can be understood as betrayal. In that picture, God can be considered "victim," while humanity in general takes the role of "perpetrator."[56] Also, Romans 3:21–26 describes God's acts to bring about change in the broken relationship, such as passing over (πάρεσις) and forbearance (ἀνοχή). As can be seen from 3:26, such acts aim to change humanity's status in the relationship with God. Therefore, given this relational situation, 3:21–26 can be regarded as one example of the restoration of a broken relationship, for which event forgiveness is indispensable.

In addition, there are other concepts that also show the relational point of view held in the passage. Although δικαιοσύνη θεοῦ in 3:21 (cf. 1:17) signifies the saving activity of God through the Christ-event, we can detect the relational implications from the cognates of δικαιοσύνη in 3:21–26. For instance, although 3:24 can be understood as denoting the declaration of innocence, it simultaneously connotes the status of being put in the right relationship when human sin is viewed as "betrayal."[57] Also, in 3:26 we cannot overlook the relational connotations of δικ- terms, because God's demonstration of δικαιοσύνη reflects his faithful attitude toward his partners (as can be seen from his forbearance [ἀνοχῇ])[58]: making righteous the one who trusts in Jesus (τὸν ἐκ πίστεως Ἰησοῦ) not only entails a forensic or ontological renewal, but it also necessarily includes the renewal of a relational status.[59]

What draws our attention is Jesus' role within this situation. Although it is clear that a primary actor in the scene is God, God's saving activity is expressed through Jesus.

---

[56] Cf. Chapter 3 of this study.
[57] For Ziesler, the restoration of the relationship is coincidental with forensic and ethical transformation (John A. Ziesler, *The Meaning of Righteousness in Paul: A Linguistic and Theological Enquiry* [Cambridge: Cambridge University Press, 1972], 192). Campbell also recognizes the relational implication of δικαιούμενοι ("humanity is being reshaped relationally and ethically") (Campbell, *Rhetoric*, 174). See also Richard K. Moore, *Paul's Concept of Justification: God's Gift of a Right Relationship* (Eugene: Wipf & Stock, 2015), 197–8 ("a right relationship"). It is hard to separate the relational connotation of δικ- terms from the OT usage of צְדָקָה in a covenantal context (e.g. Gen. 15:6). Although Paul unmistakably deals with the divine-human relationship at a universal level in Romans 1–8, Paul is based on the expanded understanding of the covenant as reflected in Romans 4 (especially 4:23–25) (*pace* Richard K. Moore, "N. T. Wright's Treatment of 'Justification' in The New Testament for Everyone," *ExpT* 125.10 [2014]: 483–6). For Wright's response, which stresses the covenantal nuance of δικ- terms, see N.T. Wright, "Translating Δικαιοσύνη: A Response," *ExpT* 125.10 (2014): 487–90.
[58] Bruce W. Longenecker, "Sharing in Their Spiritual Blessings? The Story of Israel in Galatians and Romans," in *Narrative Dynamics in Paul: A Critical Assessment*, ed. Bruce W. Longenecker (Louisville: WJK, 2002), 63.
[59] Dunn also suggests a similar point of view in his understanding of the meaning of δικαιόω ("the basic idea assumed by Paul was of a relationship in which God acts on behalf of his human partner, first in calling Israel into and then in sustaining Israel in its covenant with him") (Dunn, *Theology*, 344).

Several expressions signify that Jesus' role occupies crucial positions, particularly in terms of a forgiveness process.[60] In Rom. 3:25, Paul introduces a decisive act of God, that is, to put forward Jesus as ἱλαστήριον. Romans 3:25 not only supplements what precedes (3:24), but also expands and develops the previous idea. In particular, in 3:25, ἱλαστήριον is a metaphor that governs the whole verse and the following verse (3:26), detailing the meaning of Jesus' death for the restoration of the divine-human relationship. Therefore, given this significance of the ἱλαστήριον in Rom. 3:21–26, in order to understand the transitional movement in the entire passage, it is important to grasp what Paul means by his presentation of Jesus as ἱλαστήριον.

4.5.1 Three different outlooks on ἱλαστήριον: Expiation, propitiation and the mercy seat

In Paul's letters, the term ἱλαστήριον is a *hapax legomenon* (Rom. 3:25).[61] However, its significance can hardly be discounted, since it summarizes and characterizes what Paul explicates about the salvific meaning of Jesus' death. Therefore, because of its theological significance along with the interpretive ambiguity, the debate has continued to find out what Paul actually means by ἱλαστήριον. As a result, we can note three different outlooks on the meaning of ἱλαστήριον: 1) (means of) expiation, 2) (means of) propitiation and 3) the mercy seat.

C. H. Dodd has argued that the ἱλαστήριον in Rom. 3:25 should be understood as expiation.[62] Dodd's insistence is based on a) the translations of the Hebrew word כִּפֶּר and its derivatives into words other than those of the ἱλάσκεσθαι class, b) the Hebrew counterparts to the ἱλάσκεσθαι class being other than כִּפֶּר and its derivatives[63] and c) the cases in which כִּפֶּר and its derivatives have been translated into the words of the ἱλάσκεσθαι class. Analysis of these three categories has led Dodd to argue that unlike the pagan usage, the ἱλάσκεσθαι class in "Hellenistic Judaic" literature hardly reflects the meaning related to propitiation in the religious context.[64] Rather, the concepts behind the words are more closely related to expiation or forgiveness. Käsemann is also in favour of this view.[65] He problematizes other options (e.g. the mercy seat), indicating that it would be paradoxical if Christ became the place of the offering while at the same time being the content of the sacrifice.[66] The fact that the Roman congregations were mostly Gentiles who were not familiar with specific Jewish rites is another reason.[67]

---

[60] For instance, διὰ πίστεως Ἰησοῦ Χριστοῦ, τῆς ἀπολυτρώσεως τῆς ἐν Χριστῷ Ἰησοῦ (3:24), ἐν τῷ αὐτοῦ αἵματι (3:25) and ἐκ πίστεως Ἰησοῦ (3:26).

[61] Another occurrence in the New Testament is Heb. 9:5. The word ἱλαστήριον appears twenty-eight times in the LXX.

[62] Dodd, "Ἱλάσκεσθαι," 352–60.

[63] The four exceptional cases that can be viewed as connoting the idea of propitiation are Ps. 105:30, Zech. 7:2, 8:22, and Mal. 1:9. However, Dodd thinks that Zech. 7:2 and Mal. 1:9 reflect "a distinct tone of contempt" (cf. ibid., 355–6).

[64] Non-religious usages of c) can be found in Gen. 32:20 and Prov. 16:14.

[65] However, Käsemann thinks the notion of forgiveness is too weak (see Käsemann, *Romans*, 97).

[66] Käsemann, *Romans*, 97. See also Cranfield, 214. However, see the exception in Heb. 9:11–28 where Jesus is simultaneously described as both a high priest and a sacrifice (instead of goats and calves).

[67] See Käsemann, *Romans*, 97.

However, several scholars suggest another perspective. Leon Morris argues that the ἱλαστήριον should be viewed as a means of propitiation. Morris reacts strongly against Dodd, arguing that there are several LXX passages in which the derivatives of ἱλάσκεσθαι speak of propitiation (e.g. 1 Sam. 6:3; Ps. 105:30; Sir. 45:23; Zech. 7:2; 8.22; Mal. 1:9 [ἐξιλάσκομαι]; Exod. 32:14; 2 Kgs 24:4 [ἱλάσκομαι]).[68] Adolf Deissmann advocated this option before Morris,[69] but his main target was the traditionally accepted interpretation, that is, the mercy seat.[70] By testing several cases from the LXX and other Greek writings in which the meaning of ἱλαστήριον is far from the mercy seat,[71] Deissmann insists that "it is not correct to take the LXX's equation of words as being an equation of ideas."[72] David Hill indicates the presence of divine wrath in the OT, insisting that "in actual fact the idea of the 'wrath of God' is deeply embedded there, but it is a responsible anger, a holy reaction caused only, but inevitably, by sin and wrong-doing."[73] Also, the broader context of 1:18–3:20, which underscores aspects of human sin against God, shows that human beings are under God's wrath. For that reason, they need "the removal of wrath."[74] Morris also indicates the deficiency of the mercy seat interpretation. Morris argues that ἱλαστήριον can refer to "the ledge of the altar" (Ezek. 43:14), and that in contrast to the original circumstance of the tabernacle, "hidden from public gaze," the context of Rom. 3:25 highlights openness.[75] Others, such as Cranfield, also accept the propitiatory connotation of ἱλαστήριον. Seeing ἱλαστήριον as "propitiatory sacrifice,"[76] Cranfield also questions Dodd's analysis, indicating that "it is by no means true that all ideas of divine wrath are alien."[77] In a similar vein, McLean generally agrees with this interpretation, suggesting that ἱλαστήριον should be interpreted as "gift to God," as neither "sacrificial victim" nor "the mercy seat."[78]

---

[68] Morris, *Romans*, 179. See also David Hill, *Greek Words and Hebrew Meanings: Studies in the Semantics of Soteriological Terms* (Cambridge: Cambridge University Press, 1967) (see Chapter 2).
[69] More specifically, Deissmann sees ἱλαστήριον as "propitiatory gift," based on his observation of Dion Chrysostom, *Or.* xi and the inscriptions of Cos No. 81; 347 (Adolf Deissmann, *Bible Studies*, trans. Alexander Grieve, Second Edition. [Edinburgh: T&T Clark, 1909], 130–1).
[70] Ibid., 124–35. For instance, Luther translated ἱλαστήριον as *Gnadenstuhl*.
[71] E.g. Exod. 25:16; Ezek. 43:14; *Vit. Mos.* 3.8; *Fuga* 19; *Cher.* 8; Symmachian translation of Gen. 6:16; Jos. *Ant.* 16.7; 4 Macc. 17:22 (cf. ibid., 127–9).
[72] Ibid., 127.
[73] Hill, 25.
[74] Morris, *Romans*, 179.
[75] Cf. ibid., 181.
[76] Cranfield, 216. Cranfield finds no substantial difference between propitiation and a means of propitiation.
[77] Ibid., 215.
[78] McLean, 43–6. McLean's insistence is mainly based on the examples originally suggested by Deissmann. Similarly, Stefan Schreiber, "Das Weihegeschenk Gottes: Eine Deutung Des Todes Jesu in Röm 3,25," *ZNW* 97 (2006): 88–110 (ἱλαστήριον as "das Weihegeschenk" [but offered by God on behalf of mankind]). See also idem, "Weitergedacht: Das Versöhnende Weihegeschenk Gottes in Röm 3,25," *ZNW* 106.2 (2015): 201–15. Although some scholars refuse to accept the Hellenistic background of the concept in favour of the Jewish background (for instance Dodd or Bailey), as Finlan points out, regardless of the Roman congregation's level of biblical literacy, Paul most likely knew how ἱλαστήριον would have sounded to readers of different backgrounds (Stephen Finlan, *The Background and Content of Paul's Cultic Atonement Metaphors* [Leiden: Brill, 2004], 142–3. Here, Finlan agrees with Matthew Black, *Romans* [London: Oliphants, 1973], 69). See also Oakes, *Romans*, 155 ("he [the Pompeian Holconius as a typical Gentile] might still be more likely to hear the specific term ἱλαστήριον [3:25] in relation to Graeco-Roman stories about sacrifices ... that turned away the wrath of gods [i.e. as "propitiation"] rather than as the cover of the ark of the covenant").

There are several scholars who do not play off option 1) against 2). For instance, Dunn admits that both ideas of propitiation and expiation are implied in ἱλαστήριον, although he is inclined to see that Paul's main intent is to describe God as "offerer of the sacrifice."[79] Other interpreters, such as Barrett and Ziesler, hold a similar point of view. They acknowledge that it is unhelpful to rule out the notion of propitiation, though they point out several vulnerabilities of this interpretation.[80] Finlan also points to the close link between the notion of expiation and of propitiation, arguing that "expiation emerges from propitiation ... it is because the deity is thought to be appeased, that sin is thought to be cleansed" (cf. Lev. 16:30; Ps. 51:1–2).[81]

Traditionally, option 3) has been preferred.[82] Based on the general usage of ἱλαστήριον in the LXX as the equivalent to כַּפֹּרֶת, T. W. Manson has claimed that ἱλαστήριον can be best understood when it is interpreted as the mercy seat, which stands for "the place where God shows mercy to men."[83] In a similar vein, Stuhlmacher argues that in 3:25, Paul speaks of a new כַּפֹּרֶת, one which substitutes for the old one in Jerusalem's temple.[84] Likewise, Jewett argues that Jesus became "a new institutional vehicle of atonement."[85] Daniel Bailey also supports this point of view, arguing that "past studies of ἱλαστήριον have often allowed theological consideration to overshadow lexicography."[86] Bailey focuses on the usage of ἱλαστήριον (not its cognates [e.g. ἱλάσκεσθαι/ἐξιλάσασθαι]), which can be viewed as the mercy seat in the Pentateuch (LXX). Based on his analysis of the LXX and the context of Rom. 3:21–26, which alludes to the Song of Moses in Exodus 15, Bailey concludes that, as in Exodus, Jesus as ἱλαστήριον functions as "the centre of the sanctuary and focus of both the revelation of God and atonement of sin."[87] Although the lack of an article before ἱλαστήριον is frequently considered as counter-evidence for such an interpretation, an anarthrous

---

[79] Dunn, *Romans 1–8*, 171. Dunn also discusses the possibility of the mercy seat interpretation, suggesting that ἱλαστήριον might allude to the Day of Atonement ritual (ibid., 180). Daniel Stökl Ben Ezra argues that the continual Jewish fasting customs in the first century influenced the early Christian understanding of Jesus as *kapporet*, insisting that Christian Jews might still observe Jewish fasts, including Yom Kippur (Daniel Stökl Ben Ezra, *The Impact of Yom Kippur on Early Christianity* [Tübingen: Mohr Siebeck, 2003], 330–1).

[80] Barrett, *Romans*, 73–4; John A. Ziesler, *Paul's Letter to the Romans* (London: SCM Press, 1989), 112–13. See also Norman H. Young, "C. H. Dodd, 'Hilaskesthai' and His Critics," *EQ* 2.48 (1976): 67–78.

[81] Finlan, 137.

[82] Cf. Nico S. L. Fryer, "The Meaning and Translation of Hilastērion in Romans 3:25," *EQ* 59.2 (1987): 107.

[83] T.W. Manson, "ΙΛΑΣΤΗΡΙΟΝ," *JTS* 46 (1945): 4. Manson also rejects the idea of propitiation, thinking that it is too close to the pagan ideal of atonement. Rather, he sees that the idea of expiation has a closer association with his interpretation.

[84] Stuhlmacher, *Romans*, 60. Stuhlmacher also maintains that Rom. 3:25 derives from "the doctrinal tradition ('early-Jewish Christian tradition')" known to the early Christian communities. See Peter Stuhlmacher, "Recent Exegesis on Romans 3:24–26," in *Reconciliation, Law, & Righteousness: Essays in Biblical Theology* (Philadelphia: Fortress, 1986), 104–5.

[85] Jewett, *Romans*, 287 ("it is an early Christian version of the expectation found in the Temple Scroll [11QT] and Jubilees 1:29; 4:24–26").

[86] Daniel P. Bailey, "Jesus as the Mercy Seat: The Semantics and Theology of Paul's Use of Hilasterion in Romans 3:25," *TynB* 1.51 (2000): 155.

[87] Ibid., 157.

noun can exist in predicate position.[88] This interpretation contrasts with the pagan use of ἱλαστήριον, which is akin to "votive offering."[89] However, the fact that there are some occasions in the LXX where ἱλαστήριον does not mean the mercy seat, still remains an obstacle for that interpretation.

4.5.2 Suggesting an alternative way to understand ἱλαστήριον: ἱλαστήριον and "amends"

Each interpretation above illumines a specific aspect of the meaning of ἱλαστήριον in relation to Jesus' death. Since Paul does not give exact details about how Jesus' death functions for salvation, it is hard to choose one definite option among the three views. As Dunn notes, it is possible that the expiation of human sin relieves God's wrath, since sin triggers divine wrath (cf. 1:18; 2:5, 8; 3:5).[90] In 5:9, it is the wrath (of God) from which those who are declared righteous will be saved (δικαιωθέντες … σωθησόμεθα δι' αὐτοῦ ἀπὸ τῆς ὀργῆς). Although the whole creation is subject to God's wrath because of sin, for those who are declared righteous by Jesus' sacrifice ("expiation") such wrath no longer exists ("propitiation"). Also, it is natural for Paul, as a Jew, to borrow Jewish cultic imagery closely related to the solution to the problem of sin.[91] Thus, the multi-layered meaning of ἱλαστήριον cannot be properly explained if we adhere to only one view.

In fact, several scholars attempt to suggest a harmonized reading of ἱλαστήριον with a more or less generalized translation of the term. For instance, Richard Longenecker, agreeing with Deissmann,[92] avoids equating ἱλαστήριον with a specific object, although still taking account of the Jewish cultic background. Longenecker proposes that "ἱλαστήριον here in 3.25a is probably best understood and translated as "sacrifice of atonement," which translation keeps the important sacrificial nuances of the term without highlighting the narrower cultic symbolism and language of the OT sacrificial system."[93] Although Longenecker's suggestion is a reasonable option in terms of translation, what it still lacks is a consideration of the function of the ἱλαστήριον—can "sacrifice of atonement" explain the various functions of the ἱλαστήριον as suggested above? In a different direction, Linebaugh suggests viewing ἱλαστήριον as "place of atonement," which he argues contains "propitiatory focus

---

[88] Bailey exemplifies several cases in Philo where ἱλαστήριον appears without an article (e.g. *Mos.* 2.95, 97; *Fug.* 100) (see ibid., 158). See also Finlan, 133. Here, Finlan quotes Arland J. Hultgren, *Paul's Gospel and Mission: The Outlook from His Letter to the Romans* (Philadelphia: Fortress, 1985), 60.
[89] Bailey, 156–7.
[90] Dunn, *Romans 1–8*, 180.
[91] As Wolfgang Wiefel points out, many of Paul's recipients in Rome may have had a good knowledge of the Jewish scriptures (e.g. Jews or proselyte Gentiles). See Wolfgang Wiefel, "The Jewish Community in Ancient Rome and the Origins of Roman Christianity," in *The Romans Debate*, ed. Karl P. Donfried (Peabody: Hendrickson, 1991), 85–101. Furthermore, even though Paul points out the inability of the law as a means of salvation in the context, Paul can still utilize the OT sacrificial image as metaphor as long as it can point out the essence of the Christ-event. Such a practice does not necessarily mean that Paul endorses the OT sacrificial system (*pace* Deissmann, 129).
[92] Richard N. Longenecker, *The Epistle to the Romans* (Grand Rapids: Eerdmans, 2016), 428–9 (cf. Deissmann, 127).
[93] Longenecker, *Romans*, 429. Longenecker's translation is identical to NIV and NRSV.

without eliminating the expiatory echo," capturing "the reference to the 'mercy seat.'"[94] Nevertheless, this alternative is a more generalized translation of "the mercy seat," since the centre of gravity remains in the "place." A simple combination of "atonement" (which includes the ideas related to "expiation" and "propitiation") + "place" ("the mercy seat") cannot explain how the different ideas relate to one another. Markus Tiwald suggests an integrated interpretation, arguing that ἱλαστήριον is "*pars pro toto* expression" of Yom Kippur.[95] Thus, according to Tiwald, Jesus as ἱλαστήριον means that he is both "the eschatological atonement for our sins" and "the place of the presence of God in this world."[96] Certainly, both the concept of atonement and the place where the atonement happens are important elements for the Yom Kippur ritual. However, it is unlikely that Paul means such a highly abstract idea without an additional explanation. Furthermore, such a synecdoche exceeds the level of abstraction in context,[97] and Paul appears not to explain the meaning of Jesus' death with an exclusive focus on the OT sacrificial ritual like the author of Hebrews.

The attempts to offer an integrative interpretation show that the three options each focus on a different aspect of the salvific meaning of Jesus' death. However, these attempts cannot elucidate the core meaning of ἱλαστήριον that can integrate the three different interpretations. Since Paul may not intend for ἱλαστήριον to be interpreted arbitrarily, it is important to find a common denominator that can integrate different functions together. To approach this issue, we will pay attention to the context of Romans, rather than focusing extensively on the lexical backgrounds of ἱλαστήριον. In other words, we will primarily pay attention to the "target domain" of the concept, in order to examine to what extent the possible "source domains" suggested by previous scholars are meaningful.[98] Therefore, what matters is not an actual translation of the word, but the function of the concept in context; hence, we will leave ἱλαστήριον untranslated.[99]

Thus, based on the discussion above, we will apply the framework of IT to the process of forgiveness, since the meaning of ἱλαστήριον can be better understood within the original context of Rom. 3:21-26, where Paul examines the moment of forgiveness. As will be discussed, when we look at the text with our IT framework, we can find that the three main interpretations of ἱλαστήριον can be helpfully explicated with the concept of "amends." Not only is the IT framework useful for elucidating the various nuances of the meaning of Jesus' death in relation to the word ἱλαστήριον, but is also helpful for understanding the solution to the relational problem (i.e. betrayal) in the divine-human relationship, by describing each party's role in the course of forgiveness and reconciliation.

---

[94] Linebaugh, 147–8.
[95] Markus Tiwald, "Christ as Hilasterion (Rom 3:25). Pauline Theology on the Day of Atonement in the Mirror of Early Jewish Thought," in *The Day of Atonement: Its Interpretations in Early Jewish and Christian Traditions*, ed. Thomas Hieke and Tobias Nicklas (Leiden: Brill, 2012), 205.
[96] Ibid.
[97] For instance, Tiwald's interpretation does not match with ἀπολύτρωσις, a parallel metaphor, in terms of its level of abstraction.
[98] I borrow the terms "target domain" and "source domain" from George Lakoff and Mark Johnson, *Metaphors We Live By* (Chicago: Univ. of Chicago Press, 1980).
[99] Similarly, Michael Wolter, *Paul: An Outline of His Theology*, trans. Robert L. Brawley (Waco: Baylor University Press, 2015), 97 (n. 2).

4.5.2.1 "Amends" and expiation

Firstly, we can explain the expiatory function of the ἱλαστήριον with the concept of "amends," because through the ἱλαστήριον, a perpetrator's relational debt can be removed.[100] This function of the ἱλαστήριον becomes clearer when we consider the meaning of ἀπολύτρωσις (redemption) in 3:24. Both the ἱλαστήριον and ἀπολύτρωσις are associated with Christ, pointing out the nature of Jesus' death for salvation, though the former functions as a wider metaphor that summarizes the entire role of Jesus (especially death) in salvation. In particular, ἀπολύτρωσις can illumine a transactional connotation in the ἱλαστήριον.[101] According to Finlan:

> By saying that the redemption is in Christ Jesus, who is put forward as ἱλαστήριον, Paul links these two metaphors, equating two different kinds of transaction (economic and sacrificial), and so rejoining ideas that were originally related in Hebrew. *Kipper* (atonement) is cognate with *kopher*, which means "payment for the redemption of forfeited life ... atonement by the payment of a sum of money."[102]

Thus, it is necessary to understand the meaning of ἀπολύτρωσις in order to verify the transactional meaning implied in the ἱλαστήριον.

As several commentators acknowledge, the term ἀπολύτρωσις in 3:24 possesses an economic connotation related to the world of slavery.[103] Although there are various occasions where ἀπολύτρωσις is used differently in other contexts,[104] the word itself builds upon a strong economic foundation.[105] In fact, there are already other economic images, such as payment or purchase, found in several places where Paul explains salvation (e.g. ἀγοράζω [1 Cor. 6:20; 7:23] and ἐξαγοράζω [Gal. 3:13; 4:5]).[106] In Rom. 3:21–26, the use of terms related to the context of transaction, such as δωρεάν and χάρις, also points to the transactional facet of the salvific meaning of the Christ-event. Thus, the fact that it is through the ἀπολύτρωσις in Christ Jesus that those who believe are declared righteous, signifies that a certain transaction is involved in Christ (his death) for a change of status.[107]

We also need to remember that the transaction is primarily between God and human beings. Paul certainly does not believe that the price (redemption) is paid to

---

[100] Hannon et al., 254.
[101] Finlan, 164 ("'redemption', fundamentally an economic metaphor, but one that easily conflates with the sacrificial one").
[102] Finlan, 168. Here, Finlan is quoting Leon Morris, *The Apostolic Preaching of the Cross* (Grand Rapids: Eerdmans, 1965), 161–2.
[103] Cf. Ziesler, *Romans*, 111; Jewett, *Romans*, 282–3. Thus, it appears natural that Paul employs the slavery metaphor in the subsequent sections (Romans 6–7) to elucidate the change in human beings' status caused by the Christ-event.
[104] For instance, Jewett presents a number of options, including 1) deliverance from captivity, 2) ransoming by paying the price, 3) liberating slave by purchase and 4) a specialized soteriological concept regarding forgiveness of sins. Jewett, *Romans*, 282–3.
[105] Finlan, 163–4.
[106] Ibid., 166–7.
[107] According to Ziesler, "redemption in Christ Jesus" signifies "the transfer from one power/dominion to another, from that of sin to that of Christ" (Ziesler, *Romans*, 111–12).

the devil.¹⁰⁸ Given that "redemption" presupposes a debt, it is natural to think that redemption is paid to a creditor. So, to whom do human beings owe a debt? In our passage, the primary creditor would be God, given that the debt is a relational one incurred by the unfaithful acts of humanity (i.e. betrayal).¹⁰⁹ Thus, despite the absence of an explicit remark, redemption here deals with the restoration of the relationship, by redeeming human beings' relational debt to God.¹¹⁰

Here, we turn to the role or position of humanity in this transaction. Although it is generally true that a perpetrator offers "amends" to the victim for forgiveness and reconciliation, our passage strangely depicts God as the one who provides "amends." How can the "amends" that were not initiated by the perpetrators be effective? As will be discussed in more detail (see Section 4.6), ἱλαστήριον as "amends" is effective only when it is received and presented through the human response of faith (διὰ [τῆς] πίστεως).¹¹¹ In other words, such faith can stand in for the offenders' willingness to make "amends" for the victim's loss incurred by their disloyalty, though the "amends" do not in fact originate from the offenders. The frequent use of the term πίστις in the subsequent verses (3:26–31) makes sense when the importance of faith in the ἱλαστήριον for setting up this transaction is recognized.

To summarize, given the meaning of ἀπολύτρωσις, the function of the ἱλαστήριον regarding expiation becomes clearer. Christ as ἱλαστήριον can be regarded as "amends," an offering of "genuine atonement for one's action,"¹¹² which compensates for the interpersonal debts caused by humanity's betrayal,¹¹³ and it becomes effective through the faith of the debtors, despite the fact that the compensation is not originally provided by the debtors themselves.

---

¹⁰⁸ Ibid., 111.
¹⁰⁹ Gieniusz observes that the association between debt and sin was present in both Judaism and the NT (e.g. Mt. 6:12; Lk. 7:42) and often adopted as a framework to explain the relationship between God and human beings (Andrzej Gieniusz, "'Debtors to the Spirit' in Romans 8.12? Reasons for the Silence," *NTS* 59.1 [2013]: 65).
¹¹⁰ For another occasion that presents God as the recipient of the payment made by Christ's death, see Gal. 3:13. Here Paul uses ἐξαγοράζω. Cf. I. Howard Marshall, "The Development of the Concept of Redemption in the New Testament," in *Jesus the Saviour* (London: SPCK, 1990), 241 ("no doubt it is God … who receives the ransom"). Thus, Marshall insists that the law or the "elements" (Gal. 4:3) cannot be the recipient of ransom.
¹¹¹ Although Jewett, *Romans*, 287–8 sees Christ's blood (αὐτοῦ αἵματι) as the object of πίστεως, ἐν τῷ αὐτοῦ αἵματι can be understood as modifying ἱλαστήριον (in an instrumental sense), given that διὰ [τῆς] πίστεως is a parenthesis (cf. Dunn, *Romans 1–8*, 172). Therefore, faith is directed to ἱλαστήριον, that is, Jesus' death specified by the metaphor of blood. The NRSV translation reflects a similar idea ("whom God put forward as a sacrifice of atonement by his blood, <u>effective through faith</u>"), though it interprets ἐν τῷ αὐτοῦ αἵματι as modifying προέθετο. See Richard H. Bell, "Sacrifice and Christology in Paul," *JTS* 1.53 (2002): 20, which also links διὰ [τῆς] πίστεως with ἱλαστήριον. Although Käsemann, *Romans*, 98 argues that Paul inserted the phrase διὰ [τῆς] πίστεως into the early Christian material, Bruce Longenecker understands διὰ [τῆς] πίστεως as an original part of the formula (cf. Bruce W. Longenecker, "ΠΙΣΤΙΣ in Romans 3.25: Neglected Evidence for the 'Faithfulness of Christ'?," *NTS* 39.3 [1993]: 479).
¹¹² Hannon et al., 255.
¹¹³ There are several passages in the NT that show that redemption in Christ is closely associated with the forgiveness of sins. Cf. Mt. 20:28; Mk. 10:45; 1 Tim. 2:6; Eph. 1:7; Col. 1:14. See also Heb. 9:15.

4.5.2.2 "Amends" and propitiation

Our discussion of the ἱλαστήριον as "amends" with the function of "expiation" brings "propitiation" to our attention, since forgiveness and the restoration of a broken relationship are not possible without removing the victim's wrath. As noted above, a negative feeling or attitude (e.g. anger, wrath, etc.) is a natural response for those who experience a partner's betrayal.[114] Paul is also aware of this when he mentions God's wrath towards humanity's betrayal (cf. Rom. 1:18; 2:5, 8; 3:5; 5:9). Thus, Finlan argues that "in any monotheistic system, expiation implies propitiation,"[115] accordingly, "Paul does not envision a mechanical expiation that has nothing to do with the personal attitude of God."[116] Thiselton similarly points out the blind spot of the argument, which tries to rule out the notion of propitiation from the ἱλαστήριον, arguing that "the problem about expiation is that it depersonalizes the process, making it almost a mechanical process of cause and effect."[117]

In this respect, the concept of "amends" in IT can helpfully explain the function of ἱλαστήριον to relieve the wrath or anger of the victim. Referring to the previous definition of forgiveness, we can recognize that the function of the ἱλαστήριον, which is to lead the victim to "forego vengeance and demands for retribution," corresponds to the heart of propitiation. As argued by Morris and others, the presupposition that human sin brings about God's wrath can hardly be neglected.[118] In several places throughout Romans, Paul repeats that God will respond with wrath to those who commit evil, because sin ruins the relationship with God. In 1:18, which is parallel to 1:17 (δικαιοσύνη γὰρ θεοῦ ἐν αὐτῷ ἀποκαλύπτεται), Paul signifies that the revelation of God's wrath (ἀποκαλύπτεται γὰρ ὀργὴ θεοῦ) coincides with the revelation of God's righteousness to deal with all ungodliness and unrighteousness of human beings. Other passages (e.g. 2:5, 8 and 3:5) also show that wrath is God's response toward his unfaithful partners.[119]

As previously noted, wrath is a victim's natural response when betrayal happens.[120] Undoubtedly, God's wrath is fundamentally different from that of human beings in quality, since the wrath of God is not merely a private expression of hurt feelings. God's wrath is not an individually inclined reaction, but rather deals with the matter of righteousness at the cosmic and eschatological level.[121] However, the wrath of God is in line with our IT framework in terms of its cause and effect in the context of partnership. The wrath of God is also relational. In the previous chapter (Chapter 3), it has been shown that human sin against God can be regarded as a violation of "social

---

[114] Cf. Hannon et al., 254.
[115] Finlan, 138.
[116] Ibid., 137–8.
[117] Anthony C. Thiselton, *Discovering Romans: Content, Interpretation, Reception* (London: SPCK, 2016), 108.
[118] Cf. Barrett, *Romans*, 73–4; Ziesler, *Romans*, 112–13.
[119] Similarly, see 1 Thess. 2:16. For the disputed Pauline letters, see Eph. 5:6 and Col. 3:6.
[120] Hannon et al., 254.
[121] Linebaugh, 231.

norms," which arouses feelings of indignation of the partner.[122] Thus, "amends" will be essential in order to relieve the victim's wrath.[123]

In Rom. 3:24–26, the event of being considered righteous through faith in the ἱλαστήριον necessarily accompanies the fact that those who believe are no longer in a hostile position against God, which means the divine wrath instigated by human sin has been removed through Jesus as ἱλαστήριον. By means of the ἱλαστήριον, God's tolerance of the wrath reaches its climax,[124] and human beings can access "amends" by trusting in its effects.[125] Paul expounds the notion of salvation as escaping from the wrath of God in several other places. For instance, in Rom. 5:9, Paul writes of the salvation through Christ from wrath (σωθησόμεθα δι' αὐτοῦ ἀπὸ τῆς ὀργῆς), and a similar statement is also in 1 Thess. 1:10 (Ἰησοῦν τὸν ῥυόμενον ἡμᾶς ἐκ τῆς ὀργῆς τῆς ἐρχομένης) (cf. 1 Thess. 5:9). Even though these passages express the salvation from wrath in a future sense, believers can be saved from future wrath because they are presently in a right relationship with God.

Although in Rom. 3:21–26 "amends" are not directly offered by human beings, the actual function of such "amends" is the same as that of typical "amends." This implies that through faith in the ἱλαστήριον, "amends" become considered as having been presented by human beings to God.[126] God, as victim, may still have "righteous indignation" toward those who resist trusting his saving act through Jesus (cf. Rom. 3:3–5), but for those who believe in Christ, wrath no longer exists in the relationship with God (cf. 5:9). It should also be noted that this development does not mean that God is directly placated by Jesus' death, for this would just be another type of mechanical process. Rather, what Paul highlights here is the fact that the ἱλαστήριον associated with human faith can demonstrate humanity's willingness to take responsibility for the betrayal.

---

[122] See Section 3.3 of the present study.

[123] Hannon et al., 254. In the same way, Martin considers "God's hostility" as "the essential background" of Paul's thoughts on reconciliation, though the hostility can be considered as mutual (Martin, "Romans 5:1–11," 38; 42).

[124] Although it is somewhat clear that πάρεσις is directed toward προγεγονότων ἁμαρτημάτων, ἀνοχῇ τοῦ θεοῦ indicates God's general attitude towards humanity, which can include patience for sins. Romans 2:4–5 expresses this point well, showing that ἀνοχῇ points to the fact that God suspends judgment against unrepenting humanity.

[125] Such a reading can be rejected by a non-violent interpretation of the cross. For instance, L. Ann Jervis argues that "Paul does not describe God as punishing or making amends for sin in order to redeem humanity," seeing that Paul does not imply divine retribution in 3:21–26 in any way. Jervis discounts the significance of the propitiatory and expiatory function of Jesus' death (L. Ann Jervis, "Divine Retribution in Romans," *Int* 69.3 [2015]: 333–4). Nevertheless, as argued above, the theme of divine wrath cannot easily be ruled out from Paul's thought. Dunn also argues that it is difficult to ignore the sacrificial nuance in Paul's explication of Jesus' death (James D.G. Dunn, "Paul's Understanding of the Death of Jesus," in *Reconciliation and Hope: New Testament Essays on Atonement and Eschatology Presented to L.L. Morris on His 60th Birthday* [Exeter: Paternoster, 1974], 141). Thus, by removing the pivotal element of forgiveness from the scene, Jervis is not able to detect the fact that "making amends for sin" happens in an unconventional way.

[126] See also Stuhlmacher's translation ("[which is accessible and effective] through faith") (Stuhlmacher, *Romans*, 57).

4.5.2.3 "Amends" and the mercy seat

If Jesus as ἱλαστήριον can function as "amends" for the restoration of the divine-human relationship, embracing both expiatory and propitiatory functions, how can we understand the ἱλαστήριον as "the mercy seat" in the light of our IT framework?

What deserves our attention in relation to this question is the mediating function of the ἱλαστήριον. As previously discussed, "amends" function as "a form of situational selection" that can move a relationship with "superior behavioural options and outcomes" towards restoration.[127] As indicated by Hannon et al., this particular function provides a transitional stage through which the relationship can progress for a better quality of interactions.[128] It is noteworthy that ἱλαστήριον can also operate in a similar way, and this point becomes clearer when the Jewish cultic background of ἱλαστήριον is considered.

Given the nature of the ἱλαστήριον as a metaphor,[129] it is possible that ἱλαστήριον in Rom. 3:25 does not indicate a concrete object. Instead of employing the term ἱλαστήριον as a synecdoche,[130] Paul appears to have an interest in a particular function of the Jewish cultic practice in order to explicate the meaning of Jesus' death. Thus, with regard to the mercy seat interpretation, our attention is on the instrumental function of the ἱλαστήριον, which provides a place for communication between God and human beings. We can observe this particular aspect from several places in the OT that refer to the ἱλαστήριον within a cultic setting. Exodus 25:22 (LXX) describes the ἱλαστήριον as the place of communication where God will be revealed to Moses (γνωσθήσομαί σοι) and speak to him (λαλήσω σοι) about the Israelites. Similarly, when introducing the Yom Kippur ritual, Lev. 16:2 states that God will be seen in a cloud upon the ἱλαστήριον (ἐν γὰρ νεφέλῃ ὀφθήσομαι ἐπὶ τοῦ ἱλαστηρίου).[131] In fact, the ritual process in Yom Kippur describes the fact that it is not the ἱλαστήριον itself that directly does the work of atoning; rather, the ἱλαστήριον provides the place for atonement rituals (i.e. the place around which the ritual blood [or sin offering] is sprinkled) (cf. Lev. 16:14–17), which can be understood as a type of mediation.[132] Also, Numbers 7:89 describes the communication between God and Moses through the ἱλαστήριον, not as unilateral, but as mutual, when it states that Moses went into the

---

[127] Hannon et al., 255.
[128] Hannon et al., 255.
[129] Although Wolter agrees that Paul may be alluding to Yom Kippur with ἱλαστήριον, he does not approve that the ἱλαστήριον indicates an actual object, such as "cover" (i.e. the mercy seat). Rather, he tries to see it as "place of exculpation" or "places of expiation," arguing that the occasions in the LXX where the cover of the Ark is called the ἱλαστήριον stand for its function ("a metaphor of function"). Thus, the ἱλαστήριον in Rom. 3:25 should be understood as "an abstraction," not as "something concrete," since Paul makes "a functional analogy of Jesus' death with the ritual of blood on the *kapporaet* on the Day of Atonement" (Wolter, 105).
[130] Cf. Tiwald, 205.
[131] See also Lev. 16:13.
[132] Jarvis Williams suggests the Jewish martyrological narratives in 2 and 4 Maccabees as a few of the backgrounds against which Paul explicates Jesus' death in relation to Yom Kippur. Although it is not our main intention to identify the backgrounds of Paul's description in Rom. 3:21–26, 2 and 4 Maccabees offer an interesting example (along with the use of ἱλαστήριον in 4 Macc. 17:22, though it is general to see that 4 Maccabees is later than Romans), which reflects the idea that a death of someone can function as "amends." See Williams, *Martyrological*, 116–35.

tabernacle of witness to speak to God (λαλῆσαι αὐτῷ).¹³³ The examples above show that one of the functions of the ἱλαστήριον in the OT is to mediate between God and his people, and this mediating function provides a transitional stage in a sense that it becomes an important step by which the interactions for the management of the divine-human relationship are made.

As in the OT context, the ἱλαστήριον in Rom. 3:25 does not work in and of itself, either. Rather, the divine-human relationship encounters a transitional stage for forgiveness and reconciliation by means of the mediating function of the ἱλαστήριον just as that of "amends." In Rom. 3:25, the ἱλαστήριον is an important element through which both God and human beings as partners are able to communicate their attitude towards one another regarding the issue of forgiveness, though the spatial image here is not as prominent as in the OT. God shows his readiness to forgive—which has been consistently reflected in his forbearance (ἀνοχή)—through his act of putting forward (προέθετο) Jesus as the ἱλαστήριον. On the part of human beings, it is also through the ἱλαστήριον that human beings can demonstrate their willingness to take responsibility for their betrayal, even though the whole process is initiated by the victim, God. Therefore, the ἱλαστήριον creates a crucial transitional moment in which interactions for the restoration of the relationship are made. Bell recognizes the fact that the characterization of Jesus as ἱλαστήριον points to "the intersection of the human with the divine" in terms of Jesus' role as well as his ontological status.¹³⁴ Therefore, given this mediating nature of the ἱλαστήριον, it is reasonable that Paul continually stresses the role of faith, since the ἱλαστήριον becomes available only through faith.

Romans 5:1–2, the beginning part of Rom. 5:1–11, also discusses a similar function of the Christ-event.¹³⁵ Romans 5:1 specifies the mediating role of Jesus, claiming that humans gain peace (εἰρήνη) with God through Jesus Christ (διὰ τοῦ κυρίου ἡμῶν Ἰησοῦ Χριστοῦ). Romans 5:2 elaborates the picture, stating that it is through Jesus that human beings can access the relationship with God (δι' οὗ τὴν προσαγωγὴν ἐσχήκαμεν). The term προσαγωγή, with its particular cultic background,¹³⁶ signifies the mediating role of Jesus between God and humanity,¹³⁷ which is equally connoted in the term ἱλαστήριον. Therefore, it cannot be by chance that Paul employs a term that

---

[133] "When Moses went into the tabernacle of witness to speak to him [the Lord] [λαλῆσαι αὐτῷ] and he heard the voice of the Lord speaking to him from above the ἱλαστήριον [καὶ ἤκουσεν τὴν φωνὴν κυρίου λαλοῦντος πρὸς αὐτὸν ἄνωθεν τοῦ ἱλαστηρίου]" (Num. 7:89).

[134] Bell, "Sacrifice," 18; 22.

[135] Gupta also acknowledges the connection between the two passages, indicating the close connection between the notion of reconciliation and "the peace obtained through atonement" (Nijay K. Gupta, "Towards a Set of Principles for Identifying and Interpreting Metaphors in Paul: ΠΡΟΣΑΓΩΓΗ [Romans 5:2] as a Test Case," *ResQ* 3.51 [2009]: 178).

[136] Käsemann, *Romans*, 133 ("unhindered access to the sanctuary as the place of God's presence"). See also *TDNT*, "προσαγωγή", 3.161. Although προσαγωγή is used to indicate a person's approach to a king (e.g. Xenophon, *Cyropaedia* 7.5.45), the use of its verb form (προσάγω) in the LXX (especially in Leviticus and Numbers) reflects a meaningful connection with a cultic context. In the NT, 1 Peter 3:18 points out a similar aspect of Jesus' role (ἵνα ὑμᾶς προσαγάγῃ τῷ θεῷ).

[137] Cf. Andrew T. Lincoln, *Ephesians* (Dallas: Word, 1990), 149 (cited in Gupta, 180). Other usages of προσαγωγή found in the NT describe a similar scene, stressing Jesus' mediating role (cf. Eph. 2:18; 3:12).

has a cultic background within a context that speaks of the restoration of the divine-human relationship.

4.5.2.4 Summary

To summarize, we have noted that the concept of "amends" explains diverse aspects of ἱλαστήριον. In line with the process of forgiveness in IT, each of our suggestions about ἱλαστήριον focuses on a specific aspect of the function of "amends." Just like "amends," the ἱλαστήριον associated with faith removes humanity's relational debt caused by its act of betrayal, while it also mitigates God's wrath. Furthermore, in terms of procedure, the ἱλαστήριον provides the stage where God and humanity can communicate with each other for the purpose of steering their relationship toward a constructive direction. Therefore, we do not need to play off the three interpretations against one another if we regard the ἱλαστήριον as "amends."

4.6 "Through faith" (διὰ [τῆς] πίστεως) and mutual participation

God is the one who originally offered "amends" for humanity's betrayal; from a conventional standpoint, it is unreasonable that a victim would provide a perpetrator with an indispensable resource for the perpetrator's welfare. Because of this distinctive origin of the "amends," Paul emphasizes the particular way in which such "amends" become accessible and effective, i.e. "through faith" (διὰ [τῆς] πίστεως). In other words, by having faith in what God has done, human beings are brought into the process of forgiveness, and they become participants in a mutual process, since the "amends" effectively work together with their faith.

In this respect, the term πίστις in 3:21–26 indicates the human faith directed toward the Christ-event, though several scholars are inclined to interpret πίστις in 3:21–26 (cf. 3:22, 25, 26) as Christ's faithfulness.[138] Nevertheless, when we admit that Jesus as ἱλαστήριον works as "amends" in this context, it is unnatural to regard the term πίστις as indicating Jesus' own faithfulness, since what is highlighted is the instrumental nature of the Christ-event (especially his death).[139] The close context of 3:21–26 also supports our

---

[138] For instance, Williams, *Saving*; idem, "The 'Righteousness of God' in Romans," *JBL* 99.2 (1980): 272–6; L.T. Johnson, "Rom 3:21–26 and the Faith of Jesus," *CBQ* 1.44 (1982): 77–90; Richard B. Hays, *The Faith of Jesus Christ: The Narrative Substructure of Galatians 3:1–4:11*, Second Edition (Grand Rapids: Eerdmans, 2002), 156–62; idem, "Πίστις and Pauline Christology: What Is at Stake?," in *The Faith of Jesus Christ*, 282–4; Longenecker, "ΠΙΣΤΙΣ" (see n.1 for various supporters of the subjective genitive reading).

[139] Several scholars see that Paul is referring to God's faithfulness in 3:21–26, e.g. Karl Barth, *The Epistle to the Romans*, trans. Edwyn C. Hoskyns, Sixth Edition (Oxford: Oxford University Press, 1933), 96; A. Gabriel Herbert, "'Faithfulness' and 'Faith,'" *Theology* 58 (1955): 376 (cited in Richard N. Longenecker, *Romans*, 410–11). Although this argument corresponds to the context that stresses God's faithfulness revealed in the Christ-event (cf. 3:3 [πίστιν τοῦ θεοῦ]), this is distant from the Pauline usages of πίστις in an instrumental manner (cf. 2 Cor. 5:7; Gal. 2:16; Phil. 3:9). For instance, the adjacent parallel in 3:22 (διὰ πίστεως) can hardly be understood as indicating God's faithfulness, and it is improbable that Paul intends such divergence in the meaning of the short phrase. Noting the diversity of opinions, Finlan allows ambivalence in interpreting πίστεως, suggesting that "[I]t

reading. Given the repeated use of πίστις in 3:27–31, where there is an intense contrast between νόμος and πίστις, Christ's faithfulness is not what is at issue in this context. Furthermore, Romans 4:24–25 provides a good unabridged example of showing where πίστις is directed, showing that to be considered (λογίζεσθαι) righteous is associated with faith in the God who initiated the Christ-event (Jesus' death and resurrection).[140] It is God whom the passage indicates as the direct object of this faith; but, as the specific object of faith, what God has done in Christ cannot be separated from God himself.

If we do admit that "the story of Jesus" underlies Paul's articulation of the Christ-event,[141] Jesus' work can be regarded as a representative case in which human beings are required to participate, and accordingly Jesus as ἱλαστήριον can be seen as connoting his active work for salvation.[142] Undoubtedly, representativeness is one of the distinctive elements in Paul's understanding of Jesus.[143] In the latter half of Romans 5, Jesus' work is portrayed as the obedience (ὑπακοή) that will make many righteous (cf. 5:18–19).[144] In addition, the characterization of Jesus' work (especially his death) as obedience reflects his sincerity and faithfulness (cf. Phil. 2:6–11). Therefore, based on this narrative framework, Hays argues that πίστις in Rom. 3:21–26 should be interpreted as indicating "Christ's faithfulness in accepting death on the cross,"[145] defining Jesus' death as "an act of πίστις."[146] Svetlana Khobnya, seeing πίστις as pointing to Christ's faithfulness, also argues that "God's righteousness and faithfulness come only through the faithfulness of Christ," that is, Christ's "perfect obedience."[147] Thus, the restoration of the broken relationship between God and human beings is possible through participation in Christ's faithfulness (πίστις).[148] In this respect, the fact that

---

is even possible that the faithfulness of God, Jesus, and believers are all included in the metaphor [ἱλαστήριον], faith being a current that flows between and connects these persons" (Finlan, 147). Similarly, Teresa Morgan understands πίστις in the context of the tripartite relationship between God, Christ and humanity, arguing that Paul's concept of πίστις indicates "the relationship of trust/belief between God, Christ, and the faithful, the pledge or assurance secured by Christ" (Teresa Morgan, *Roman Faith and Christian Faith: Pistis and Fides in the Early Roman Empire and Early Churches* [Oxford: Oxford University Press, 2015], 291; see also ibid., 282–302). However, as will be argued, the main problem of this interpretation is that Christ's role as an active mediator is not so prominent in Rom. 3:21–26 that it is difficult to speak of Christ's faithfulness in the context, though Morgan correctly draws attention to the relational connotation of *pistis/fides*.

[140] Cf. Rom. 10:9.
[141] Cf. Douglas A. Campbell, "The Story of Jesus in Romans and Galatians," in *Narrative Dynamics in Paul: A Critical Assessment*, ed. Bruce W. Longenecker (Louisville: WJK, 2002), 120.
[142] For instance, on 3:25, Johnson argues that "the faith of Jesus and the pouring out of his blood, together, form the act of expiation" (Johnson, 80).
[143] Dunn, "Death," 35–40.
[144] Johnson, 80.
[145] Hays, "Πίστις," 284.
[146] Ibid., 282. One of the exegetical grounds for Hays' argument is the fact that an objective genitive reading of πίστεως Ἰησοῦ Χριστοῦ in 3:22 will make εἰς πάντας τοὺς πιστεύοντας in the same verse redundant (ibid., 283). However, it is still possible to see that with εἰς πάντας τοὺς πιστεύοντας, Paul is not making a simple repetition but emphasizing the universal applicability of faith in Jesus Christ (cf. πάντας/οὐ γάρ ἐστιν διαστολή).
[147] Svetlana Khobnya, *The Father Who Redeems and the Son Who Obeys: Consideration of Paul's Teaching in Romans* (Cambridge: James Clarke & Co, 2014), 104–5.
[148] Khobnya, 107; 113. Cf. idem, 82–3. For a further discussion about the transmission of the relationality of the Jesus-God relationship to the divine-human relationship, see Chapter 7 (7.4.2.1) of the present study.

πίστις is an essential element for the restoration of the divine-human relationship is still sustained, regardless of the subject of faith to which πίστις primarily refers. Therefore, as Hooker suggests, it might be unhelpful to adhere to a robust dichotomy between Christ's πίστις and human πίστις, since πίστις can be both Christ's faith and believers' faith,[149] though Hooker is careful not to overlook the latter's dependence upon the former.[150] However, this faithfulness displayed by Jesus appears to not be the primary focus of Rom. 3:21–26, where God is described as a main actor. Unlike in Romans 5, Jesus' active role does not surface here.[151] Rather, as we have noted, Jesus as ἱλαστήριον, a central metaphor used of Jesus' death in this passage, accentuates the instrumental significance of Jesus' death.

Also, having faith in the ἱλαστήριον can signify one's active participation in the relationship with God. Gorman rightly argues that the meaning of πίστις cannot be restricted to trust,[152] but the term points to a deeper dimension, which Gorman names "co-crucifixion," i.e. one's own participation in the faithfulness of Jesus, characterized by obedience and love.[153] However, such a deeper understanding of faith does not necessitate interpreting πίστις in Rom. 3:21–26 as Christ's faithfulness, as Gorman argues.[154] Rather, when we regard the ἱλαστήριον as "amends," we can realize that πίστις in 3:25 does not mean a simple acknowledgement, but can be basically identified with the expression of a willingness to take responsibility for the acts that caused betrayal. Also, given that making "amends" is accompanied by behavioural efforts to restore and develop the partnership in a constructive manner,[155] the active participation characterized by a lifestyle committed to God can be regarded as grounded in the πίστις associated with the ἱλαστήριον. In this respect, Hay's comprehensive definition

---

[149] Morna D. Hooker, "Another Look at Πίστις Χριστοῦ," *STJ* 69.1 (2016): 62. See also idem, "Πίστις Χριστοῦ," in *From Adam to Christ: Essays on Paul* (Cambridge: Cambridge University Press, 1990), 184–5.

[150] Hooker, "Another Look," 62.

[151] Morgan, 290.

[152] Gorman also acknowledges the role of faith as a human response, which constitutes a significant part of justification, indicating the importance of "a required subjective response, or mode, that effects justification/reconciliation." See Michael J. Gorman, *Inhabiting the Cruciform God: Kenosis, Justification, and Theosis in Paul's Narrative Soteriology* (Grand Rapids: Eerdmans, 2009), 57. See also ibid., 81 ("justification is on the basis of divine initiative followed by human response"). However, Gorman criticizes what he calls the "minimalist definition of faith" that usually restricts faith to "trusting, acknowledgement, and consent" (ibid., 82).

[153] Gorman, *Inhabiting*, 79–85. See also Robert C. Tannehill, *Dying and Rising with Christ: A Study in Pauline Theology* (Berlin: Töpelmann, 1967), 230; Morna D. Hooker, "Interchange and Atonement," in *From Adam to Christ*, 26–41; Powers, 82–110.

[154] See Gorman, *Inhabiting*, 100 [n. 168]. However, he does not deal with 3:25. Hay also notices the difficulty to interpret πίστις in 3:25 as Christ's faithfulness. See David M. Hay, "Paul's Understanding of Faith as Participation," in *Paul and His Theology*, ed. Stanley E. Porter (Leiden: Brill, 2006), 74. Jeanette Hagen poses a similar question: "Does viewing faith as participation necessitate a subjective reading of πίστις Χριστοῦ?" (Jeanette M. Hagen, "Faith as Participation: An Exegetical Study of Some Key Pauline Texts" [PhD Thesis, Durham University, 2016], 49). Barclay also recognizes that to accept πίστις as indicating Jesus' faithfulness is not a precondition to speak of the participatory meaning of faith. Rather, he correctly argues that "the πίστις of 3:21–26 is better understood as that of believers, signalling their participation in, and derivation from, the Christ-event" (Barclay, *Gift*, 477). Similarly, Dunn's emphasis on the representativeness of Jesus' death is not accompanied with the interpretation of πίστις as faithfulness of Christ (Dunn, "Death," 35–6).

[155] Hannon et al., 255.

of faith helpfully explains what having faith in Jesus as ἱλαστήριον implies overall. Hay claims that "Paul's concept of faith is best understood as the mode by which Christians participate in Christ, a mode with both individual and corporate dimensions, and one that combines elements of cognitive assertion, trust, and faithfulness."[156] The fact that God has already provided the means for making "amends" does not in itself accomplish forgiveness and reconciliation, but it is only "the law of faith" (νόμου πίστεως [3:27]) through which the process of forgiveness and reconciliation becomes complete.[157]

4.7 Conclusion

To sum up, in the light of the process of forgiveness in IT, we have identified that Jesus' as ἱλαστήριον works as "amends" in the process of forgiveness in the divine-human relationship. Although, unlike a conventional case, the "amends" in Rom. 3:21–26 are not originally provided by the offender, the effect of such "amends" can be the same when the "amends" are associated with faith. The fact that the ἱλαστήριον can be viewed as "amends" has two significant implications.

Firstly, the concept of "amends" can explain the diverse facets of ἱλαστήριον, i.e. expiation, propitiation and the mercy seat. We have noted that the three aspects of the ἱλαστήριον match the functions of "amends" in the process of forgiveness. The expiatory and propitiatory functions are what "amends" can do for an offender and a victim, respectively, while the mediating function of the mercy seat creates a transitional stage as "amends" does.

Secondly, the fact that the ἱλαστήριον can function as "amends" denotes that the process of forgiveness in the divine-human relationship in 3:21–26 consists of mutual participation. Even though the originator of the "amends" is not the perpetrator but, surprisingly, the victim, human beings as perpetrators can participate in the process of forgiveness through having faith in what God has done for them. The fact that God intends mutual participation even from the beginning of the restored relationship anticipates a more mature level of interaction at a later stage.

The fact that it is God who initiates such a process cannot be contested. However, this does not necessarily imply that the process of forgiveness and reconciliation is carried out automatically. As argued above, it is crucial to show one's willingness to take responsibility for the act of betrayal by having faith in Jesus as ἱλαστήριον. However, such

---

[156] Hay, "Faith," 46. Benjamin Schliesser's definition of πίστις, "personal relationship of trust, submission, assent of certain contents, knowledge, confession, perseverance," also appropriately extends the meaning of πίστις on the part of human beings. However, Schliesser's suggestion that in Rom. 3:21–4:25 πίστις is also a means through which "the objective reality of salvation manifested by God" appears to give too much weight to the divine πίστις, because such a usage of πίστις is not so prominent in the context. See Benjamin Schliesser, *Abraham's Faith in Romans 4* (Tübingen: Mohr Siebeck, 2007), 408–9.

[157] Acts 10:43 shows that there is a parallel idea in the early Christian traditions that indicates a similar point regarding the function of faith and forgiveness (ἄφεσιν ἁμαρτιῶν λαβεῖν διὰ τοῦ ὀνόματος αὐτοῦ πάντα τὸν πιστεύοντα εἰς αὐτόν). Cf. Tobias Hägerland, *Jesus and the Forgiveness of Sins: An Aspect of His Prophetic Mission* (Cambridge: Cambridge University Press, 2011), 102.

a meaning of having faith in Jesus cannot be restricted to a simple cognitive activity. In this respect, Gorman rightly stresses the importance of believers' active participation ignited by God's saving activity. Gorman states that "the atonement produces not merely *beneficiaries* but *participants*: participants in the cross and therefore also participants in the life-giving self-giving of God."[158] Given the participatory nature of having faith in Jesus as ἱλαστήριον, it will be our next task to explore the motivation for such participation.

---

[158] Michael J. Gorman, *The Death of the Messiah and the Birth of the New Covenant: A (Not So) New Model of the Atonement* (Eugene: Cascade, 2014), 237 (emphasis original).

5

The Relational Significance of Jesus' Death (2)—The Meaning of God's Self-Sacrifice in Christ's Death (Rom. 5:1–11)

5.1 Introduction

As shown in the previous chapter, the process of forgiveness and reconciliation in Romans necessitates mutual interaction between God and human beings. Therefore, in dealing with the Pauline concept of reconciliation, several scholars have indicated the necessity of the human response to God's initiative. Marshall observes three stages of reconciliation in Rom. 5:1–11 and 2 Cor. 5:[1] 1) "the reconciling act of God in the death of Jesus," 2) "the proclamation of reconciliation by the 'servants' of reconciliation" and 3) "the acceptance of God's message by men, when they accept his act (i.e. Jesus' death) by faith."[2] The entire process of reconciliation is not complete "until all three stages have taken place."[3] In a similar vein, Moo identifies "two aspects or moments" of reconciliation, in which the acceptance by human beings should follow what God has completed through Christ.[4] These moments are when, according to Martin, "human responsibility is called into play" because God's grace in reconciliation must be "received."[5] In Jewett's analysis, Paul frequently mentions "human volition" when he deals with the issue of human enmity and reconciliation (cf. Rom. 5:1).[6] Cranfield also

---

[1] Marshall argues that Romans 5 and 2 Corinthians 5 reflect the same idea in terms of the concept of reconciliation (Marshall, *Saviour*, 266).
[2] Ibid., 269–70. Marshall's argument about human acceptance is based on his observation of the verb καταλλάσσω in the passive voice form in 5:10 (cf. 2 Cor. 5:20), which is similar to the pattern of "X gives up his own anger against Y" except for the emphasis on God's initiative (ibid., 262–6).
[3] Ibid., 270.
[4] Moo, *Romans*, 311.
[5] Martin, *Reconciliation*, 148. Cf. E. Dinkler, *Eirēnē: Der Urchristliche Friedensgedanke* (Heidelberg: Winter, 1973), 34–5 (n. 108) ("the gift of God's peace is to be matched by our seeking to live in that relationship" [cited in ibid.]).
[6] Jewett, *Romans*, 348. According to Jewett, 2 Cor. 5:20 is an example that supports a subjunctive ἔχωμεν. William Sanday and Arthur C. Headlam, *A Critical and Exegetical Commentary on the Epistle to the Romans*, Tenth Edition (New York: Charles Scribner's Sons, 1905), 120; C.H. Dodd, *The Epistle of Paul to the Romans* (New York: Harper & Row, 1932), 72; Longenecker, *Romans*, 548–9 also support the subjunctive reading (ἔχωμεν), indicating a better text-critical support for this reading (ℵ* A B* C D K L 33 81 630 1175 1739*). See also Neil Elliott, *The Rhetoric of Romans: Argumentative Constraint and Strategy and Paul's Dialogue with Judaism* (Sheffield: JSOT Press, 1990), 226–8.

indicates a similar point, arguing that Paul does not see "men's part as merely passive" since human beings are demanded to be reconciled (2 Cor. 5:20).[7]

Thus, given the necessity of human response for the sake of reconciliation, it is also important to understand how such a response can be made by the human partners who previously had enmity against God. Although the aforementioned scholars have correctly identified one of the crucial stages of reconciliation, the question of how partners who used to be on hostile terms can totally transform their attitudes requires further treatment. In what way can the human party, who had once betrayed God, respond positively? What is the motivation? These questions also concern the way in which the divine initiative relates to human response in terms of faith (πίστις). We have noted that human beings can respond to God's initiative for forgiveness and reconciliation through having faith in the ἱλαστήριον, which functions as "amends." Although several scholars have noted that it is the act of the Spirit through the proclamation of the Gospel by which human faith (πίστις) is elicited,[8] the way in which the divine activity elicits human faith has not yet been entirely illuminated. Given that the process of reconciliation consists of two-way communication, in which the human response of faith is one of the key stages, grasping the correct picture of the Pauline concept of reconciliation necessitates analysis of how the response from the human party is made.[9]

Therefore, we will focus on the relational implications of Christ's death in Rom. 5:1-11, arguing that God's self-sacrificial attitude expressed in the Christ-event can influence the whole personality (i.e. cognition, emotion and habit) of the human partners in order to elicit the response of faith for the sake of reconciliation.[10] Romans 5:1-11 tells the story of the restoration of the broken relationship with a unique

---

Elliott supports the subjunctive reading on the basis of the rhetorical significance of Romans 5 for the whole letter. *Pace* Cranfield, *Romans*, 257; Martin, *Reconciliation*, 148. Martin's argument is based on his view that Paul possesses an "anti-nomistic strain." However, the subjunctive interpretation does not need to be seen as "nomistic," because what it fundamentally indicates is the significance of the reception that Martin himself stresses.

[7] Cranfield, 266.
[8] Despite the different spectrums, it is generally acknowledged that the divine outworking is important for eliciting "faith" as a human response. Cf. David M. Hay, "Pistis as 'Ground for Faith' in Hellenized Judaism and Paul," *JBL* 108.3 (1989): 475 ("faith not as a general human capacity but as a reaction made possible 'from outside' believers by the disclosure of a crucified Messiah"); Wright, *Faithfulness*, 952-60; Martyn, "Apocalyptic," 251-2 ("God's good news of Jesus Christ is also the power that elicits faith"); Barclay, *Gift*, 461 ("this power is linked to the revelation of God's righteousness ... which elicits faith"); Watson, *Hermeneutics*, xl ("if divine speech is to be effective, it must evoke a human response").
[9] Martin tries to distance reconciliation from faith (πίστις) since, in Romans 5, faith is attached to justification, not reconciliation, which needs to be received (cf. 5:11 [καταλλαγὴν ἐλάβομεν]) (Martin, *Reconciliation*, 152). Nevertheless, we do not need to rule out the meaning of faith for the acceptance of reconciliation, given that faith and acceptance are interchangeable with one another, just as the gift of justification is also described as something to be received (cf. τῆς δωρεᾶς τῆς δικαιοσύνης λαμβάνοντες [5:17]). In fact, faith can elaborate the manner in which one receives reconciliation, and it does not override the nature of "the free forgiveness of God" (see Martin, "Romans 5:1-11," 46).
[10] Martin suggests that the difference of 5:1-11 from 3:24-26 originates from Paul's intention to enlarge the scope of the meaning of Christ's death to the universal level in order to communicate with Gentile hearers, without restricting it to the sphere of Jewish cultic activity (Martin, *Reconciliation*, 153-4).

emphasis on the self-sacrificial love of God that enabled reconciliation.[11] Although what appears to be mainly stressed in 5:1–11 is the certainty of future salvation based on God's love manifested through reconciliation, thick descriptions about reconciliation in the passage give us helpful clues for identifying the process by which hostile humanity makes a prosocial response toward God.

We will firstly look at the significance of a partner's self-sacrificial acts in a dyadic relationship from the IT perspective. We will also refer to the IT model of transformation to understand the process through which one can change one's attitude toward a partner. The process of "self-presentation" in IT will also be applied to identifying how God's demonstration of self-giving love influences the transformation of his human partners' motivation, notably by eliciting a response characterized by faith. The meaning of "gift" in Romans will also be discussed, as it provides helpful evidence for recognizing that God's self-giving act in Christ entails positive expectations for his human partners' response for the sake of developing the relationship, including their acceptance by faith of what God has done in Christ.

5.2 Understanding God's self-sacrifice in Christ from an interpersonal perspective

IT is interested in showing how self-sacrificial behaviour for a partner positively influences the management of an ongoing relationship. In two points, what IT explains about such behaviour brings a fresh perspective to our understanding of the relational implications of God's sacrifice in Christ's death. Firstly, Rusbult, Arriaga and Agnew identify that self-sacrificial acts accompanied by the loss of one's own interest can testify of one's trustworthiness to the partner:

> Correspondence defines opportunities for the display of important motives. It is possible for John to demonstrate his trustworthiness in relatively non-correspondent situations, in that such situations "test" trustworthiness – if John behaves cooperatively, thereby promoting Mary's interests at the expense of his own interests, it becomes clear that he is trustworthy.[12]

We can also observe something similar in God's self-sacrifice in Christ. Although it was human beings' choice to leave the relationship with God, God took this situation, which could not guarantee any positive outcomes, as an opportunity to demonstrate (συνίστημι) his love and trustworthiness to his human partners (Rom. 5:8; cf. 3:25–26). Therefore, it is on the basis of God's trustworthiness that Paul can affirm the certainty of future salvation for those who are already reconciled with God (5:9–10).

Secondly, although self-sacrificial acts for a partner's benefit usually necessitate one's own loss, IT explains that in the long term such a choice can bring about positive

---

[11] Martin, *Reconciliation*, 145–7; Moo, *Romans*, 305–6.
[12] Rusbult, Arriaga and Agnew, 369.

results for the future of the relationship, by enabling the relationship to be sustained for further development. Rusbult, Arriaga and Agnew put it as follows:

> Willingness to sacrifice is positively associated with dyadic adjustment and probability of persisting (Van Lange, Rusbult, et al., 1997). Thus, although sacrificial behaviour necessitates forgoing direct self-interest, the willingness of committed individuals to sacrifice—when it becomes necessary to do so—yields clear benefits in ongoing relationships.[13]

From a conventional viewpoint, God's choice to make a sacrifice seems irrational. Self-sacrifice for the sake of "sinners" (cf. 5:8) is not a valuable investment, and in this sense God's choice would have sounded very strange to Paul's contemporaries.[14] However, it is possible for a voluntary heroic death to be deemed worthwhile—even if it is scarcely the case that one would do so—if done for the sake of those who are worthy to be saved.[15] Applying this logic to the case of God's sacrifice in Christ's death (see Figure 5.1), the quality of God's outcome for his decision ought to be undoubtedly negative. In other words, from a conventional point of view, the outcomes that follow God's self-sacrificial act cannot exceed CL.[16] In our context, CL can be the same as the quality of outcome expected from a heroic death for righteous and good people, since this occasion is treated as the criterion for comparison.[17]

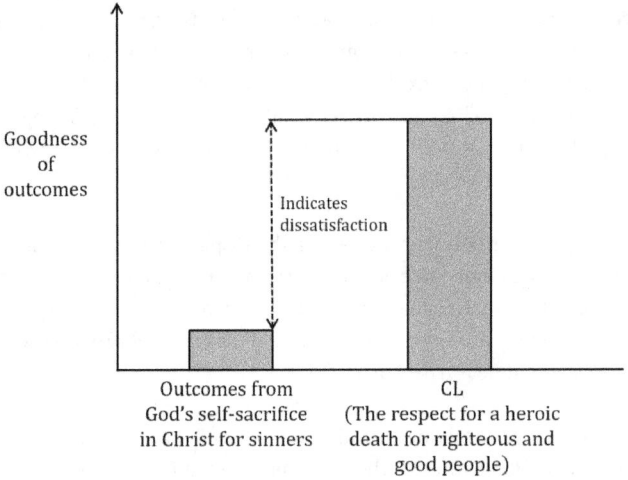

Figure 5.1 Expected outcomes for God by his self-sacrificial act (conventional point of view).

[13] Ibid., 379.
[14] Cf. *Somn.* 2.175-7 (cf. McFarland, *Grace*, 184–5); *Ben.* 1.1.9 (cf. Barclay, *Gift*, 73).
[15] Cf. Jewett, *Romans*, 360 (see n. 158).
[16] In this case, CL-alt for God is not clear.
[17] "CL is the standard against which one evaluates outcomes from a certain relationship" (Kelley and Thibaut, *Interdependence*, 8–9). For attempts to understand the vicariousness of Christ's death against the background of heroic deaths in the Graeco-Roman literature, see Gathercole, *Defending*, 103–4; Breytenbach, "For Us," 73; Henk S. Versnel, "Making Sense of Jesus' Death: The Pagan Contribution," in *Deutungen Des Todes Jesu Im Neuen Testament*, ed. Jörg Frey and Jens Schröter (Tübingen: Mohr Siebeck, 2005), 213–96.

However, if we understand God's self-giving act in the light of what IT proposes, although God's act in Christ requires a considerable amount of cost, this does not necessarily mean final loss. Rather, there can still be positive expectations about the future of the relationship, through which positive outcomes become available for both partners. Also, given the fact that forgiveness of betrayal "is positively associated with couple well-being,"[18] God's act of self-sacrifice for the restoration of the broken relationship can be interpreted as an effort to make a better future for the relationship.

5.2.1 The pattern of "martyrdom"

The self-sacrificial nature of God's act in Christ's death becomes clearer when viewed with a pattern of "martyrdom" that explains the situation in which A's altruistic act benefits B at the expense of A's own outcomes.[19] Kelley et al. conceptualize this particular situation as follows: "the personal sacrifice required to bring about the solution that makes the partner happiest is the basis for characterizing the situation as one that offers the opportunity to be a 'martyr.'"[20] The outcome tables for the pattern of "martyrdom" are presented as below (see Figure 5.2).

The table on the left reflects the pattern of "martyrdom." Here, B is subject to A's JC. This means that in order to attain the best outcomes, B should vary their choices as A varies their choices, either a1 or a2. An explicit pattern of "martyrdom" is observed when B chooses b1 and A chooses a2. This occasion displays the characteristic of "martyrdom," because A relinquishes positive outcomes by choosing a2 when B chooses b1, whereas there is no reason for A to choose a2 since a1 always guarantees the best outcome to A. Thus, A's sacrificial choice (a2) is a *sine qua non* for B's best outcomes when b1 is the only option for B.

As can be seen in the table on the right, God's self-sacrificial act in our text also reflects the pattern of "martyrdom." Based on the textual data, one can imagine that God will attain the worst immediate outcomes ($\alpha 2$ or $\alpha'2$) if he decides to make a self-sacrifice for the good of his disloyal partners. However, if he chooses not to do so, he

	Options (2X2) (for A, for B)	Outcomes		Options (2X2) (for God, for human beings)	Outcomes
1	(a1, b1)	(10, 0)	1	(not to sacrifice, to return)	($\alpha 1, \beta 1$)
2	(a1, b2)	(10, 5)	2	(not to sacrifice, not to return)	($\alpha'1, \beta 2$)
3	(a2, b1)	(0, 5)	3	(to sacrifice, to return)	($\alpha 2, \beta'1$)
4	(a2, b2)	(0, 0)	4	(to sacrifice, not to return)	($\alpha'2, \beta'2$)
	Martyr			Martyr (applied)	

Figure 5.2 Outcome tables for the pattern of "martyrdom."[21]

---

[18] Rusbult, Arriaga and Agnew, 380.
[19] Kelley et al., 90.
[20] Ibid., 219.
[21] Based on Table 2.8 (case II) in ibid., 48.

might preserve his critical resource (i.e. his Son) (with the outcomes of α1 or α'1). God's actual choice is striking because he decided to sacrifice himself even when it was not certain whether his disloyal partners would react in a positive manner (cf. 5:6). However, such a decision is vital for human beings' best outcome (β'1: e.g. justification, reconciliation, salvation from the wrath and boasting in God [cf. 5:9–11]) if they choose to return to God, the only positive option. If they do not return, they will be put in the worst situation (β'2).[22] However, from God's side, to choose to sacrifice means suffering an immediate and serious loss. In this respect, the relational situation of the divine-human relationship in 5:1–11 can be characterized as a case of God's "martyrdom" toward his human partners.

5.3 "Self-presentation" and "attribution": The process of communication for "transformation"

As shown above, our reading through the lens of IT suggests that God's self-sacrificial act in Christ exhibits both his positive expectations for his human partners' response and his trustworthiness. The communication process in IT helps us to understand how God's self-sacrificial gesture can work for the transformation of the human partners' motive, which was previously driven by immediate self-interest, into a prosocial one. The results of which enable the relationship to persist with long-term goals.[23] Given that the broken status of the relationship was caused by the human partners' self-centred attitude, such an attitude requires transformation for the purpose of reconciliation. As will be shown, the result of changes in cognitive, emotional and habitual dimensions can be summarized in the concept of faith (πίστις) as a human response to God's reconciling act.

The process of communication consists of two procedures: "self-presentation" on the part of one person; and "attribution" on the part of the other.[24]

5.3.1 Self-presentation

"Self-presentation" forms a part of the communication process, through which one's attitude towards a partner is conveyed.[25] Rusbult and Van Lange explain the function of self-presentation:

> Self-presentation describes individuals' attempts to communicate their abilities, motives and dispositions to partners. Conveying that one cares for or loves another is most directly (and perhaps most convincingly) communicated by departing from one's interests in order to enhance that person's outcomes.[26]

---

[22] One can imagine the nature of β'2 from the subsequent passages (5:12–21), in which eternal life clearly contrasts with death.
[23] See Section 2.2.6 of the present study for the transformation process.
[24] Rusbult and Van Lange, "Interdependence," 361–2.
[25] Ibid., 361.
[26] Ibid., 362.

In a similar manner, Christ's death can work as the "self-presentation" of God's love and faithfulness to his human partners.[27] God's act in Christ, which risks loss for the welfare of his human partners, communicates the depth of his love and trustworthiness.

The importance of such a communicational activity also derives from the fact that the intention behind one's own actions cannot be fully conveyed without presenting information about one's abilities, motives and dispositions. Thus, Rusbult and Van Lange explain the problem of incomplete or missing self-presentation:

> Because we do not always hold complete information about our partners' given outcomes, we sometimes mistakenly assume that acts resulting from transformation of a situation reflect the partner's simple preferences. For example, John's acts of loyalty, kindness or sacrifice may not be visible if Mary fails to recognize the cost he incurred.[28]

Following this explanation, it seems that one of Paul's aims in 5:6–11 is to emphasize the fact that God's self-sacrifice in Christ is not based on his "simple preference," but incurred considerable cost to him.[29] The miserable existential condition of human beings (e.g. the weak, ungodly, sinners, enemies of God) makes God's sacrifice more extraordinary.[30] The meaning of the sacrifice is not entirely recognizable if the original conditions of both God and humanity are not fully understood.[31]

5.3.2 Attribution

Self-presentation is followed by attributional activity. If "self-presentation" concerns what God has done for his human partners, attributional activity deals with how the human partners comprehend his "self-presentation" and respond to it. According to IT, attributional activity is the attempt "to uncover the direct meaning and broader implication of a partner's actions, developing expectations regarding future behavior and seeking to explain prior behavior in terms of underlying dispositions."[32] Thus, a partner's past actions and situational responses inform one's attributional activity and attitude towards the partner.[33]

Both self-presentation and attributional activity are involved in the transformation process (see Figure 5.3). One's self-presentation is conveyed in a way that it is cognitively

---

[27] Martin, "Romans 5:1–11," 40.
[28] Rusbult and Van Lange, "Interdependence," 362.
[29] Martin, "Romans 5:1–11," 45.
[30] By using the first-person plural from Rom. 5:1, Paul situates his readers and himself in the perspective of human beings in general. Such a move is inaugurated from 4:24, which specifies the identity of "us." Cf. N.A. Dahl, "Two Notes on Romans 5," *ST* 5.1 (1951): 40.
[31] For Paul's immediate hearers, the "self-presentation" of God is conveyed by Paul's statements. Paul's act of delivery can be deemed as a rhetorical strategy to persuade his recipients and to elicit his intended responses from them. Cf. Wright, *Faithfulness*, 886. Campbell also recognizes that "Paul's proclamation mediates God's own word ... his speech is a vehicle through which God speaks and begins to rule" (Cf. Campbell, *Deliverance*, 161).
[32] Rusbult and Van Lange, "Interdependence," 361.
[33] Ibid.

Sequence 1	Given situation: Direct self-interest
Sequence 2	Activation of relevant interpersonal orientations (e.g. interpersonal dispositions, relationship-specific motives, social norms)
Sequence 3	Influence of the interpersonal orientations on cognition, emotion and habit [Effected by partner's "self-presentation"]
Sequence 4	Transformation of motivation
Sequence 5	Effective situation: Broader considerations
Sequence 6	Behaviour

Figure 5.3 Transformation process and the influence of the communication process.[34]

and emotionally influential.[35] The subsequent attributional activity involves cognitive and emotive evaluations of the partner's self-presentation through the processes of "discerning what a given situation is 'about,'" evaluating one's own behavioural options,[36] and verifying "the partner's needs and predicting his or her motives."[37] Also, in accordance with what information is conveyed and evaluated, one is able to make a decision to depart from a given situation and internalize a prosocial attitude that seeks long-term relations.

In our case, God's self-presentation confirms his commitment and faithfulness toward his human partners, capable of being particularly influential on the cognitive and emotional planes. In terms of the cognitive aspect, by demonstrating his motives through his self-sacrificial acts in a non-correspondent situation, God's self-presentation provides a good foundation for the human partners' attributional activity of trusting in God.[38] Moreover, representing its essence, which runs counter to the conventional way of calculation (cf. 5:6–8), God's self-presentation cognitively challenges human partners to reconfigure the way by which they perceive a given situation and their own behavioural options. Whereas the betrayal was made for the sake of self-interest and autonomy, God's self-presentation through his altruistic act can renovate human calculation by affecting the human partners' values system in a cognitive way. Romans 5:3–5 (εἰδότες ὅτι) represents the transformed cognition of those who are in the reconciled relationship with God. It is characterized by a prosocial attitude that is oriented toward long-term management. With this new attitude, present tribulations are no longer counted merely as loss and the value of perseverance to

---

[34] Based on Figure 1 in ibid., 359.
[35] Ibid.
[36] Ibid., 360.
[37] Ibid.
[38] Similarly, Morgan notes that to trust in God/gods in antiquity is not seen as a "leap of faith" (Morgan, *Faith*, 149–56; 180; 187; 241–3; 260–1).

persist in the relationship with God is highly esteemed (5:3-4), based on remembering what God has done for them (5:5).

God's self-presentation through Christ's death also entails emotional weight.[39] For instance, Paul's stress on God's love (ἀγάπη) cannot be appropriately understood if an emotional aspect is discounted. In 5:5 and 5:8, divine love characterizes God's saving activity through the Spirit and Christ. What is communicated through God's self-presentation is God's love for us (τὴν ἑαυτοῦ ἀγάπην εἰς ἡμᾶς); furthermore, the future hope of salvation is grounded in God's love (5:5, 9; cf. 8:35, 39).[40] It is noteworthy that the troubles that hinder the human partners' fidelity to God also have emotional content (e.g. shame [5:5]).[41] We can observe that love (ἀγάπη) plays a crucial role throughout Paul's letters in motivating the life committed to God. As Paul confesses in Gal. 2:20, it is the love of God's Son expressed in his self-sacrificial death to which Paul responds by devoting his own life to God.[42] Similarly, it is the love of Christ (ἡ ἀγάπη τοῦ Χριστοῦ) revealed in the Christ-event that urges (συνέχει) Paul and his fellow workers to reorientate the purpose of their lives (2 Cor. 5:14-15; cf. Rom. 15:30). Käsemann also emphasizes the power of God's love to transform one's whole personality, stating that "when God's love has seized us so totally and centrally, we no longer belong to ourselves; a change in existence has taken place."[43]

As shown above, we can see that as a result of the cognitive and emotive influences of God's self-presentation, what the transformation process produces is a new relational attitude of human beings toward God, one that is characterized by faith. Through the transformation of the self-centred way, the human partners are now able to internalize their own fidelity and commitment to God.[44] Given the comprehensive nature of faith (cf. Section 4.6), such a transformed relational attitude elicited by God's self-presentation can be included in what faith means, working as a response that accepts God's opening gesture for reconciliation.

Habit formation is an equally influential factor on the transformation process. IT sees that "as a consequence of adaptation to repeatedly encountered patterns, people develop habitual tendencies to react to specific situations in specific ways, such that transformation transpires with little or no conscious thought."[45] Although such a process is not directly activated by self-presentation, the process is still an important means by which the human partners' transformation is fortified.

In Romans 6, Paul's exhortations about bodily obedience point to a process of developing habitual tendencies to confirm believers' new relational status as no longer slaves of Sin but slaves of God (cf. 6:19-23). The concept of body (σῶμα [6:6, 12]) or

---

[39] Rusbult and Van Lange, "Interdependence," 361.
[40] Powers, 92-3.
[41] Ben C. Blackwell, *Christosis: Pauline Soteriology in Light of Deification in Irenaeus and Cyril of Alexandria* (Tübingen: Mohr Siebeck, 2011), 156.
[42] Cf. David deSilva, "'We Are Debtors': Grace and Obligation in Paul and Seneca," in *Paul and Seneca in Dialogue*, ed. Joseph R. Dodson and David E. Briones (Leiden: Brill, 2017), 172 ("God's love shown in Christ... has the power to quicken gratitude even in the soil of the ingrate's heart").
[43] Käsemann, *Romans*, 135.
[44] Cf. deSilva, "Debtors," 176.
[45] Rusbult and Van Lange, 'Interdependence', 360-1. Cf. Rusbult, Arriaga and Agnew, 372-3; Rusbult and Van Lange, "Why," 2056-7.

members (τὰ μέλη [6:13, 19; cf. 7:5, 23]) in Romans 6 exhibits "corporeality" while also indicating the whole personality.[46] Thus, Paul encourages that those who have experienced baptism into Christ—a baptism which has nullified a specific bodily characteristic (i.e. τὸ σῶμα τῆς ἁμαρτίας) that had negatively influenced one's relational identity—ought to practise self-control over their bodies in order to maintain their new status (cf. 6:12–13).

Engberg-Pedersen and Barclay also recognize the significance of bodily obedience for the purpose of confirming one's identity. They commonly borrow Pierre Bourdieu's notion of "habitus,"[47] which indicates the importance of bodily practice in the formation of one's whole personality.[48] Barclay argues that "the new Christian habitus can be expressed and reinforced only in practice; it requires to be embodied, not simply conceptualized,"[49] and that "everything one does every moment of time contributes to the formation of one habitus or another."[50] In this respect, Engberg-Pedersen and Barclay closely resemble Rusbult and Van Lange, who argue that the transformation process through habituation can reveal "the unique self."[51]

In Romans 12–15, Paul elaborates on the principle of Rom. 6, i.e. the process of the habituation of bodily practices within the community (cf. 12:1). Because they are facing various issues among members of the community, Paul's hearers are urged to react to these issues in a manner congruent with transformation, by renouncing any self-centred orientation and acting in others' interests (cf. 12:10, 14–21; 13:8–10; 14:7–8, 13, 19; 15:1–2, 7).[52] In that way, the relational attitude transformed as a result of the self-presentation of God (i.e. faith) is reinforced through repeated bodily practices as manifest in the relationships with fellow believers, which consequently will strengthen the tendency to yield themselves to God in any situation. To put it differently, what habituating this tendency of transformation reinforces also has to do with faith—particularly, its communal aspect, i.e. "the building up of the community in love and self-sacrifice" (cf. 12:3–8; 14:23 cf. 14:7).[53] Such implications of one's own faith for the community also concretizes the cognitive and emotional aspects of faith, since the different dimensions and functions of faith cannot be separated from one another.[54]

To summarize, God's self-giving act in Christ as his self-presentation elicits his human partners' response characterized by faith for reconciliation and development of

---

[46] Ernst Käsemann, "On Paul's Anthropology," in *Perspectives on Paul*, 21–2.
[47] Pierre Bourdieu, *Outline of a Theory of Practice* (Cambridge: Cambridge University Press, 1977), 82–3 ("a system of lasting, transposable dispositions which, integrating past experiences, functions at every moment as a *matrix of perceptions, appreciations, and actions* and makes possible the achievement of infinitely diversified tasks") (cited in Barclay, "Under," 70).
[48] Troels Engberg-Pedersen, *Cosmology and Self in the Apostle Paul: The Material Spirit* (Oxford: Oxford University Press, 2010), 141–2; Barclay, "Under," 69–73; Barclay, *Gift*, 504–8.
[49] Barclay, "Under," 72.
[50] Ibid., 75.
[51] Rusbult and Van Lange, "Why," 2055–6.
[52] Ben C. Dunson, "Faith in Romans: The Salvation of the Individual or Life in Community?," *JSNT* 34.1 (2011): 22; 34–8.
[53] Ibid.
[54] Ibid., 40–1.

the relationship, affecting their attributional activity at the cognitive and emotive levels.[55] The transformed attitude toward God—from a self-centred attitude ("given situation") to a prosocial one ("effective situation")—is reinforced through the habituation process, especially in a communal setting that requires bodily practices. Given the width of the meaning of faith in Paul, which covers mental (e.g. trusting), relational (e.g. fidelity or loyalty) and participatory (e.g. behavioural participation) dimensions,[56] what the transformation process eventually produces is the human partners' faith.[57] Thus, having faith in Christ is the human response ignited by God's demonstration of his faithfulness and love. In this respect, we trace the divine origin of human faith but can still characterize faith as a human response.

5.4 The results from the transformation: Positive outcomes for God and for the (long-term) relationship

Given that God's self-giving act as self-presentation can trigger the human partners' response of faith, which is indispensable for completing the reconciliation process, what positive outcomes can be made for God in that reconciled relationship as originally expected? In other words, in what way do human agents contribute to their partner and to the ongoing relationship by responding to their partner's positive expectations implied in the self-sacrificial act?

Even with the loss incurred from self-sacrifice, there are still positive outcomes for God. The demonstration of his righteousness—as faithfulness[58] and divine justice[59]—through Christ does yield some positive outcomes for God with regard to his fame, since righteousness has been considered as one of the reasons for praise.[60] But, more importantly, we also find positive outcomes for God from the reconciled relationship that originates from his human partners' response of faith. Moreover, given that faith can be seen as an expression of willingness to offer "amends," then such an expression contains not only a mental dimension but also a practical and behavioural aspect just as an act of making "amends" does. In this regard, Paul's "ethical

---

[55] Cf. Burnett, 222-4. ("cognitive and emotional elements" are "inherent" in faith).
[56] Cf. Hay, "Faith," 46.
[57] Identifying mental and behavioural changes in the course of the transformation process that results in "faith" as a relational attitude, our investigation demonstrates the point similar with Morgan's argument that "interiority, relationality, and action are inseparable wherever *pistis/fides,*" which is based on the examination of various ancient sources (e.g. Graeco-Roman, Jewish and Christian) (Morgan, 472).
[58] Jouette M. Bassler, *Navigating Paul: An Introduction to Key Theological Concepts* (Louisville: WJK, 2007), 53. Jewett also sees the righteousness of God revealed in Christ's death as "divine faithfulness to covenantal partners" (Jewett, *Romans,* 289).
[59] Bassler, 62.
[60] See Ps. 95:12–13; 96:1–2; 97:9; 98:4–5 (LXX). Similarly, deSilva understands the demonstration of God's righteousness in Christ's death in terms of the patronage system, in which benefactors demonstrate "virtuous character" through their generosity, thereby accruing a positive reputation (David deSilva, *Honor, Patronage, Kinship & Purity: Unlocking New Testament Culture* [Downers Grove: IVP Academic, 2000], 130).

exhortations" are noteworthy,[61] because we can observe that believers' proper lives, as a continuation of human response to God's self-presentation, can bring about positive outcomes for God.[62]

For instance, Rom. 12:1–2 claims that believers' lifestyle transformed in a prosocial manner can elicit God's pleasure. Paul exhorts the Roman believers to present their bodies as "a living sacrifice" (θυσίαν ζῶσαν), which is "holy [and] pleasing to God" (ἁγίαν εὐάρεστον τῷ θεω [12:1]). Becoming a "living sacrifice" involves a lifestyle that derives from a transformation marked by "the renewal of mind" (τῇ ἀνακαινώσει τοῦ νοὸς [12:2]). By experiencing such transformation, one is then able to discern what is "good and pleasing and perfect" (τὸ ἀγαθὸν καὶ εὐάρεστον καὶ τέλειον) for the partner. The cultic background of "worship" (λατρεία) also informs us that Rom. 12:1–2 epitomizes a partner (God)-oriented lifestyle.[63] Also, as Gupta notes, the use of παρίστημι in 12:1 demonstrates a close link between Rom. 12:1–2 and Rom. 6 in terms of the issue of "serving."[64] Furthermore, because "the mercies of God" (τῶν οἰκτιρμῶν τοῦ θεοῦ), a ground for Paul's exhortation, also basically point to God's gift-giving (i.e. Christ's death),[65] we can once again identify Christ's death as the essential factor in the transformation process, and also as an exemplar of the other-oriented lifestyle (cf. 15:1–3).[66]

At this point, despite differences in origins, there are similarities between Paul's idea of transformation and the process of transformation in IT that make them mutually illuminating. Firstly, in both cases, transformation takes place in the mind, which embraces both the cognitive and emotive dimensions of mental activity.[67] Of course, one cannot miss the habitual/behavioural aspect of transformation since Paul's imperatives—"do not be conformed" (μὴ συσχηματίζεσθε) and "be transformed"

---

[61] "Ethics" in a modern sense has a limitation to define the Pauline paraenesis (e.g. Romans 12–15), as the paraenesis is grounded in Paul's distinct experience of the Christ-event and his subsequently formed identity. Cf. Nijay K. Gupta, *Worship That Makes Sense to Paul: A New Approach to the Theology and Ethics of Paul's Cultic Metaphors* (Berlin: de Gruyter, 2010), 117. Victor Paul Furnish, *Theology and Ethics in Paul* (Louisville: WJK, 2009), 106 argues that the nature of the Pauline paraenesis intertwines both theological and ethical dimensions.

[62] Although Paul mainly stresses the principle of obedience in Romans 6, concrete examples of his principle are observable in the later chapters of the letter, in the so-called "ethical" sections. See especially Rom. 12:1–2; 14:7–8, 18. Cf. 2 Cor. 5:9; Eph. 5:10; Phil. 4:18; Col. 3:20; Tit. 2:9.

[63] Concerning Paul's own example of service, see Rom. 1:9 (Paul himself as a worshipper [ὁ θεός, ᾧ λατρεύω ἐν τῷ πνεύματί μου]). See also 15:16 in which Paul's self-identity and the duty are articulated with cultic expressions.

[64] Gupta, *Worship*, 119; 127–32; Barclay, "Under," 69. See Rom. 6:13, 16, 19 for the use of παρίστημι.

[65] Barclay, *Gift*, 508–9. Similarly, Victor Paul Furnish, "Living to God, Walking in Love: Theology and Ethics in Romans," in *Reading Paul's Letter to the Romans*, ed. Jerry L. Sumney (Atlanta: SBL, 2012), 194 ("this phrase connects his appeal . . . that he has said about Christ").

[66] Horrell notes the significance of the paradigm of Christ's self-giving as a "fundamental motivation and pattern" for Paul's ethical exhortations. See David G. Horrell, "Paul's Narratives or Narrative Substructure?: The Significance of 'Paul's Story,'" in *Narrative Dynamics in Paul* (Louisville: WJK, 2002), 166. Cf. Gupta, *Worship*, 125 ("sacrificing one's body" necessitates "a cost of conformity to Christ's suffering and death").

[67] Jewett's definition of the Pauline concept of νοῦς as "a constellation of thoughts and assumptions which fills the consciousness and provides the criteria for judgements and actions" helps us understand νοῦς as governing the totality of mental functions. See Jewett, *Anthropological*, 367; 385; 450 (cf. Rom. 1:28; 7:23, 25; 11:34; 14:5; 1 Cor. 1:10; 2:16; 14:14, 15, 19; Phil. 4:7).

(μεταμορφοῦσθε)—urge his hearers to exert their willpower toward embodying these attitudes. Secondly, the goal of both types of transformation is to enable one partner to have a committed attitude towards the other (e.g. to please one's partner). If the human partners' former attitude, the object of the transformation, is characterized by ignorance of the partner (God) (cf. Rom. 1:28), the core of the transformation in the mind is active acceptance of whatever pleases their partner.[68]

A similar pattern is found in 14:7–9 and 14:18. 14:7–9 reflects believers' transformed attitude towards God. The life of those reconciled with God is no longer driven by self-interest, but is now motivated to live and die for the sake of the Lord. Paul elaborates on the meaning and purpose of the Christ-event in Rom. 14:7–9, establishing a principle for coping with the problem of "the weak and the strong" in the community. Christ died and lived again in order that his human partners could become capable of living and dying for him, which summarizes the essence of Christ's lordship (14:9). Thus, every distinction derived from human standards is relativized in the light of this major principle (cf. 14:1–6). Similarly, in 2 Cor. 5:15, Paul claims that Christ died for all humanity in order to elicit a prosocial response from the human partners—"so that those who live might live no longer for themselves, but for him who died and was raised for them" (ἵνα οἱ ζῶντες μηκέτι ἑαυτοῖς ζῶσιν ἀλλὰ τῷ ὑπὲρ αὐτῶν ἀποθανόντι καὶ ἐγερθέντι [2 Cor. 5:15, NRSV]).[69] Therefore, the transformed lifestyle as a proper response to God's self-sacrifice is basically a partner-oriented one, always pursuing the partner's benefit.[70] In addition, in Rom. 8 we see how the relationship develops and creates positive outcomes for the relationship at the cosmic level.[71] As will be shown, the development of the divine-human relationship to that level is based on the reconciliation initiated by God's self-sacrificial act in Christ's death.

5.5 Contextual evidence: Christ's death as a gift[72]

Paul's portrayal of the Christ-event as a gift throughout Rom. 3:21–5:21 (χάρις [3:24; 5:15, 17, 20, 21]/χάρισμα [5:16]/δώρημα [5:16]/δωρεά [5:15, 17]),[73] also points to the nature of God's self-sacrifice as an act of communication that aims to elicit a positive

---

[68] George H. Van Kooten, *Paul's Anthropology in Context* (Tübingen: Mohr Siebeck, 2008), 388–9 also finds a link between the two different types of minds (a debased mind [ἀδόκιμον νοῦν, 1:28] and the transformed mind [12:2]) in terms of "metamorphosis." See also Craig S. Keener, *The Mind of the Spirit: Paul's Approach to Transformed Thinking* (Grand Rapids: Baker Academic, 2016), 155 who finds a stark contrast between "the corrupted mind" (1:18–32) and "the renewed mind" (12:1–3).
[69] Hays also connects Rom. 12:1–2 and 2 Cor. 5:14–21, seeing both texts as describing the same vision (Richard B. Hays, *The Moral Vision of the New Testament: A Contemporary Introduction To New Testament Ethics* [Edinburgh: T&T Clark, 1997], 35).
[70] In the same vein, Paul wants his recipients to imitate his own lifestyle of devotion to the Lord, bearing the risk of all kinds of shame and danger for the sake of Christ (1 Cor. 4:6–16; 11:1; cf. Phil. 3:17).
[71] See Chapter 7 of the present study.
[72] For studies on the meaning of gift in Paul in terms of the interaction between God and human beings, see the review of scholarship on χάρις in Chapter 1.
[73] Χάρις in 5:2 does not appear to directly address the Christ-event, although it basically points to the effect of the Christ-event.

response from the human partners for developing the relationship. The studies of the concept of "gift" in Paul commonly argue that "gift" carries the expectation of mutual interactions, including a response from the recipient.[74] Barclay argues that Paul "draws on the ancient assumption that gifts are vehicles of power, creating obligations and allegiances through their very character as gift."[75] Thus, as believers' obligation, "Christian obedience" is a response to the gift of God in Christ.[76] What makes Paul's notion of gift distinct is not because the gift is "unconditional" by nature, but because it is given regardless of the worth of its recipients (i.e. "unconditioned gift").[77] David deSilva also points out that Paul's concept of gift entails the expectation about the recipient's welcoming response:

> God should give such a gift with the expectation that the recipients would respond in ways that aligned with what would be understood as a grateful response, rather than with no expectation that the gift would impact their lives in a significant way so as to establish (at last) an ongoing, mutual relationship between them and a just and holy God, is entirely in keeping with the ancient ethic of gift-giving.[78]

Here, deSilva recognizes that the recipients' positive response is essential for managing an ongoing relationship. Engberg-Pedersen also touches on a similar point, arguing that "personal involvement" in the form of friendship created by gift-giving is also present in Paul's notion of gift.[79]

Several scholars note that the response to the divine gift can be expressed in the form of human gift-giving. Joubert argues that human gift-giving can be regarded as one of the ways to respond to God's gift, arguing that the corollary of "God's eschatological gift of new life through Christ's sacrifice" is to place "all believers in debt to him [God]."[80]

---

[74] This concept of "gift" is also found among Paul's contemporaries. Stephen Joubert points out that it is impossible to rule out Paul's own *Umwelt* from Paul's conceptualization of the gift based on the Christ-event (Stephan Joubert, *Paul as Benefactor: Reciprocity, Strategy and Theological Reflection in Paul's Collection* [Tübingen: Mohr Siebeck, 2000], 216–17). Briones acknowledges the similarity between Paul and Seneca (*De beneficiis*) regarding the meaning of χάρις. According to Briones, the notions of "mutual obligation" and "other-oriented self-interest" are still meaningful in Paul's understanding of χάρις as it is in Seneca, though for Paul it is redefined in Christ (Briones, *Financial*, 42–56). Similarly, Thomas R. Blanton, "The Benefactor's Account-book: The Rhetoric of Gift Reciprocation According to Seneca and Paul," *NTS* 59.3 (2013): 400; 413–14. Barclay, investigating the various sources of Second Temple Judaism (e.g. Wisdom, Philo, Hodayot, Pseudo-Philo's LAB, 4 Ezra), argues that "none of them perfect the non-circularity of grace, the notion that God gives without expectation of return" (e.g. gratitude and praise), and neither does Paul in Romans (Barclay, *Gift*, 314; 500; 558; 569). McFarland notes that both Philo and Paul acknowledge the importance of the recipient's expression of gratitude as a response toward gift (cf. *Legat.* 118; *Post.* 33–39; *Spec.* 2.234; *Plant.* 130; Rom. 1:21; 14:6) (McFarland, 183–9; 211–12; 219–21). deSilva also argues that "God's grace [χάρις] would not have been of a different kind than the grace with which they were already familiar," though he admits that it is distinctive in terms of "quality and degree" (deSilva, *Honor*, 122).
[75] Barclay, *Gift*, 497.
[76] Ibid., 517.
[77] Ibid., 500.
[78] deSilva, "Grace," 42.
[79] Engberg-Pedersen, "Gift-Giving," 18–20.
[80] Joubert, *Benefactor*, 138.

Therefore, it is to respond to such divine benefaction to participate in Paul's call for the collection (cf. 2 Cor. 8:1–6).[81] Similarly, McFarland also notes that Paul regards human gift-giving as "participation within the divine gift economy."[82] Briones also recognizes that human giving is a route of both receiving God's gift and returning gratitude to God.[83]

To summarize, we can recognize that there exists an expectation of the human partner's proper response latent in God's sacrificial act in Christ, according to Paul's articulation of the Christ-event (especially death) as a gift. Also, such an expectation includes the prospective development of an ongoing relationship. The studies of the concept of gift in Paul are significant for demonstrating that a framework of interpersonal relationships plays an important role for Paul in portraying the interactions between God and humanity.[84] What distinguishes our approach utilizing IT is that the studies of gift start from a specific expression by which the Christ-event is conceptualized, whereas our approach pays more attention to the contents of the Christ-event. Nevertheless, the fact that the act of gift-giving requires one to relinquish a private resource, indicates that there are points of intersection between the two types of approaches. In any case, both a self-sacrificial act for a partner and gift-giving anticipate a positive response, and this illuminates the relational implication of the Christ-event.

5.6 Conclusion

To conclude, by focusing on God's self-sacrificial act in Christ's death as a means of "self-presentation," we have discussed how it is possible for the human partners once hostile to God to accept what God has done by faith for reconciliation. Christ's death, as "self-presentation" of God's trustworthiness, has the power to transform the human partners' cognition, emotion and habit; it also evokes a transformation of motivation characterized by an obedient lifestyle committed to God, which can be summarized in the concept of "faith." It is also this transformation process through which hope for the future of the relationship becomes a reality. Paul's depiction of the Christ-event as "gift" also indicates that God's self-giving act in Christ anticipates a response that can strengthen the ties of the divine-human relationship. Given the purpose of God's commitment to his human partners, God's sacrifice in Christ's death cannot be completely explained if it is considered as merely unilateral benevolence; rather, it is an act of communication for eliciting a response from a partner that can make the relationship persistent and beneficial. It is on this ground that positive outcomes for the relationship become available, both for God and for

---

[81] Ibid., 138–9.
[82] McFarland, 212.
[83] Briones, *Financial*, 218–24; cf. idem, "Mutual Brokers of Grace: A Study in 2 Corinthians 1.3–11," *NTS* 56.4 (2010): 554.
[84] Cf. Stephen C. Mott and Gerald F. Hawthorne, "The Power of Giving and Receiving: Reciprocity in Hellenistic Benevolence," in *Current Issues in Biblical and Patristic Interpretation* (Grand Rapids: Eerdmans, 1975), 60–72.

human beings. In this respect, Christ's death lays the foundation for a mutually beneficial relationship.

Nevertheless, our investigation with IT does not claim that human beings are able to contribute something positive in the relationship with God by themselves; neither do we argue that the human response is to simply repay or "match" what God has done.[85] Rather, our analysis shows how God faithfully creates and leads the relationship, transforming his human partners into capable agents who are invited to contribute some paint strokes to the grand picture of God's plan for the cosmos. For Paul, it is an important fact that, despite the existential gap, God chose human beings to be his partners (cf. Rom. 8:28)[86] who can bring either negative or positive outcomes to the relationship. We will discuss how the human role is significant for the accomplishment of the shared goal, i.e. the cosmic vision of salvation, in Chapter 7. Before delving into this topic, we will examine the opposing relationship in which human beings have been involved, namely, the relationship with Sin as a cosmic entity. By investigating this relationship, which is antithetical to the divine-human counterpart, we will elucidate another meaning of the Christ-event, viz. its effect on Sin's dominion over humanity. Such an investigation will provide an answer to the question of how a fallen humanity under Sin's dominion becomes able to respond to God.

---

[85] Cf. deSilva, "Debtors," 170 ("[T]he obligation to respond is not an obligation to *match* the gift" [emphasis original]).

[86] See also Rom. 1:6, 7. Paul's understanding of his own apostleship underscores a similar point (cf. Rom. 1:1; 1 Cor. 1:1; 2 Cor. 1:1; Gal. 1:15; Phil. 1:1).

6

History of Slavery and History of Salvation: An Investigation of the Sin-Human Relationship (Rom. 5:12–8:11)

6.1 Introduction

In the previous two chapters, we discussed the relational significance of Christ's death for the restoration of the divine-human relationship. In this chapter, we will analyze the Sin-human relationship, a case antithetical to the divine-human relationship, in order to understand the other side of the meaning of Christ's death. As noted in Chapter 3 (Rom. 1:18–3:20), humanity's betrayal of God caused an alternative relationship, i.e. the relationship with Sin as a personified power hostile to God. Granted this situation, terminating the Sin-human relationship is an essential precondition of the remedy for the brokenness of the divine-human relationship. Therefore, in the present chapter, by investigating the Sin-human relationship in Rom. 5:12–8:11, we will explore 1) the main reason for humanity's lack of ability to escape from the relationship with Sin, and subsequently 2) how Christ's death is effective for introducing change to the Sin-human relationship. Romans 7 will be our primary focus because it illustrates the human situation under Sin's oppression in detail through the monologue of the "I" (ἐγώ).

To begin with, we will see how Paul conceives of Sin, drawing attention to Sin's identity as a personified cosmic force opposing God and as a cruel slave master. The metaphor of slavery used to portray Sin's oppression offers an important key to define the relational structure of the Sin-human relationship. Such observations invite the IT framework of "non-voluntary relationship," which will help us recognize the relational dynamic that sustains Sin's dominion over humanity and the meaning of Christ-event for freeing humans from that situation. By analyzing the relational structure of the Sin-human relationship, we will also suggest a solution to a complex exegetical issue of the point in time that Rom. 7:7–25 reflects.

6.2 The identity of Sin in Romans 5–8

In order to map the geography of the Sin-human relationship, we will examine how Paul construes the identity of Sin throughout Romans 5–8. There are two literary strategies that Paul utilizes to colour the portrait of Sin. One is the personification of Sin as a cosmic power, and the other is the depiction of the Sin-human relationship with a slavery metaphor.

6.2.1 Sin as a personified cosmic power

Paul's treatment of Sin (ἁμαρτία) as a personified cosmic entity is prominent in Romans. As Martyn points out, Sin is described as one of the main actors alongside God and human beings in Paul's narrative of salvation.[1] Sin is an active agent that exerts its power over humanity (Rom. 5:12, 21; 6:12; 7:8–9, 11, 17, 20), and its work is depicted as having influence on the whole cosmos (Rom. 5:12–21; cf. 1 Cor. 15:20–28).[2] Although several scholars are reluctant to admit the existence of Sin as a personified cosmic force in Romans,[3] it is hard to deny that throughout Rom. 5–8 Paul presents Sin as one of the main actors in the drama of the history of salvation from Adam to Christ.[4]

Gaventa points out that one of the main reasons for the scholarly lack of interest in Sin as a personified cosmic power is because ἁμαρτία is often treated as "a feature of human activity or human experience."[5] For example, Moo argues that what is personified in Rom. 5:12–8:13 is "a principle" or "network" constituted by "individual acts of sin."[6] A similar tendency is observed when Stephen Westerholm argues that what is at issue in Rom. 6:16–23 is the "personification of patterns of life, not supernatural forces,"[7] though he does not entirely deny the fact that in some places Paul's depiction of Sin is close to the shape of a demonic force (e.g. 5:12). However, Paul's use of ἁμαρτία as human transgression (cf. Romans 1–3) is not incompatible with the depiction of Sin as a personified power.[8] There are some points in Rom. 5 (e.g. 5:13, 20) when ἁμαρτία seems to indicate human transgression. Nevertheless, this does not necessarily exclude the fact that Paul personifies ἁμαρτία as a cosmic power in the context.[9] Rather, the various uses

---

[1] Martyn, "Epilogue," 178–82.
[2] Beverly Roberts Gaventa, "The Cosmic Power of Sin in Paul's Letter to the Romans," *Int* 58.3 (2004): 236–7; idem, "Neither Height nor Depth: Discerning the Cosmology of Romans," *STJ* 64.3 (2011): 269–77. Cf. Fitzmyer, *Romans*, 411–12.
[3] E.g. Stowers, *Rereading*; Troels Engberg-Pedersen, *Paul and the Stoics* (Louisville: WJK, 2000), 225–46.
[4] Death (θάνατος) is another personified subject in Rom. 5:12–21 that is closely associated with Sin (cf. 1 Cor. 15:56). However, we will primarily focus on Sin, since it is treated as a representative of anti-divine agents throughout Rom. 5:12–8:11.
[5] Gaventa, "Cosmic," 229–31.
[6] Moo, *Romans*, 319 (n. 25) ("it is not clear that Paul personalizes sin, viewing it as a 'demon'"). See also Dunn, *Romans 1–8*, 272.
[7] Stephen Westerholm, "Paul's Anthropological 'Pessimism' in Its Jewish Context," in *Divine and Human Agency*, 79. See also Miller, 104–9 who understands that Paul is talking about the "passions" in 6:12–23. Cf. Emma Wasserman, "Paul among the Philosophers: The Case of Sin in Romans 6–8," *JSNT* 30.4 (2008): 401–10.
[8] Gathercole also suggests that sin and Sin coexist in Romans, being closely interrelated with one another. He sees that both sin in Romans 1 and Sin in Romans 7 function as a means of divine revelation (Simon J. Gathercole, "Sin in God's Economy: Romans 1 and 7," in *Divine and Human Agency*, 158–72).
[9] *Pace* Cranfield, 273.

of the word ἁμαρτία can demonstrate a close link between Sin as a personified power and sin as tangible human practice in Paul's thought.[10] Moreover, given the fact that the terms related to παράβασις or παράπτωμα that indicate human transgression are increasingly employed when Paul begins to personify ἁμαρτία, we can recognize that Paul is sensitive to the distinction between the demonic force and human transgressions in this context. The use of the singular form of ἁμαρτία throughout 5:12–8:11 can also be deliberate.[11]

Also, if we sustain a relational perspective on this issue, we can recognize that Sin's role as an anti-divine cosmic entity is an important element for the relational dynamics in the cosmos and the conflicts present in the text. If Paul describes Sin at a purely metaphorical level or merely as human transgression, what Paul says about the divine-human relationship in Rom. 5–8 will be ambiguous,[12] because Paul explains the divine-human relationship through the sets of contrast with the Sin-human relationship of these chapters, though this does not assume ontological symmetry between God and Sin. Moreover, we need to note that there are several hints throughout Romans that show that Paul is conscious of the activity of an anti-divine power (cf. 1:18–32; 3:9).[13] De Boer also points out that both 1:16–17 ("the personification of God's righteousness") and 3:9 ("the personification of Sin") anticipate the presentation of Sin as a "cosmological power."[14] In some places Paul explicitly announces such a cosmic power with a particular name (cf. 16:17–20),[15] which he also does in his other letters.[16]

However, accepting the existence of Sin as a cosmic power does not necessitate that we ascribe all human transgressions to Sin as a demonic power in our interpretation.[17] Sin is not a power that can exercise its dominion regardless of human beings' cooperation.[18] Paul warns his readers: "Do not present your members to Sin as instruments of unrighteousness" (μηδὲ παριστάνετε τὰ μέλη ὑμῶν ὅπλα ἀδικίας τῇ

---

[10] Dodson, 137.
[11] Moo, *Romans*, 319.
[12] Gaventa claims that Paul is using an "ontological metaphor," not purely metaphorical or figurative language, in identifying the cosmic agents (i.e. Sin, Death and "Rectification") (Beverly Roberts Gaventa, "The Rhetoric of Violence and the God of Peace in Paul's Letter to Romans," in *Paul, John, and Apocalyptic Eschatology: Studies in Honour of Martinus C. de Boer*, ed. Jan Krans et al. [Leiden: Brill, 2012], 72–3). See also Dodson, 137. Although Dodson does not present his opinion on the issue of whether Sin is a real entity or not, he thinks a personified Sin forms a counterpart of the divine-human relationship in the context in a literary level.
[13] For Sin's identity implied in 1:18–32, see Chapter 3 (3.2.3) of the present study.
[14] Martinus C. de Boer, "Paul's Mythologizing Program in Romans 5–8," in *Apocalyptic Paul*, 19.
[15] Gaventa, "Rhetoric," 62–3 advocates the originality of Rom. 16:17–20, arguing that the human situation illustrated with "rhetoric of violence" necessitates the divine action as expressed in that passage.
[16] Satan (cf. 1 Cor. 5:5; 7:5; 2 Cor. 2:11; 11:14; 12:7; 1 Thess. 2:18); 2 Cor. 4:4; 6:14; 1 Thess. 3:5; 1 Cor. 10:20–21. Cf. de Boer, "Mythologizing," 13.
[17] The present argument is an answer to Westerholm's concern about the imprudence of overemphasizing Sin as a personified power (Westerholm, 79). Bultmann viewed Paul's articulation of cosmic drama as influenced by Gnosticism. See Rudolf Bultmann, "New Testament and Mythology," in *Kerygma and Myth: A Theological Debate*, ed. Hans Werner Bartsch, trans. Reginald H. Fuller (New York: Harper & Row, 1961), 1–8.
[18] *Pace* Martinus C. de Boer, *The Defeat of Death: Apocalyptic Eschatology in 1 Corinthians 15 and Romans 5* (Sheffield: JSOT Press, 1988), 85–91; idem, "Apocalyptic as God's Eschatological Activity in Paul's Theology," in *Paul and the Apocalyptic Imagination*, 51–9.

ἁμαρτία [6:13; cf. 6:11, 19]). This admonition indicates the fact that human beings play their own role in their interactions with Sin. We have already noted that various types of transgressions originate from the affiliation between Sin and human beings (cf. 1:24–32), in which human beings' role is not merely to passively conform to and remain steady in the relationship.[19] In this respect, Dodson correctly points out Paul's reasoning on the responsibility for transgressions, arguing that "to demonstrate that all unredeemed humanity abides under the regime of Sin, he [Paul] presents it as a ruler who shares the blame for evil. However, when the apostle desires to personify Sin for the sake of ethical exhortation, he develops Sin into an internal master who can and should be rejected."[20]

6.2.2 Sin as a malicious slave master

The metaphor of slavery portrays the tyrannical side of Sin's character.[21] Although Paul can utilize different images and aspects of slavery throughout Romans 6–8,[22] including the case related to "voluntary slavery",[23] Paul's description of Sin's dominion corresponds to the dark side of Graeco-Roman slavery practices. Although some scholars stress the positive aspects of slavery in the Graeco-Roman world,[24] the master-slave relationship in that society often involved the one party's (i.e. master's) oppression and abuse of the other (i.e. slave). For instance, Tacitus's famous story about how the murder of Pedanius Secundus by one of his slaves resulted in the execution of all the household slaves illustrates how vulnerable slaves' lives were (*Ann.* 14.42–45). Apuleius's descriptions of

---

[19] Cf. Section 3.2 of the present study.

[20] Dodson, 135–6. Dodson argues that the relational framework that he terms "partnership paradigm" shows that Paul does not ascribe the problem of sin solely to one party, either evil powers or human beings (so also the author of Wisdom) (ibid., 185–9).

[21] Cf. J. Albert Harrill, *Slaves in the New Testament: Literary, Social, and Moral Dimensions* (Minneapolis: Fortress, 2006), 17–34. Oakes also points out the prevalence of the slavery metaphor in Romans 7, indicating its relevance for the particular situation of Paul's hearers (cf. Oakes, *Romans*, 147).

[22] A number of studies note the complexity of slavery in ancient Graeco-Roman society. See Dale B. Martin, *Slavery as Salvation: The Metaphor of Slavery in Pauline Christianity* (New Haven: Yale University Press, 1990), xxii–xxiii; J. Albert Harrill, "Slavery," in *DNTB* (Downers Grove: IVP, 2000), 1124–8; idem, *Slaves*, 5; Hendrik Goede, "Constructing Ancient Slavery as Socio-Historic Context of the New Testament," *HTS Teologiese Studies/Theological Studies* 69.1 (2013): 1–7. Some scholars highlight the positives dimensions of slavery in antiquity, whereas others stress the negative aspects (John Byron, "Paul and the Background of Slavery: The Status Quaestionis in New Testament Scholarship," *CBR* 3.1 [2004]: 116–39).

[23] Dale Martin argues that one of the distinctive types of slavery in ancient Graeco-Roman society is "slavery as a means of social mobility" (Martin, *Slavery*, xxii). Martin argues that for the purpose of "social mobility," "even voluntary self-enslavement was conceivable among some portion of the population" (cf. *Ep.* 47.17) (Martin, *Slavery*, 36–42). Romans 6:16 can be seen as reflecting the background of "voluntary slavery" (cf. Dunn, *Romans 1–8*, 340–1). Byron rejects the Graeco-Roman background of self-sale, and argues that what Paul discusses in Romans 6 is not the matter of choosing freedom or enslavement, but of changing masters, suggesting that the Exodus imagery is a more relevant background. See John Byron, *Slavery Metaphors in Early Judaism and Pauline Christianity: A Traditio-Historical and Exegetical Examination* (Tübingen: Mohr Siebeck, 2003), 211–19. However, if we accept that Paul does not necessarily apply all dimensions of a metaphor when he adopts it, the Graeco-Roman voluntary slavery motif can still be a useful device to highlight the importance of one's decision.

[24] For example, Scott Bartchy, Francis Lyall and Dale Martin (see Byron, "Background," 117–19; 121–3).

slaves in *The Golden Ass* (*Metamorphoses*) also reflect similar points.[25] Slaves were physically vulnerable, abused and treated like animals.[26] In a similar vein, borrowing Orlando Patterson's phrase, Combes argues that being a slave means "social death."[27] Every type of slavery presupposes the restriction of freedom.[28] Slavery is not only a physical condition but also affects one's social status, bringing about total alienation from family and society.[29] Furthermore, if a slave owner is malicious, the situation becomes much worse; the personality and character of the master practically defines the quality of a slave's life.[30]

Paul depicts that Sin dominates over humanity just as a cruel slave owner does. Sin is characterized as one who imposes its rule (βασιλεύω) through death (5:14, 17, 21). This not only implies that death is the final outcome of humanity's relationship with Sin, but also shows that Sin's dominion is fear, just as in many negative cases of master-slave relationships.[31] Death was in no way an abstract idea but a very palpable issue for Paul's audiences, especially for those who were living in harsh conditions.[32] Sin's dominion of fear is also observed in 8:15. Whereas believers' relationship with God is analogous to a father-child relationship, the slavery under Sin is characterized by fear (οὐ γὰρ ἐλάβετε πνεῦμα δουλείας πάλιν εἰς φόβον). The terms related to rule (βασιλεύω/κυριεύω), servitude (δουλεύω) and sale (πιπράσκω) in Romans 6–7 also display the unhealthy relational dynamics of the Sin-human relationship. In 6:15–23,[33] we can see that Sin brings negative outcomes to human beings, revealing its tyrannical and exploitive character.[34] Sin leads humanity to lawlessness (ἀνομία [6:19]), and the ultimate outcome from this relationship is death (θάνατος [6:23]; cf. 7:11). Moreover, Sin oppresses human beings so that they cannot

---

[25] For a detailed analysis of the text, see Keith Bradley, "Animalizing the Slave: The Truth of Fiction," *JRS* 90 (2000): 110–25.

[26] J. Albert Harrill, "Paul and Slavery," in *Paul in the Greco-Roman World: A Handbook*, ed. J. Paul Sampley (Harrisburg: Trinity Press International, 2003), 582. Harrill estimates that Bradley's study on *The Golden Ass* rejects the positive views on slavery (J. Albert Harrill, "Slavery and Inhumanity: Keith Bradley's Legacy on Slavery in New Testament Studies," *BibInt* 21 [2013]: 506–14). For other negative examples, see Seneca, *De Ira* 3.40 (cited in John M.G. Barclay, "Paul, Philemon and the Dilemma of Christian Slave-Ownership," *NTS* 37.2 [1991]: 166–7).

[27] I.A.H. Combes, *The Metaphor of Slavery in the Writings of the Early Church: From the New Testament to the Beginning of the Fifth Century* (Sheffield: JSOT Press, 1998), 87–9; Orlando Patterson, *Slavery and Social Death: A Comparative Study* (Cambridge: Harvard University Press, 1982) (see Byron, "Background," 123).

[28] Jewett, *Romans*, 416.

[29] Byron, "Background," 120. For instance, Juvenal, *Sat.* 11 (cited in Barclay, "Slave-Ownership," 167 [n. 26]).

[30] Barclay, "Slave-Ownership," 166–7. Cf. Patterson, 26 ("the master had power over all aspects of his slave's life").

[31] Cf. Barclay, "Slave-Ownership," 167.

[32] Cf. Oakes, *Romans*, 141–3.

[33] In 6:15–23, Paul not only personifies Sin but also righteousness. God is the one whom the personified righteousness indicates. Thus, Paul offers two sets of comparison in order to show how the relationship with two different partners can result in drastically contrastive outcomes. Cf. David J. Southall, *Rediscovering Righteousness in Romans* (Tübingen: Mohr Siebeck, 2008), 83–111; 113–47.

[34] For the constant influence of the slavery metaphor throughout Romans 7–8, see 7:6, 25 (δουλεύω); 8:15 (πνεῦμα δουλείας). Cf. 8:21(τῆς δουλείας τῆς φθορᾶς).

freely choose how to act (cf. 7:14–20).³⁵ As we will see, understanding the slavery metaphor is important for defining Sin's identity as well as the relational dynamics that sustain the miserable conditions of humanity's relationship with Sin. Furthermore, it is through the slavery metaphor that we can recognize why throughout Romans 6–7 Paul utilizes the concept of death when dealing with the issue of obtaining freedom from Sin's dominion.

6.3 Romans 7 in the light of IT–The issue of the "I" (Rom. 7:7–25)

As we have discussed, Paul describes Sin as a personified cosmic force that exerts dominion over humanity as a malicious slave master does. In Romans 7, the Sin-human relationship is spelled out in more detail through the monologue of the "I" (ἐγώ). Although a few scholars insist on the existence of a disjunction between 7:7–13 and 7:14–25,³⁶ there are several elements that sustain the unity of 7:7–25, and the issue of Sin's oppressiveness is one of the elements that can be continuously witnessed throughout.³⁷ Therefore, the activity of Sin still remains as a focal point.³⁸ Although Paul aims to make an apologia for the law,³⁹ such an aim is achieved by presenting a subtle picture of how Sin oppresses the "I." Therefore, by focusing on how Sin operates in the dilemmatic situation of the "I"—a situation characterized by the dissonance between what the "I" pursues and what the "I" actually does—we will be treating one of the main issues in this text.

Romans 7 is one of the difficult passages in the letter that has puzzled many scholars, in particular, regarding the identity of the "I."⁴⁰ Given that Sin's activity is portrayed by

---

[35] As will be argued below, the "I" in Romans 7 can be seen as a generic human being, identical to the humanity in Romans 5–6.

[36] Cranfield, 342; Stowers, *Rereading*, 259; Longenecker, *Romans*, 639. However the distinctions are not decisive enough to make a clear division. For instance, the present tense in 7:14–25 can make the agony of the "I" lively and vivid, helping the readers relate that agony to themselves. Cf. Stuhlmacher, *Romans*, 109.

[37] The presence of the speaker "I" also supports the continuity between 7:7–13 and 7:14–25.

[38] Cf. Paul W. Meyer, "The Worm at the Core of the Apple: Exegetical Reflections on Romans 7," in *The Word in This World: Essays in New Testament Exegesis and Theology*, ed. John T. Carroll (Louisville: WJK, 2004), 69–70 ("the central protagonist in the whole of 7:7–25 ... is not the law at all but sin as a personified power").

[39] Dunn, *Romans 1–8*, 376.

[40] For instance, the "I" represents 1) a person who is defeated by "passions and desires" as in the Hellenistic moral psychology (Emma Wasserman, *The Death of the Soul in Romans 7* [Tübingen: Mohr Siebeck, 2008]); 2) general humanity without Christ (Rudolf Bultmann, "Romans 7 and the Anthropology of Paul," in *Existence and Faith: Shorter Writings of Rudolf Bultmann*, ed. S.M. Ogden [London: Hodder & Stoughton, 1961], 147–57; Käsemann, *Romans*, 192–7 ["mankind under the law"]); 3) Paul's experience as a Jewish boy (Robert H. Gundry, "The Moral Frustration of Paul before His Conversion: Sexual Lust in Romans 7:7–25," in *Pauline Studies: Festschrift for F.F. Bruce* [Exeter: Paternoster, 1980], 228–45); 4) Paul's pre-Christian (conversion) experience (Jewett, *Romans*, 443–5); 5), both Paul's pre-Christian (7:7–12) and post-Christian (7:13–25) experiences; 6) Paul's post-conversion experience (Cranfield, 345–7; Dunn, *Romans 1–8*, 382–3; 389–90 [with an emphasis on "eschatological tension"]); 7) an intrinsic situation of a sinful human being who confronts the law after the Christ-event (Mark A. Seifrid, "The Subject of Rom 7:14–25," *NovT* 34.4 [1992]: 313–33); 8) the experience of Israel (Wright, *Climax*, 196–200; Moo, *Romans*, 428–31; Kruse, 319–21; John K. Goodrich, "Sold under Sin: Echoes of Exile in Romans 7:14–25," *NTS* 59.4 [2013]:

the monologue of the "I," we must identify on whose behalf the "I" is speaking. Scholars generally have different interpretative tendencies regarding understanding the two issues surrounding the identity of the "I": 1) Does the "I" directly refer to Paul's personal experiences? If not, what kind of subject does the "I" represent?; and 2) Which point in time does the situation of the "I" represent?[41]

Recently, there seems to be widespread agreement that Paul does not directly describe his autobiographical experience in Romans 7.[42] The "I" can be a rhetorical device that indicates people in general, similar to the Greek convention of *prosōpopoiia* (speech-in-character)[43] or *Stilform* (stylistic form).[44] This point of view, however, does not necessarily rule out the possibility that Paul's own experiences influenced the description of the "I."[45] Thus, we can understand that Paul tries to say something dramatically, which can be meaningful for all his hearers, borrowing the voice of the "I."

Also, when using the voice of the "I," Paul does not restrict its relevance to a specific ethnic group, Jews or Gentiles.[46] The references to Adam and the law, the elements closely related to the identity of the "I,"[47] are still relevant for both Jews and Gentiles. The allusion to Adam implies that Paul wants to make the monologue of the "I" meaningful for all human beings.[48] Just as in 5:12–21, an earlier passage where Paul refers to the story of Adam, here Paul broadens the scope of his argument to embrace a cosmic and universal scale. Also, the fact that Paul tends to treat the law in a universal manner in Romans 5–8 should be mentioned. Paul's choice of the tenth commandment (7:7) can be seen as a deliberate attempt to make the agony that the "I" experiences in relation to the law relevant for all people.[49] In Paul's contemporary culture, having

---

476–95); 9) a gentile Christian who tries to keep the law (Stowers, *Rereading*, 273–84; Harrill, *Slaves*, 26–30); 10) a Jewish Christian (L. Ann Jervis, "'The Commandment Which Is for Life' [Romans 7.10]: Sin's Use of the Obedience of Faith," *JSNT* 27.2 [2004]: 193–216; Hae-Kyung Chang, "The Christian Life in a Dialectical Tension? Romans 7:7-25 Reconsidered," *NovT* 49.3 [2007]: 257–80); 11) a religious Jewish person; 12) a generic human being (but mostly a Jewish person) described in "the two way tradition" that highlights the capability of human agency (cf. Ben Sira) (Maston, *Divine and Human Agency*, 127–52); and 13) a rhetorical device adopted from the Psalter reinterpreted in the light of the gospel (Beverly Roberts Gaventa, "The Shape of the 'I': The Psalter, the Gospel, and the Speaker in Romans 7," in *Apocalyptic Paul*, 77–92). These lists complement Kruse, 314–21.

[41] Cf. Jewett, *Romans*, 441; Longenecker, *Romans*, 651.

[42] The influence of Stendahl and Sanders who try to distance this passage from Paul's experience of conversion can be seen as formative for this viewpoint. See Stendahl, "Introspective"; Sanders, 443.

[43] Cf. Stowers, *Rereading*, 264–9. As Jewett points out, the overlap between Paul (Rom. 7:7) and Epictetus (*Diatr.* 1.12) is notable (Jewett, *Romans*, 443–4).

[44] Werner G. Kümmel, *Römer 7 Und Die Bekehrung Des Paulus* (Leipzig: J.C. Hinrichs, 1974), 119–32.

[45] Pace Kümmel, 85–97. Cf. Theissen, 194; Moo, *Romans*, 427–8; Jewett, *Romans*, 441. Stendahl's famous objection—which is based on his interpretation of Paul's "robust conscience" in Phil. 3:6—does not necessarily prove that Paul had no inner conflict in any way similar to the "I" in Romans 7. Rather, the passage contains a highly rhetorical argument in which a hint of hyperbolism can be perceived. Cf. John M. Espy, "Paul's 'Robust Conscience' Re-Examined," *NTS* 31 (1985): 164–5.

[46] Cf. Gaventa, "I," 88.

[47] Dodd, *Paul's Paradigmatic "I,"* 230.

[48] Cf. Käsemann, *Romans*, 196; Ziesler, *Romans*, 181–4. For a detailed analysis of the allusion to Adam's story, see Francis Watson, *Paul, Judaism, and the Gentiles: Beyond the New Perspective* (Grand Rapids: Eerdmans, 2007), 279–87.

[49] For this inclusiveness of the tenth commandment see, John A. Ziesler, "The Role of the Tenth Commandment in Romans 7," *JSNT* 33 (1988): 46; Oakes, *Romans*, 146.

ἐπιθυμία was widely recognized as sinful.[50] Also, we need to remember that the Roman congregations consist of both Jews and Gentiles.[51] Therefore, Paul needed to make his message relevant and meaningful for both Jews and Gentiles.[52] If 7:7–25 spoke only about the Jews' experience (or, conversely, the Gentiles'), we cannot properly identify Paul's universal vision of salvation and his concept of human beings' location within it in the subsequent passage (i.e. Romans 8). In this respect, we understand the "I" as primarily representing humanity in general, and thus the universal manner in which Paul articulates the issue of Sin and salvation is also sustained.

The second question is particularly relevant to our primary aim in the present chapter. In order to identify the temporal situation of the "I," we must understand how the "I" as a generic human being interacts with Sin. We have discussed that Sin exercises dominion like a cruel slave master in the relationship with humanity. In Rom. 7:15 (cf. 7:19), a characteristic description—"For I do not do what I want, but I do the thing I hate" (οὐ γὰρ ὃ θέλω τοῦτο πράσσω, ἀλλ' ὃ μισῶ τοῦτο ποιω)—exemplifies the slavery under Sin, in which one's freedom is totally restricted by a governing power. We will summarize this particular situation in two points. Firstly, the situation portrays an oppressive relationship between an abusive partner (Sin) and a helpless counterpart (the "I"). Secondly, despite the abuse, the victimized partner (the "I") is unable to leave the relationship. This type of relationship is a typical case of "non-voluntary dependence" as defined by IT. Based on this observation, we will bring the IT framework into our discussion of Romans 7, finding answers to the questions of why the "I" cannot leave the relationship despite its awareness of the harms from the relationship, and of the manner in which the Christ-event relates to this situation. As a corollary, of course, we will also offer a suggestion to the issue of the point in time of the dilemmatic situation of the "I."

6.3.1 "Non-voluntary relationship" in IT

Why are some people unable to leave an unsatisfactory relationship, but choose to remain in it? Thibaut and Kelley define this as a "non-voluntary relationship," in which "the person is forced to stay even though he would prefer not to."[53] IT studies attempt to explain this paradoxical phenomenon with respect to the expectation of "outcomes," drawing attention to the significance of the relational structure of the relationship, which regulates one's choice. As IT points out, a phenomenon such as "persistence in an abusive relationship"—a dramatic example of "non-voluntary" relationship—is not fully

---

[50] See Jewett, *Romans*, 447–8. In Rom. 1:24, "the lusts of the hearts" (ταῖς ἐπιθυμίαις τῶν καρδιῶν) is a characteristic portrayal of the state of sinful Gentiles. Dunn, *Romans 1–8*, 51 notes that 1:24 is simultaneously a character of corrupted humanity in general.
[51] Cf. Wiefel, "The Jewish Community."
[52] Sometimes Paul might need to deal with some issues related to ethnicity. For instance, the issue of circumcision (2:17–29) and the issue of eating (Romans 14). But even in these occasions, Paul tries to give general principles that are applicable for both ethnic groups (cf. 2:28–29; 14:7–8, 17, 23).
[53] Thibaut and Kelley, 169.

explicable if we merely attribute it to personal traits (e.g. low self-esteem or learned helplessness).[54] Thus, Thibaut and Kelley, in their classical work on IT, contend that:

> The person remains in relationships of this sort [i.e. unsatisfactory relationships] because heavy costs are in some manner associated with being in better ones. A person would not, of course, prefer to enter the "better" ones if the heavy costs were intimately and inevitably associated with the rewards to be attained there.[55]

Thibaut and Kelley's explanation indicates that one may continue to depend on the abusive partner despite unsatisfactory outcomes and it is "the nature of an actor's dependence" (i.e. "structural dependence") that causes such a phenomenon.[56] Likewise, Rusbult and Van Lange indicate that "the extent that people are more dependent upon their jobs or relationships, they are more likely to persist."[57]

An actor's dependence upon an abusive partner is reinforced by several factors, such as 1) the level of satisfaction in the relationship, 2) the quality of alternatives, and 3) the size (or amount) of investment in the current relationship, which affects the degree of commitment in the relationship.[58] According to Rusbult and Van Lange:

> People have been shown to persist in relationships because they are strongly committed to the relationship – not only because they feel satisfied, but also because their alternatives are poor and they have invested heavily in a relationship. Thus, Mary may persevere in an abusive relationship not necessarily because she has low self-esteem or has acquired a pattern of learned helplessness, but rather, for reasons resting on structural dependence – because she is heavily invested in remaining with her partner or poor alternatives.[59]

More specifically, we can discuss this unreasonable persistence in terms of the level of dependence. Despite the poor outcomes from the current relationship (lower than the original expectation, namely, CL), if an alternative choice (CL-alt) appears worse than the current outcomes, or if there are no alternatives, i.e. when "the relationship is dissatisfying but involves high dependence," one cannot help but remain in the current relationship.[60] Thus, the victimized person has no option but to stay with an abusive partner. Relationship C in Figure 6.1 displays the typical relational structure of "non-voluntary dependence," whereas the other two (relationships A and B) represent situations of "voluntary dependence."[61] In both relationships A and B, one experiences

---

[54] Rusbult and Van Lange, "Why," 2060–1.
[55] Thibaut and Kelley, 169.
[56] Rusbult and Van Lange, "Why," 2061.
[57] Ibid.
[58] Caryl E. Rusbult and John M. Martz, "Remaining in an Abusive Relationship: An Investment Model Analysis of Nonvoluntary Dependence," *PSPB* 21.6 (1995): 561.
[59] Rusbult and Van Lange, "Why," 2061.
[60] Rusbult, Arriaga and Agnew, 362.
[61] Ibid., 361–2.

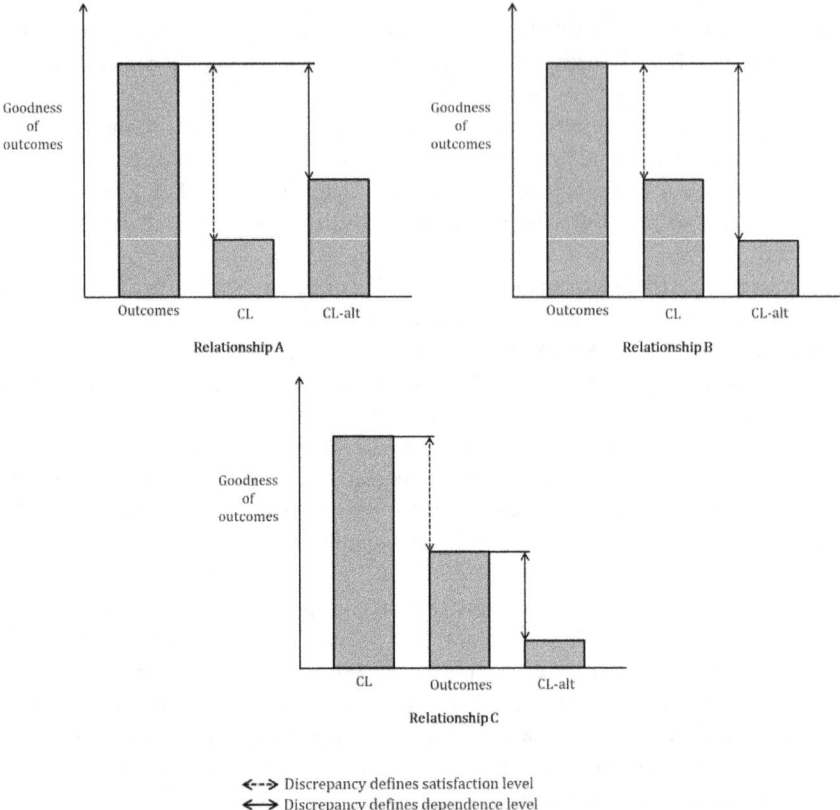

Figure 6.1 Patterns of voluntary versus non-voluntary dependence.[63]

satisfaction because the outcomes from the relationships are higher than both CL and CL-alt[62]; however, one cannot be satisfied in relationship C, because the outcomes from the relationship cannot meet CL. Ironically, in the case of relationship C, one's dependence level is high, because the quality of CL-alt is lower than the currently available outcomes, in which case one persists in the relationship.

6.3.2 Reading the monologue of the "I" in the light of "non-voluntary relationship" in IT

As discussed above, what is prominent in Romans 7 is the helplessness of the "I." The "I" remains in the relationship with its cruel partner, doing what it does not want to do. Why is the "I" unable to leave the relationship? By referring to the connotation of

---

[62] The difference between relationships A and B is that in B the CL-alt is poorer than CL and therefore one's level of dependence is relatively higher than in A. Also, the degree of satisfaction is generally higher in A than in B, as the gap between outcomes and CL is greater in A than in B (see ibid., 361).

slavery in the text, we can say that it is because the "I" has been "sold under Sin" (πεπραμένος ὑπὸ τὴν ἁμαρτίαν [7:14]), like a slave, and thus has been deprived of the freedom to leave.[64]

When we look at this situation through the lens of our IT framework, however, we can recognize that there is more to say concerning the reasons that the "I" cannot escape its own dilemma. According to the IT framework of "non-voluntary relationship (dependence)," we can see that the "I" stays under the oppression of Sin because of a high level of commitment, which increases because of the absence of a proper alternative. From this perspective, what detains the "I" is a relational structure. Although there are other factors that may influence an actor's persistence in a relationship, the satisfaction level in the relationship with Sin cannot be positive, and it is also difficult to estimate how much investment the "I" has put into the relationship with Sin. What alternative choices does the "I" have, and what is the quality level of these alternatives?

6.3.2.1 An alternative option for the "I" and the required cost: The reason for remaining in the abusive relationship with Sin (Rom. 7:1–6)

The "I" may have some positive expectations when tempted by the ἐπιθυμία provoked by Sin's activity through the law (7:8).[65] Accordingly, there is the possibility of a discrepancy between the original expectation and the actual outcome that the "I" obtains. Nevertheless, the "I" cannot choose an alternative option. The "I" seems to know about God and "the law of God" (νόμῳ τοῦ θεοῦ [7:22]), which can be deemed as good (ἀγαθός [cf. 7:18–19, 21]). This denotes the possibility for an alternative choice, one that is closely related to God. If the alternative relationship is the one with God, it is apparent that the new relationship guarantees a better "reward" than the current relationship with Sin. But what is the "cost" of such an alternative relationship? Even though it is difficult to quantify the amount, we can evaluate the quality of the cost: it is "death," which is what Paul is implying in 7:1–6.

In Rom. 7:1–6, Paul articulates an important principle for understanding the situation of the "I" and the alternative option, especially concerning the cost required for choosing the alternative option. In 7:1–3, Paul explains that for a wife to be free

---

[63] Based on Figure 14.1 in ibid., 361–2.
[64] The phrase πεπραμένος ὑπὸ τὴν ἁμαρτίαν does not necessarily mean that the "I" became a slave of Sin purely by coercion. Rather, the phrase illustrates a situation of confinement. Although Paul describes the "I" as having been killed and also deceived by the law (7:8–10), he does so in order to highlight Sin's active work, not to deny the culpability of the "I". In fact, ἐπιθυμία is not purely Sin's work, but is internalized in the "I" (cf. 7:8). Similarly, in 5:12–21, it was "the one man's trespass" (τοῦ ἑνὸς παραπτώματι [5:17]) that formed a close association between "one man" and Sin. Therefore, we cannot attribute all human sin to Sin personified. Similarly, Jewett also insists that "human assent to sin is the necessary precondition to being enslaved by it . . . the sinful distortion of the motivation to obey the law is so willingly endorsed by the ego that seeks the honor of superior performance" (Jewett, *Romans*, 467).
[65] Weima terms this function of the law as its "causative function," finding a meaningful link between 5:20 and 7:5, 8–11 (Jeffrey A.D. Weima, "The Function of the Law in Relation to Sin: An Evaluation of the View of H. Räisänen," *NovT* 32.3 [1990]: 231–3).

from the bondage under her husband, the husband must die.⁶⁶ This principle of the freedom through death is applied in 7:4–6 to explain the fact that those who died to the law are no longer bound to it. Likewise, such a principle is also applicable to the Sin-human relationship. In fact, Paul treats the relationship between human beings and the law in Romans 6–7 in a manner very similar to the way he articulates the Sin-human relationship. As seen in 7:8, Sin is dependent upon the law for its own functionality. Also, in a few places, the law and Sin appear to be interchangeable. For instance, Paul elsewhere affirms believers' new status, claiming that "we died to Sin" (ἀπεθάνομεν τῇ ἁμαρτίᾳ [6:2; cf. 6:11]); while in 7:4 he declares that "you died to the law" (ὑμεῖς ἐθανατώθητε τῷ νόμῳ). Moreover, in 6:14–15, Paul indicates that the opposite of grace (χάρις) is the law (νόμος); whereas, in 5:21, Sin (ἁμαρτία) takes a position antithetical to χάρις. Also, Paul's endeavour to make an apologia for the law from 7:7 mirrors his self-awareness that his exhortations present the law as very close to Sin; the apologia does not intend to deny the close link between Sin and the law. Thus, given Paul's view on the connection between the law and Sin, it is reasonable that the principle in 7:1–6 is applicable to the Sin-human relationship. Dunn also recognizes that death is the common means for escaping from the dominion of both Sin and the law.⁶⁷ In this respect, along with Romans 6 (cf. 6:2, 6–7), 7:1–6 confirms that death is the only means for escaping the dominion of Sin, viz. an essential condition for moving into the alternative relationship with God.⁶⁸

So, what are the total calculations of outcomes involved in this situation (see Figure 6.2)? Although the exact quality of CL is not apparent in the text, we can guess that the law can affect the shape of CL, since the law in the context can stand for what is good (ἀγαθός/καλός) (cf. 7:12, 13, 16, 18–19, 21). However, it is evident that the outcomes from the relationship with Sin cannot meet CL. Several descriptions given by the "I" indicate this fact. Sin's acts evidently do harm to the "I," (cf. 7:11), and the freedom of the "I" is totally restricted in the relationship with Sin (7:15). Rather, the "I" is made to do what it thinks is evil (7:19), thus the "I" feels a deep sense of despair (7:24), a profound dissatisfaction. With regard to CL-alt, given the quality of its "cost" (i.e. death), the alternative choice can be estimated as almost impossible, since death will nullify everything. If the "I" dies, they cannot even receive the reward from an alternative relationship. Consequently, the "I" can do nothing except remain in the current abusive relationship. The fact that death is the only means to escape from the grip of Sin is understandable, given the fact that Paul is

---

[66] As several commentators have noted, what Paul stresses in 7:1–3 is the principle of the freedom through death, not an analogy for 7:4–4 (*pace* Sanday and Headlam, 172–4). Cf. Dunn, *Romans 1–8*, 368; Fitzmyer, *Romans*, 455; Jewett, *Romans*, 428–9.

[67] Dunn, *Romans 1–8*, 368. See also Justin King, "Rhetorical Chain-Link Construction and the Relationship between Romans 7.1–6 and 7.7–8.39: Additional Evidence for Assessing the Argument of Romans 7–8 and the Identity of the Infamous 'I,'" *JSNT* 39.3 (2017): 265–9.

[68] However, the meaning of death in 7:9–11 should be treated in a different way. As Ziesler, *Romans*, 187 contends, given the Adamic motif prominent in these passages, this death can refer to "the death that followed breaking the command (cf. Gen. 3:19)." Of course, there is a rhetorical move in Rom. 7:9–11. In contrast to Christ's death, Sin attempts to revive itself, killing the "I." This description also connotes the activeness of Sin and the passiveness of humanity under Sin's rule. Cf. Cranfield, 351–2; Witherington III, 190–1.

using slavery metaphor to depict the Sin-human relationship. Patterson notes that slaves can acquire freedom by death, though this is an (almost) impossible choice. Patterson puts it:

> The slave, it will be recalled, was someone who by choosing physical life had given up his freedom. Although he could, of course, have kept his freedom and died, man lacked the courage to make such a choice.[69]

Combes also indicates that death can be a way of manumission.[70] Therefore, given the unbearable cost for the alternative choice, CL-alt is poorer than both CL and the outcomes from the relationship with Sin.

The fact that the "I" in 7:7–25 cannot leave the abusive relationship because of the excessive cost and the low quality of CL-alt, gives us an important clue for identifying the temporal background of the circumstances surrounding the "I." When is such an alternative choice impossible for the "I" who here represents human beings? The answer is clear. It is before the Christ-event. The monologue of the "I" is the representation of the situation of generic humanity (cf. 5:12–21) who used to be under the slavery of Sin (cf. 6:19–21). The absence of a promising alternative can confirm that in 7:7–25, Paul is dramatizing the experience of human beings under the oppression by Sin without Christ, from the Christian point of view.[71] This interpretation is not a novel one, but has been suggested by several scholars, although their points of

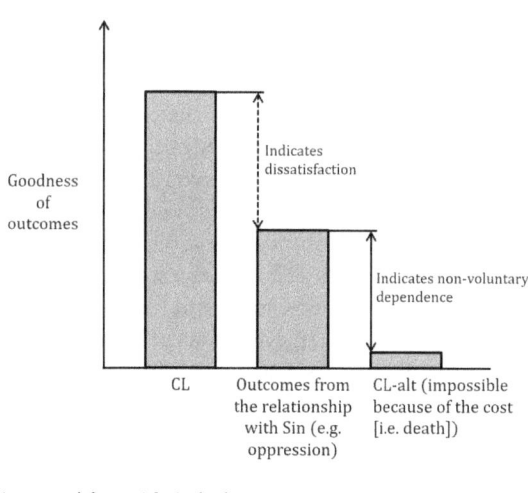

Figure 6.2 Pattern of the "non-voluntary dependence" of the "I" upon Sin.

---

[69] Patterson, 71.
[70] Combes, 88. However, Combes also notes the possibility of an exception (see n. 72).
[71] Cf. Sanders, 442–3.

emphasis are various.[72] However, our approach draws attention to another method of reaching this conclusion, showing that the specific way in which the "I" interacts with Sin is exclusive to a certain period.

6.3.2.2 *The solution for the abusive relationship – The implication of the Christ-event for the termination of the Sin-human relationship (Rom. 6:1–11; 8:1–11)*

So, if the "I" stands for humanity in general, which has suffered in the relationship with Sin before the Christ-event, how do we understand the meaning of the Christ-event in relation to that situation? What kind of change does the Christ-event bring about to the Sin-human relationship? Other psychological approaches diagnose the issue of "non-voluntary dependence" from an *intrapersonal* perspective (e.g. personal disposition),[73] thereby finding solutions in a similar manner (e.g. psychotherapy to raise self-esteem or to remove learned helplessness).[74] However, IT is unique in finding the solution for such unreasonable dependence from an *interpersonal* (external) point of view. According to Rusbult and Van Lange, in order to end "non-voluntary dependence," it is essential to change the relational structure that sustains such a relationship and to lessen the victim's level of dependence by providing an alternative choice.[75] Empirical studies about abuse in a partner relationship attest to the importance of the interventions that will influence interpersonal structures to solve such a pathological relational problem.[76] Not only psychotherapies but also the interventions that can affect the victim's CL-alt are required to solve the problem of "non-voluntary dependence."

A solution based on IT studies can be helpful to expound the meaning of the Christ-event for the Sin-human relationship. The phenomenon of persistence in the abusive relationship with Sin does not arise only because of the weaknesses of human beings. Rather, as argued above, the main reason that human beings cannot escape from the abusive relationship is because there is no appropriate alternative for them because of the alternative's exorbitant cost. However, as can be seen in 7:25, the Christ-event becomes the decisive turning point, because it provides a powerful alternative as a solution to the problem of the relationship with Sin.

The freedom mentioned in 8:2 is the liberation of human beings from the abuse and oppression of Sin. The following comment in 8:3 elaborates upon the meaning of the

---

[72] For instance, Ziesler, *Romans*, 181–4; Stuhlmacher, *Romans*, 114–16; Byron, *Slavery*, 230–1; Leander E. Keck, *Romans* (Nashville: Abingdon, 2005), 180–1; Jewett, *Romans*, 441–5. Byron sees this chapter describing "involuntary enslavement," unlike in Romans 6. Jewett is inclined to accept Paul's biographical element. Ziesler focuses on the allusion to Adam's story in Romans 7.
[73] For instance, one's "masochistic tendencies of pathological personalities," "low (depressed) self-esteem" and "learned helplessness" have been regarded as accountable for such phenomena (cf. Rusbult and Van Lange, "Why," 2060–1; Rusbult and Martz, 559).
[74] Rusbult and Van Lange, "Why," 2061.
[75] Ibid.
[76] For example, "to enhance economic alternatives by providing continuing education, job training, short-term financial assistance, legal advocacy, a means of transportation" (Rusbult and Martz, 569).

Christ-event for such liberation. The statement that "God condemned Sin in the (his son's) flesh" (κατέκρινεν τὴν ἁμαρτίαν ἐν τῇ σαρκί), points out the fact that Jesus' death is "the decisive enactment by God" to bring Sin's oppression to an end.[77] Thus, it is the Christ-event (in particular, his death) that has a vital effect on liberating human beings from the slavery under Sin. The fact that the actual means of liberating victimized humanity from the abusive relationship is death, corresponds to the condition set to escape from Sin, as mainly discussed in 7:1–6. The main reason that human beings represented by the "I" cannot leave the abusive relationship with Sin is because of the poor quality of CL-alt because of the unrealistic cost to be paid for the alternative choice. One cannot even hope to pay the cost for the alternative choice, since the choice of death will make everything meaningless. Nevertheless, on behalf of human beings who have entered this paradoxical situation, God has paid the cost by means of his own Son's death (8:3). Patterson also points out the same meaning of Jesus' crucifixion in relation to the slavery metaphor:

> He [Jesus] annulled the condition of slavery in which man existed by returning to the original point of enslavement and, on behalf of the sinner about to fall, gave his own life so that the sinner might live and be free.[78]

As a result of Christ's death, the shape of CL-alt that used to be negative and practically impossible turns positive. However, this radical turn of events holds true only if one participates in Christ's death (cf. 6:3–5; 7:4).

Thus, the significance of baptism makes good sense in this framework (cf. 6:1–11). Paul indicates that it is "the baptism into Christ's death" (τοῦ βαπτίσματος εἰς τὸν θάνατον [6:4]) that makes what Christ has done effective for human beings. Through baptism, believers are united with Christ in his death, so that, although the death is not actually theirs, they can enjoy the same effects that come from Christ's death, i.e. liberation (cf. 6:2, 6–7). Moreover, just as Christ was raised from the dead by God, unification with Christ's death through baptism will also lead believers to possess his resurrection (6:4–11). And it is with the resurrection life, the life to God (6:10–11), that human beings can enjoy a proper relationship with God, a relationship characterized by righteousness (δικαιοσύνη [6:13]).[79]

Furthermore, the Christ-event is closely associated with the empowerment of believers by the Spirit. As mentioned above, a victim must be appropriately equipped to choose an alternative partner or way of life.[80] By having the capability to choose rather freely, the previously victimized person becomes much less dependent upon the abusive partner. Paul claims that receiving the Spirit is an event associated with believing in Christ, through whom God has demonstrated his love for humanity (cf. 5:5). The Spirit empowers believers so that they can actively resist the enticement of Sin. The Spirit opposes the flesh (σάρξ), whose position is almost synonymous to Sin

---

[77] Dunn, *Romans 1–8*, 422.
[78] Patterson, 71.
[79] Cf. Samuli Siikavirta, *Baptism and Cognition in Romans 6–8* (Tübingen: Mohr Siebeck, 2015), 168.
[80] Rusbult and Martz, 569.

(8:4–8),[81] and the dwelling of the Spirt attests to one's new identity in relation to Christ (8:9). The Spirit helps believers to maintain their distinctive identity, which indicates an intimate relationship with God, namely, their becoming "sons of God" (υἱοὶ θεοῦ [8.14]). Thus, believers are able to cry out (κράζω) to God for help, further bearing witness to their new identity (8:15–16). As seen in 8:26, the Spirit also aids believers with intercession. In addition, it is the Spirit through whom the power of God resurrects the dead (8:11).[82] In this way, the Spirit enables believers to manage the relationship with God, to resist temptation from "the flesh," and to renounce their old habits in the relationship with Sin (cf. 8:13). As Paul exhorts, there still exist some risks for those who are already in Christ to resume their previous relationship with Sin, namely, following "the flesh" again (cf. 8:12). Nevertheless, the Spirit grants believers the ability to avoid and overcome it by helping them to pursue much better outcomes (e.g. ζωὴ καὶ εἰρήνη [8:6]) in the relationship with God. It is now that the victims are able to do what they think is good with the help of the Spirit.

6.4 Conclusion

As the result of our investigation, it has become clearer that what Paul describes in Romans 7, utilizing the voice of the "I," is the human experience under the power of Sin before the Christ-event. Sin, as a personified cosmic force, detains humanity under its oppression, just as a cruel slave master does. Human beings, however, cannot escape from this master-slave relationship because of the unrealistic cost (i.e. death) for an alternative choice. Our interpretation of the human history of slavery under Sin sheds new light on the meaning of the Christ-event, which itself inaugurates the history of salvation. The Christ-event has brought about a crucial change, breaking the relational structure of and decreasing the dependence level in the Sin-human relationship. Since the cost is paid on behalf of human beings, they are now able to choose the alternative option of a relationship with God. The empowerment by the Spirit, which is also a corollary of the Christ-event, enables them to stay away from the previous exploitive master.[83] In this respect, Romans 7 can be an effective means to exhort Paul's hearers not to return to the relationship with Sin. By reminding his hearers of how life under Sin's oppression was, Paul can warn them that it is irrational to go back to the relationship with Sin.

---

[81] The flesh (σάρξ) is an entity that is closely linked with ἐπιθυμία. However, as can be seen from a few of the occurrences of σάρξ in Romans 7 (7:5, 14, 18, 25), σάρξ does not exactly overlap with Sin, despite its close connection with it. Rather, Paul's usage of σάρξ throughout Romans 7–8 shows that σάρξ points to a specific domain controlled by Sin. Pace Jewett, *Anthropological*, 156-7 ("an independently active power").

[82] Cf. Rom. 1:4.

[83] Thus, we can sequence the changes in the relationships implied in the text (5:12–8:11) with regard to "the history of slavery" and "the history of salvation" as follows: 1) Ensnared by ἐπιθυμία (through the law) → 2) Settled in the relationship with Sin → 3) Persistence in the abusive relationship with Sin because of the lack of an available alternative → 4) Breaking of the human dependence upon Sin by the Christ-event (and the empowerment of the Spirit) → 5) Still remains the temptation from Sin, but one can keep the relationship with God following the Spirit.

The scholars who are involved in the "apocalyptic interpretation of Paul" have underlined the liberating effect of the Christ-event, recognizing the significance of the Sin-human relationship in the context of salvation. For instance, several scholars have attempted to explain the meaning of the Christ-event in Romans at a cosmic level (and in Pauline theology, too), seeing that the defeat of Sin is the most important result of the crucifixion.[84] However, some scholars appear to undermine the role of human beings with their emphasis on a powerful divine invasion, setting up an unhelpful dichotomy between divine and human agencies.[85] As we have argued, however, we must preserve the importance of the role of human beings in order to explain the beginning and the maintenance of their relationship with Sin. If we remove this from the scene, then Paul's exhortations throughout Romans 6–8 will be unintelligible. Therefore, by focusing on the importance of human partners in the next chapter, we will ask how the human role is important for the completion of God's cosmic and eschatological drama in Rom. 8:12–39. To do so, we will peer into what kind of development is portrayed in the relational structure and, ultimately, what kind of outcomes come to the fore over the course of divine-human interactions.

---

[84] Cf. de Boer, *Defeat*; Gaventa, "Cosmology"; Susan Eastman, "Apocalypse and Incarnation: The Participatory Logic of Paul's Gospel," in *Apocalyptic and the Future of Theology*, 165–82. See also the review of "apocalyptic Paul" in Chapter 1.

[85] For instance, de Boer sets up a dichotomy between "forensic eschatology" that prioritizes human agency and "apocalyptic eschatology" and puts emphasis on divine agency, arguing for the relevance of the latter for Paul (de Boer, *Defeat*, 85–8; idem, "Apocalyptic"). However, Wright finds that such a division is not warranted in both Second Temple Jewish thought and Paul, claiming that "the cross, at its heart, is for Paul both penal in force and cosmic in scope" (N.T. Wright, "Apocalyptic and the Sudden Fulfillment of Divine Promise," in *Paul and the Apocalyptic Imagination*, 117–18; 132).

7

Investment for the Future: The Meaning of Endurance Throughout Suffering (Rom. 8:12–39)

7.1 Introduction

At the climax of Romans 5–8, the divine-human relationship enters a deeper level by bearing the relational features that are characteristic of "interdependence." In 8:12–39, although God's saving action is a core element that drives universal salvation, Paul's focus does not move away from the human actors. Paul envisages that the human partners will act as important co-agents with God for the sake of the ultimate purpose for the cosmos, as expected for Abraham.[1]

In fact, there are several elements that constitute the whole picture of cosmic salvation, including non-human creation (cf. 8:19–22), despite differences in their roles and significance. However, some scholars tend to regard the human role in Romans 8 as passive. For instance, Gaventa contends:

> While all that God has made is in the veritable pangs of labor awaiting God's glorious apocalypse, there is nothing creation or humanity can do to bring it to completion. Even though believers have already received the first glimpse of what is on the horizon, they cannot make the day come one moment faster. Instead, they wait for what God will do.[2]

---

[1] Cf. Rom. 4:13–14. The word κληρονόμος makes a meaningful connection between Romans 4 and 8 together with the cosmic scale of the passage. Cf. Mark Forman, *The Politics of Inheritance in Romans* (Cambridge: Cambridge University Press, 2011), 102–35; Wright, *Faithfulness*, 814; 841; 1509. In this vein, we can see that Paul is elaborating the promise in Rom. 4:13 in Rom. 8:17. Cf. Adolf Schlatter, *Gottes Gerechtigket: Ein Kommentar zum Römerbrief* (Stuttgart: Calwer, 1935), 267 (cited in Forman, 103). *Pace* James C. Walters, "Paul, Adoption, and Inheritance," in *Paul in the Greco-Roman World: A Handbook*, ed. J. Paul Sampley (Harrisburg: Trinity Press International, 2003), 66. Walters tends to undermine the continuity between the inheritance in Abraham and the inheritance by adoption in favour of the "apocalyptic" character implied in the concept of adoption, arguing that Abraham's Jewishness is not relevant for such an "apocalyptic" context. Nevertheless, Paul has already notified that he does not use the example of Abraham as a case relevant to the Jewish people only, expanding the meaning of being Abraham's descendants (Rom. 4:16–25); therefore, the concept of inheritance in Romans 4 can still be a factor in Paul's understanding of being heirs of God in Romans 8.
[2] Beverly Roberts Gaventa, *Our Mother Saint Paul* (Louisville: WJK, 2007), 59.

According to Gaventa, the role of humanity in Romans 8 is "to wait — eagerly, expectantly, hopefully, yes — but to wait."[3] When discussing the necessity of God's initiative for the accomplishment of this cosmic vision, Judith Gundry also stresses that "their [believers'] activity [e.g. believing] is not negated, nevertheless, it is not mentioned" in the text.[4]

These scholars are correct in noticing the fact that God is the decisive actor in salvation. Nevertheless, the human role in Romans 8 cannot simply be defined as passive. Several expressions in the passage that describe what believers have to do signal that waiting is not merely a passive activity (cf. 8:23).[5] Believers are to suffer with Christ (συμπάσχω [8:17]), and in the course of waiting, believers are also to cry out to God with the help of the Spirit (8:15-16, 26-27). Also, these activities can be included in the endeavour to put to death "the deeds of the body" (τὰς πράξεις τοῦ σώματος) by the Spirit (8:13). Moreover, given the fact that God's saving act in Christ requires and instigates mutual human participation for the restoration of the relationship (cf. 3:21-26; 5:1-11), we can expect that the relational dynamics of the divine-human relationship are in a more developed form in Rom. 8:12-39, the place where Paul describes the climactic stage of the relationship.

Thus, by delving into 8:12-39 in this chapter, we will ask how the divine-human relationship enters a new dimension of relationality, in particular, with regard to believers' roles in Paul's cosmic vision of salvation. We will especially pay attention to the meaning of the suffering that believers ought to undergo. We will firstly frame the situation in Rom. 8:12-39 with the concept of "outcome" in IT and identify the coherence between cost and reward. Then we will investigate the relational meaning of endurance throughout suffering in two ways—as 1) the expression of fidelity and as 2) an investment for the future. For the latter, we will refer to IT concerning a specific relational situation termed the "investment situation." We will also discuss further what kinds of strategies are utilized in order to sustain believers' association with God.

7.2 Framing suffering and glory: Suffering as "cost" and glory as "reward" (Rom. 8:17-18)

Instead of simply celebrating the great liberation from Sin, Paul tries to maintain tension throughout Romans 8 by drawing attention to the believers' present situation. There is a facet of believers' lives that involves endurance (ὑπομονή) when undergoing sufferings (παθήματα) (cf. 8:17-18). These sufferings arise from the circumstances in which the hostile entity against God and believers is still operating. Since this hostile

---

[3] Gaventa, *Mother*, 56.
[4] Judith M. Gundry Volf, *Paul and Perseverance: Staying in and Falling Away* (Louisville: WJK, 1990), 13.
[5] Cf. Luzia S. Rehman, "To Turn the Groaning into Labor: Romans 8.22-23," in *A Feminist Companion to Paul*, ed. Amy-Jill Levine and Marianne Blickenstaff (Cleveland: Pilgrim, 2004), 76 ("it [waiting] is restless; all senses are focused on one event that is anticipated every new day"). See also David Catchpole, "Who and Where Is the 'Wretched Man' of Romans 7, and Why Is 'She' Wretched?," in *The Holy Spirit and Christian Origins: Essays in Honor of James D.G. Dunn*, ed. Graham N. Stanton, Bruce W. Longenecker and Stephen C. Barton (Grand Rapids: Eerdmans, 2004), 175-6.

cosmic power still attempts to exert its influence on believers, putting the deeds of the body—a domain where Sin operates—to death may involve struggles, resistance and suffering.[6] Paul recognizes that his lifestyle and ministry dedicated to God as an apostle involves affliction (θλῖψις) (cf. 2 Cor. 1:4, 8; 2:4; 4:17; 6:4; 7:4; Phil. 4:14; 1 Thess. 3:7), which is also true for his fellows (cf. 2 Cor. 8:1–2; Phil. 1:29; 1 Thess. 1:6; 3:3). In other words, affliction or suffering is an inevitable experience for those who aim to maintain a dedicated relationship with God.

As can be seen in 8:17–18, Paul sees that the enduring of sufferings is oriented toward a certain destination, i.e. glory (δόξα). The concept of glory in Romans 8 has an eschatological and cosmic connotation. Glory stands for the image of resurrection life (cf. 8:23), and the connection between the glory and life is already present in several places in Romans.[7] It is frequently noted that Rom. 8:17–18 has a close connection with 5:3–4, wherein affliction (θλῖψις) is a necessary path to reach hope (ἐλπίς).[8] The function of affliction in Rom. 5:3–4 cannot simply be restricted to an "educative function."[9] Hope (ἐλπίς), the final goal, is not merely a psychological state, but has a strong salvific implication.[10] The hope mentioned here is "the hope of the glory of God" (ἐλπίδι τῆς δόξης τοῦ θεοῦ [5:2]).[11] Similarly, the close connection between hope and glory is also prominent in Romans 8, wherein the meaning of hope becomes more concrete (i.e. the hope of resurrection) (cf. 8:18–39).[12]

As can be seen in Rom. 8:21, "the glory of the children of God" (τῆς δόξης τῶν τέκνων τοῦ θεοῦ) is not restricted to the human boundary, but it is also significant for non-human creation.[13] Several scholars have noticed that Romans 8 appears to have a meaningful connection with Genesis 1–3 with regard to the link between humanity and non-human creation.[14] Ryan Jackson also rightly indicates that "Romans 8, in

---

[6] Cf. Barclay, *Gift*, 505–6.
[7] See Rom. 1:23; 2:7–10; 5:1–2. See Preston M. Sprinkle, "The Afterlife in Romans: Understanding Paul's Glory Motif in Light of the Apocalypse of Moses and 2 Baruch," in *Lebendige Hoffnung – Ewiger Tod?!: Jenseitsvorstellungen im Hellenismus, Judentum und Christentum*, ed. Michael Labahn and Manfred Lang (Leipzig: Evangelische Verlagsanstalt, 2007), 221–6.
[8] Dunn, *Romans 1–8*, 466; Moo, *Romans*, 505; Jewett, *Romans*, 506. In Romans 5, the term θλῖψις is equivalent to παθήματα (see also 2 Cor. 1:4–5 where θλίψει ἡμῶν is identified with τὰ παθήματα τοῦ Χριστοῦ).
[9] Siu Fung Wu, *Suffering in Romans* (Eugene: Pickwick Publications, 2015), 58; 63. For the educative value of sufferings in both Graeco-Roman and Jewish worlds, see ibid., 42–4. See also Brian J. Tabb, "Paul and Seneca on Suffering," in *Paul and Seneca in Dialogue*, ed. Joseph R. Dodson and David E. Briones (Leiden: Brill, 2017), 94–5; 101–3, who observes that Paul's understanding of the purpose of suffering differs from Seneca's idea, which mainly stresses an educative function because of his unique emphasis on missiological and eschatological implications.
[10] Wu, 63.
[11] NRSV adds in "sharing" ("hope of sharing the glory of God").
[12] Cf. N.T. Wright, *The Resurrection of the Son of God* (Minneapolis: Fortress, 2003), 248–59.
[13] Cf. John Duncan, "The Hope of Creation: The Significance of 'Εφ' Ἐλπίδι (Rom 8.20c) in Context," *NTS* 61.3 (2015): 424–6.
[14] Harry Alan Hahne, *The Corruption and Redemption of Creation: Nature in Romans 8:19–22 and Jewish Apocalyptic Literature* (London: T&T Clark, 2006), 187 (see n. 89); Edward Adams, *Constructing the World: A Study in Paul's Cosmological Language* (Edinburgh: T&T Clark, 2000), 152–5; 174–9; Wu, 70–6; Blackwell, *Christosis*, 163–7; Moo, *Romans*, 515–16; Jewett, *Romans*, 513; Brendan Byrne, "An Ecological Reading of Rom. 8.19–22: Possibilities and Hesitations," in *Ecological Hermeneutics: Biblical, Historical and Theological Perspectives*, ed. David G. Horrell et al. (London: T&T Clark, 2010), 89 (see also idem, *Romans* [Collegeville: Liturgical Press, 1996], 255–7).

particular, provides evidence that Paul's soteriology inextricably links the salvation of people with the salvation of the world."[15] Thus, glory as an ultimate goal cannot be properly understood if its meaning is restricted to the salvation of human beings. John Yates also notices the significance of "God's chosen people" for Paul's cosmic vision. Comparing Ezekiel 36 with Romans 8, Yates argues that "in both Ezekiel and Romans the renewal of the created world is dependent on the renewal of God's chosen people through the indwelling spirit."[16] "The renewal of God's chosen people" is not a human goal, but rather involves God's purpose for the whole cosmos.

Several OT and Second Temple Jewish writings also admit a close link between humanity and the rest of creation in terms of both corruption and an eschatological restoration.[17] For instance, the Greek Life of Adam and Eve (GLAE) also reflects a close link between human sin and the corruption of creation (cf. Chapters 10–12; 24), intimating that the resurrection will bring about the recovery of their authority over the creation (cf. 39:1–3).[18] However, it is Paul's idiosyncratic thought that human beings are invited to participate in the process of reaching the goal (i.e. glory) by means of undergoing sufferings. They are called as partners of God according to this purpose (cf. 8:28), as Adam was originally called to be obedient.[19] It is through this process that the relationship will reach its climax.[20]

Grounded in this observation, we can articulate the correlation between suffering and glory with the IT framework of "reward in relation to cost" (i.e. "outcome"). According to Paul, experiencing sufferings can be a necessary "cost" for believers, while glory will be given as a "reward" in return for the "cost." What is striking is the result of Paul's calculation. Romans 8:18 gives a glimpse into the cost-reward mentality with which Paul considers the connection between suffering and glory.[21] Paul even claims that the sufferings (παθήματα) of the present life ("cost") are tolerable because the sufferings are not worthy (οὐκ ἄξια) in comparison with the future glory (τὴν

---

[15] T. Ryan Jackson, *New Creation in Paul's Letters: A Study of the Historical and Social Setting of a Pauline Concept* (Tübingen: Mohr Siebeck, 2010), 150.

[16] John W. Yates, *The Spirit and Creation in Paul* (Tübingen: Mohr Siebeck, 2008), 153.

[17] For instance, Isa. 11:6–9; 43:19–21; 55:12–13; Ezek. 34:25–31; Hos. 2:18; Zech. 8:12; 2 Apoc. Bar. 29:1–8; AW (Apocalypse of Weeks in 1 Enoch Book 5); BP II (Books of Parables [1 Enoch Book 2, the second parable]); 4 Ezra 8:51–54; GLAE (Apocalypse of Moses); Jubilees. See Hahne, *The Corruption and Redemption*, 159–65; 215–16; Byrne, "Ecological," 88.

[18] For the link between Romans and GLAE, see Ben C. Blackwell, "The Greek Life of Adam and Eve and Romans 8:14-39: (Re-)creation and Glory," in *Reading Romans in Context: Paul and Second Temple Judaism*, ed. Ben C. Blackwell, John K. Goodrich and Jason Maston (Grand Rapids: Zondervan, 2015), 108–14. Although Blackwell's investigation revolves around the similarity between the two texts (e.g. the solidarity between humanity and other creation), Sprinkle also observes some differences. For example, although the glory in GLAE mainly connotes immortality ("a primordial condition of man"), glory in Romans focuses more on "eschatological restoration," which implies "escalation" (Sprinkle, "Glory," 231–2).

[19] Cf. Rom. 5:12–21.

[20] Sprinkle correctly expounds a relational dimension of salvation in Romans (i.e. salvation as the restoration of the divine-human relationship), when he argues that it is necessary for God to "envelope" human beings into his own glory in order that he may "enjoy perfect fellowship with humanity." Therefore, glory here functions as "a bridge" between God and human beings (Sprinkle, "Glory," 226, 228; 233).

[21] *Pace* Moo, *Romans*, 508–9 ("to be sure 'suffering' . . . is still present, but Paul is not so much interested in its relationship to glory").

μέλλουσαν δόξαν) ("reward"). In other words, the degree of cost (the degree of sufferings) does not exceed the quality of the reward (the degree of glory). By focusing on the term λογίζομαι, Dunn also notes that Paul is deliberately calculating the values of suffering and glory.[22] Therefore, in Paul's estimation, the final outcomes turn out to be clearly "positive." Such a calculation mirrors Paul's particular value system, which appears to transcend a conventional way of thinking as Paul's rhetoric in 8:24–25 does.

A similar hierarchy of value is also in operation in Paul's other letters. In 2 Cor. 4:17–18, Paul compares the degree of affliction (θλῖψις) ("cost") with the quality of glory (δόξα) ("reward"), affirming that the "cost" does not match the "reward" in terms of both duration (παραυτίκα – αἰώνιος) and weight (ἐλαφρός – βάρος). Paul sees that it is the affliction itself that actually produces (κατεργάζομαι) the glory (2 Cor. 4:17). The relationship between affliction and glory linked by the verb κατεργάζομαι can be found in a similar context in Romans (cf. Rom. 5:3),[23] and is in the background when Paul insists on the necessity of suffering with Christ in order to be glorified with him (Rom. 8:17). This particular correlation between suffering and glory leads us to an additional question of how the "cost" yields the "reward": In what way can suffering lead human partners to the ultimate goal of their relationship with God?

7.3 Relational implication of enduring suffering (1): An expression of fidelity

We have already noted that the divine-human relationship cannot be managed without some necessary cost. In the previous chapters, Paul has underlined the cost (i.e. Christ's death) that God paid to restore the broken relationship. In the context of Romans 8, cost and reward are accompanied by the decision to faithfully remain in the relationship with God. To put it differently, believers have to pay a cost by enduring suffering in order to maintain the reconciled relationship with God.

We can guess from 8:35–36 that sufferings (παθήματα) in Romans 8 are not merely mental or abstract. Nor would it be sufficient to see them simply as sufferings in general spread in the world.[24] Rather, the sufferings refer to concrete cases that arise on account of the Roman believers' faith in Christ, which can be viewed as their endeavour to remain faithful to the relationship with God.[25] We can see that the list of sufferings in 8:31–39 are meant to be hindrances to the relationship between God and believers. The verb χωρίζω in 8:35 and 39 has a prominent relational connotation as in 1 Cor. 7:10–16 where Paul speaks of a marriage relationship. The personified subjects that attempt to separate believers from God and his love—such as persecution (διωγμός [8:35]),[26]

---

[22] Dunn, *Romans 1–8*, 467–8; Thiselton, 173.
[23] ἡ θλῖψις ὑπομονὴν κατεργάζεται.
[24] Pace Moo, *Romans*, 508–9; 511.
[25] Cf. Adams, 183.
[26] In Acts 8:1; 13:50 διωγμός describes concrete cases of persecution. For similar cases, see 2 Cor. 12:10; 2 Thess. 1:4; 2 Tim. 3:11.

sword (μάχαιρα [8:35]) or rulers (ἀρχαί [8:38])[27]—allude to the perils placed by earthly authorities before the Roman believers because of their particular faith.[28] From the exhortation in 12:14 (εὐλογεῖτε τοὺς διώκοντας [ὑμᾶς]), we see that persecution was already a reality in the Roman believers' lives.[29] The characterizations of their antagonists' work—e.g. opposing (καθ' ἡμῶν [8:31]), accusing (ἐγκαλέω [8:33]) and condemning (κατακρίνω [8:34])—show that their antagonists are diametrically opposed to God's work for believers (e.g. ὑπὲρ ἡμῶν [8:31]; δικαιόω [8:33]; ἐντυγχάνει ὑπὲρ ἡμῶν [8:34]). In this sense, the antagonists not only oppose believers but also God himself, and their activities are attempts to harm the alliance between the two newly reconciled parties.

The nature of the antagonists is not restricted to a physical realm. Some of them are non-human and supernatural (e.g. ἄγγελοι; δυνάμεις [8:38]). Paul is still conscious of the hostile cosmic power that is in operation in the cosmos, though in a limited domain (cf. 8:1-13). Thus, believers' sufferings can be viewed as the fruits of eschatological tension (cf. 8:10).[30] Believers who are now in the reconciled relationship with God will face such threats or temptations from the malicious previous partner. In this situation, for believers to endure sufferings can be regarded as resistance against those who attempt to separate them from God, a struggle that is necessary for keeping fidelity toward the new partner.

We can witness an interesting parallel in 2 Corinthians 4-5, in which Paul lists the sufferings that he had to face for Jesus' sake (cf. 2 Cor. 4:7-12). As in Romans 8, such sufferings are also considered as a preparation for glory "beyond all measure" (καθ' ὑπερβολὴν εἰς ὑπερβολὴν [2 Cor. 4:17]).[31] Furthermore, Paul and his fellow workers' endurance through such sufferings can be deemed as a fitting response to Christ who died for all humanity (cf. 2 Cor. 5:15). This is the lifestyle that fulfils the original expectations for relationship as implied in Christ's self-sacrificial death. In this sense, enduring sufferings is a crucial way to maintain the relationship with God.[32]

---

[27] Although a spiritual connotation of this term is still probable, ἀρχαί can also refer to earthly authorities under control by anti-God forces (cf. 1 Cor. 2:6, 8). Cf. Jewett, *Romans*, 552. As Barclay argues, it is fundamentally an association with the anti-God forces that imposes the negative characteristic on earthly authorities, not the authorities per se, and the close proximity between the two subjects in 8:31-39 implies that such a connection is functioning in the passage (John M.G. Barclay, "Why the Roman Empire Was Insignificant to Paul," in *Pauline Churches*, 385-6).

[28] Cf. Jewett, *Romans*, 546. See also Sylvia C. Keesmaat, *Paul and His Story: (Re)Interpreting the Exodus Tradition* (Sheffield: Sheffield Academic, 1999), 74-7; 120-2.

[29] Adams argues that it is probable that the Roman believers faced hostility from wider society, e.g. "political vulnerability, being subject to the contempt and suspicion of outsiders." Such hostile attitudes and behaviours may have been "the social preconditions of Nero's persecution." Separation from the Jewish community partly effected by the Claudian edict is another possible reason for such a condition. Adams, 209-18.

[30] Cf. Käsemann, *Romans*, 226.

[31] As in Romans, glory (δόξα) in 2 Corinthians also connotes the glory of resurrection (cf. 2 Cor. 4:14; 5:1-5). Cf. Murray J. Harris, *The Second Epistle to the Corinthians* (Grand Rapids: Eerdmans, 2005), 362.

[32] Frances M. Young, "Understanding Romans in the Light of 2 Corinthians," *STJ* 43.4 (1990): 438-41 recognizes both 2 Corinthians and Romans espouse similar ideas with regard to vocation and obedience. See also Jackson, 165.

7.4 Relational implication of enduring suffering (2): In the light of the "investment situation" in IT (Rom. 8:12–30)

Enduring suffering is not only important for preserving the relationship per se, but is also vital for achieving a common goal set within the relationship. This is because the achievement of the goal is dependent upon a successful management of the relationship. In this respect, the situation in Romans 8, which requires endurance through suffering, can be viewed as one of the examples of "investment situation" in IT.[33] Rusbult defines the "investment situation" as:

> Investment situations are extended situations in which each person, at each of a series of preliminary steps, must make an "investment" in order to move toward a desirable goal.[34]

In this particular situation, several conditions need to be met in order to reach the goal. The illustration below notes such conditions for a successful management of the "investment situation":

> In seeking to establish a successful business, the owners proceed through a series of preliminary steps at which they invest time and effort in order to reach their goal ... forgo short-term financial profits and re-invest early earnings in development activities, including employee training and construction projects. In the situations considered here, those of mutual investment, both owners must engage in these activities. If either loses heart and backs out of the venture, their investments are lost and the company fails. If both persist and jointly work their way through the early steps, making suitable choices and effective investments of time, effort and resources, they may achieve a desirable goal.[35]

There are two main conditions for a successful end to situations such as the one above: 1) forgoing immediate interests and 2) mutual commitment. Kelley et al. emphasize the importance of the second condition, stating that "the effort must be mutual, and the relationship aborts if either partner fails to persist toward the goal."[36] We can observe how "interdependence" in terms of outcomes is established in a relationship by observing the degree to which mutual commitment is significant for the relationship, since the fact that mutual commitment is important for good outcomes of both partners means that there is a high degree of "mutuality of dependence" in the relationship.[37]

Several points in the text indicate that the divine-human relationship in Rom. 8:12–30 can be conceptualized as an "investment situation." Firstly, Romans 8:12–30

---

[33] Cf. Kelley et al., 285–303.
[34] Ibid., 285.
[35] Ibid.
[36] Ibid., 285–6.
[37] Rusbult, "Interdependence Theory," 330. See Chapter 2 of this study (2.2.5.2).

portrays a situation in which the goal of the relationship is not achieved right away, but a time of waiting (but not in a passive manner) is required of both parties. In the "investment situation," it is crucial to undergo the "delay of gratification," keeping one's single-minded attitude toward the original partner.[38] Secondly, the correlation of cost as "investment" (enduring sufferings) and reward (sharing future glory) is importantly stated in Rom. 8:12-30. Thirdly, the situation of Rom. 8:12-30 involves mutual interactions. We have noted that the endurance throughout sufferings can be regarded as a human response to manage the proper relationship with God who is already in action. The issue of mutuality will be dealt with in more detail as we proceed.

Thus, on the basis of such an observation, we will explore the meaning of endurance throughout sufferings, asking to what extent the believers' role is significant for carrying the "investment situation" in their relationship with God to a successful conclusion. The two important conditions for a successful management of the "investment situation"—forgoing immediate interests and mutual commitment—will provide a guideline for our discussion.

7.4.1 Forgoing immediate interests (Rom. 8:12-17)

In Romans 8, one aspect of endurance Paul mentions is forgoing one's immediate interests. For believers, pursuing immediate interests involves an instant gratification, which becomes available when they choose not to tolerate suffering. Avoiding suffering itself can be regarded as fulfilling one's immediate interests. More specifically, pursuing immediate interests has a positive correlation with engaging in an alternative relationship. Kelley et al. describe the influence of a third party as one of the factors that can induce one's failure to forgo immediate interests:

> There are also important instances in which pursuit of a goal requires forgoing alternative activities, in that the appearance of attractive alternatives (more promising ways to spend money, a more attractive or compatible partner for one of the romantic pair) can disrupt the persistence pattern of investment that is necessary to reach a rewarding goal.[39]

From 8:12-17 we can recognize that the lifestyle "according to the flesh" (κατὰ σάρκα) can seduce believers by offering a seemingly more attractive reward and promising immediate interests through the formation of an alternative relationship (i.e. the relationship with Sin).[40] Given that perseverance in suffering (cf. 8:14-17) depicts the lifestyle of those who are led by the Spirit (ὅσοι πνεύματι θεοῦ ἄγονται), one's own immediate interests can be considered as the outcomes from an opposing lifestyle, i.e. the way of life "according to the flesh" (cf. 8:12-13). Paul does not elaborate

---

[38] Kelley et al., 288.
[39] Ibid.
[40] Although the Sin-human relationship in Romans 7 epitomizes the human situation before the Christ-event, Paul reminds his hearers that they have an obligation to persist in rejecting their previous way of life, since the temptations from Sin through the flesh are still present (cf. 8:1-17).

on "the works of the flesh" (τὰ ἔργα τῆς σαρκός) in Romans as he does in Galatians (cf. Gal. 5:19–21).[41] Nevertheless, we see a picture of the life "according to the flesh" in Rom. 13:13–14: moral dissoluteness (e.g. κῶμος, μέθη, κοίτη, ἀσέλγεια) and discord with others driven by self-centredness (ἔρις, ζῆλος) characterize the lifestyle that makes "provision for the flesh" (τῆς σαρκὸς πρόνοιαν). This sort of lifestyle does not fundamentally differ from what Galatians 5 describes, i.e. indulging the impulse to pursue immediate and self-centred interests.

Therefore, in situations where the temptation of an alternative source of satisfaction comes to the human agent, the capability for sufficient "self-control" will determine successful persistence.[42] As Kelley et al. state:

> When preliminary steps present the interactants with tempting alternative situations, they must possess sufficient self-control to forgo the alternatives and persist in single-minded movement toward the goal.[43]

The concept of self-control has been studied in various academic contexts, having different philosophical connotations.[44] However, the meaning of self-control[45] in IT is rather narrow in the interpersonal situation described above. Self-control here can be defined as the ability to renounce alternatives and to maintain a consistent attitude toward the original partner and shared goal.[46] Stowers brings in the Stoic concept of "self-mastery" to explain the issues Roman congregations faced, arguing that Paul's main aim in the letter is to show that Christ is a better means than the Torah of achieving "self-mastery."[47] Therefore, for Stowers, Paul's letter to the Romans is "a story of the loss and recovery of self-control."[48] However, we find that what Paul is stressing with regard to the importance of self-control throughout Romans 6–8 is a relational matter, not one that is directed toward the self as Stowers sees. Paul's admonition to practise self-control—"not to live according to the flesh" and to "put to death the deeds of the body" (cf. 8:12–13, see also 6:11–13)—is designed to persuade believers to maintain their relationship with God properly (cf. 8:14–17). Although an exercise of such self-control is accompanied by sufferings,[49] to overcome these hardships and to forgo the temptations are inevitable when one seeks to persist in the affiliation with God. In this respect, the notion of self-control in IT can provide a more suitable explanation for what Paul urges than the Stoic concept that holds a different

---

[41] However, the antithetical relationship between the Spirit (πνεῦμα) and the flesh (σάρξ) is also present here (cf. Rom. 8:7; Gal. 5:17).
[42] Kelley et al., 288.
[43] Ibid.
[44] For instance, Stowers, *Rereading*, 42–82; idem, "Paul and Self-Mastery," in *Paul in the Greco-Roman World*, 524–50; Michelle V. Lee, *Paul, the Stoics, and the Body of Christ* (Cambridge: Cambridge University Press, 2006), 65–6; Engberg-Pedersen, *Stoics*, 52–3.
[45] For Paul's direct use of the term, see Gal. 5:23 (ἐγκράτεια) (see also 1 Cor. 7:5[ἀκρασία]).
[46] Kelley et al., 299.
[47] Stowers, *Rereading*, 42–6.
[48] Ibid., 42.
[49] Cf. Volker Rabens, *The Holy Spirit and Ethics in Paul: Transformation and Empowering for Religious-Ethical Life* (Tübingen: Mohr Siebeck, 2013), 213.

orientation.[50] Although Enberg-Pedersen, who also draws upon the Stoic notion of self-control, appears to recognize the relational facet of self-control in Romans when he sees the failure to exert self-control in 1:18–3:20 as "a failure in the proper directedness toward God",[51] the framework of mutual partnership is not as prominent in his point of view as in our IT concept.

In our case in Romans, the ability to exercise self-control for the sake of forgoing immediate interests is not generated from believers themselves, but becomes possible by divine empowerment. However, this empowerment is neither automatic nor unilateral. Rather, it is described as a process of cooperation that does not exclude believers' active participation. Rabens observes that 8:13–14 exhibits "an interplay between divine and human activity."[52] Thus, it is of importance to examine in what manner Paul stresses the active engagement of believers in the "investment situation," the successful management of which also requires mutual commitment.

7.4.2 Necessity of mutual commitment (Rom. 8:18–30)

When it comes to mutuality in the "investment situation," there are several distinctive expressions that describe believers' mutual involvement in Paul's cosmic vision in Romans 8. Mutual engagement is essential in the "investment situation," because each party ought to fulfil its own role in order to proceed in the relationship toward the goal. Kelley et al. describe the necessity of mutuality as follows:

> The requirement that the investment be mutual can be seen by the fact that at each step, further movement toward the goal requires that both people select the investment option ... The investment at each step is indicated by the negative outcome that each person experiences (the cost incurred) in selecting that option. *If either or both people fail to select the investment option at any step, they do not make the next necessary move toward the goal and, instead, leave the investment situation altogether.*[53]

On God's part, the option to invest has already been selected, as seen in the Christ-event. Accordingly, it is imperative for believers to afford their due investment in order to move the relationship ahead to the goal. Thus, we will analyze how Paul stresses the necessity of mutual commitment by looking at two distinctive types of expressions. One is his use of the language of familial relationships, and the other is his use of συν- compounds.

---

[50] When discussing the meaning of ἡ ἐνεστῶσαν ἀνάγκη in 1 Cor. 7:26, Barclay expounds a similar principle of "investment": the rule of investment originates from the relational identity of believers, because it is "reconfigured human allegiances" effected by the Christ-event that gives a new order of priority in deciding where to invest. As investment into one means disinvestment into the other, Barclay argues that Paul's exhortation of disinvestment cannot parallel the Stoic concept of "indifference" (i.e. the detachment of the inner self from outside). See John M.G. Barclay, "Apocalyptic Allegiance and Disinvestment in the World: A Reading of 1 Corinthians 7:25–35," in *Paul and the Apocalyptic Imagination*, 257–74.
[51] Engberg-Pedersen, *Stoics*, 207–9.
[52] Rabens, 214–15.
[53] Kelley et al., 286 (emphasis mine).

7.4.2.1 The use of familial language

By defining the divine-human relationship as a "father-son (child)" relationship (cf. 8:14–17, 21), Paul not only ties God and believers together more intimately but also emphasizes the necessity of both parties' responsibility for the relationship. Firstly, we can see the familial ties in the believers' cry of "*Abba*, Father" (αββα ὁ πατήρ) in 8:15. Although the use of the Aramaic word *Abba* (αββα) is not restricted to the NT circle,[54] a comparison between the two NT passages where αββα ὁ πατήρ appears[55] shows that Paul employs this particular phrase to express believers' specific position in the relationship with God. In Mark 14:36, Jesus uttered αββα ὁ πατήρ before his passion. Given the possibility that Paul was aware of the Markan tradition,[56] he may have wanted to remind his audience of Jesus' utterance by using the very same phrase. Interestingly, the background of Jesus' utterance in Mark 14:36 is similar to that of believers, i.e. a situation of undergoing suffering. Just as when Jesus called on his father, believers' utterance is made in times of suffering as a call for help. As will be discussed shortly, another interesting parallel between Jesus and believers (cf. 8:17, 29) heightens the possibility that Paul's employment of Jesus' utterance is intentional; by so doing, he identifies believers' position with Jesus himself.[57]

Rabens also detects this particular relational connotation created by the phrase αββα ὁ πατήρ, arguing that the intimacy represented by the phrase extends to include "the imitation of the Son's religious-ethical life before God."[58] The relationship believers have with God is identified with Jesus' relationship with God. They suffer and cry out like Jesus, and consequently they will be glorified like Jesus (cf. 8:17).[59] Also, just as Jesus has demonstrated his commitment to God through his obedience (cf. 5:15–19),[60] believers' commitment (i.e. enduring suffering) is also directed toward God, their "father." Thus, with this identification, Paul opens the path to transmit the mutuality found in the Jesus-God relationship into the relationship between God and believers.

In addition, the necessity of mutual commitment originates from the distinctive identity of believers: "sons of God" (υἱοὶ θεοῦ [8:14]) by "adoption" (υἱοθεσία [8:15, 23]),[61]

---

[54] Jewett, *Romans*, 499.
[55] For another appearance of αββα ὁ πατήρ in the NT, see Gal. 4:6.
[56] Stuhlmacher, *Romans*, 129; Rabens, 234; Longenecker, *Romans*, 703.
[57] A similar point can also be observed in Gal. 4:6. As in Rom. 8:15, here Paul also identifies believers with Jesus as sons (υἱοί) of God who have received the Spirit of the Son, so they can cry αββα ὁ πατήρ. Also, by identifying believers with Jesus, Paul speaks on the theme of inheritance (cf. Gal. 3:29; 4:1, 7).
[58] Rabens, 235.
[59] A similar logic of reward with a Christological basis is found in Phil. 2:9–11 (cf. 3:20–21). Cf. Peter Oakes, *Philippians: From People to Letter* (Cambridge: Cambridge University Press, 2001), 201–4.
[60] Although there is no direct parallel in Romans to passages such as Phil. 2:6–11, we can find that the logic found in "the Christ hymn" in Philippians is also roughly situated in Romans, e.g. Jesus' suffering (8:17; cf. Phil. 2:7–8), obedience to God (5:19; cf. Phil. 2:8) and glorification (1:4; 8:17; cf. Phil. 2:9–11). It is also notable that Rom. 1:3–4, which may use a "credal material," has a meaningful link with Phil. 2:6–8 (cf. Gal. 4:4; Col. 1:15–17) (Kruse, 48).
[61] As Scott has demonstrated, it is now widely acknowledged that the term υἱοθεσία refers to "adoption," as it occurred in Hellenistic society, not "sonship" in general (James M. Scott, *Adoption as Sons of God* [Tübingen: Mohr Siebeck, 1992], xiv; 13–57).

"children of God" (τέκνα θεοῦ [8:16]), "heirs" (κληρονόμοι [8:17]) or "co-heirs" (συγκληρονόμοι [8:17]).[62] In both the Jewish and the Graeco-Roman traditions, mutual obligation was an important element in the father-son relationship.[63] For instance, as Jewett notes, Israel has the responsibility as "sons of God" to maintain their particular identity (cf. Deut 14:1–2).[64] Similarly, in the classical Greek world, the son who held the right of inheritance had certain obligations to fulfil towards his parents.[65] Ada Cohen also points out that both obligation and affection were important elements that bound the family together in ancient Greece.[66] In Roman society, each member of the household was expected to fulfil an obligation in accordance with the individual's position in the family. For instance, obedience was required of children to their father, while the father was to take care of his children with love.[67] Judith Grubbs expounds the mutuality of relational dynamics within the Roman family in terms of *pietas*.[68] Grubbs argues that the concept of *pietas*, a "quintessential Roman family value," entails two distinctive aspects in chorus—a "sense of duty and responsibility to family members" and an "affective aspect."[69] According to Grubbs, such an ideal was applied to the Roman laws in the second and third centuries of the Empire, which enacted the existence of mutual obligation between father and sons, in particular, with regard to financial support.[70]

Such a cultural context aids in construing the relational implication of Paul's use of familial language. Burke argues that "the ethical responsibility for God's son to live circumspectly pervades Paul's thesis of adoption."[71] Romans 8:12 preannounces that what follows will be mainly about the obligation that corresponds with believers' new

---

[62] James Walters correctly points to the close association between adoption and inheritance in Paul (cf. Rom. 8:12–25; Gal. 4:1–7) just as it existed in Graeco-Roman conventions. See Walters, "Adoption," 56.

[63] For our study, we will not draw a sharp line between the Graeco-Roman and Jewish backgrounds while discussing Paul's use of these terms, as there are points upon which two different cultures converge. Cf. Cranfield, 397. See also Trevor J. Burke, *Adopted into God's Family: Exploring a Pauline Metaphor* (Nottingham: Apollos, 2006), 46. For the Jewish background of adoption, see Scott, 61–117.

[64] Jewett, *Romans*, 497. Jewett also exemplifies other texts such as Exod. 4:22; Hos. 2:1, 11:1; Sir. 4:10; Pss. Sol. 17:26–27; Jub. 1:24–25. For other Jewish texts, see also Rabens, 221–2.

[65] Hugh Lindsay, "Adoption and Heirship in Greece and Rome," in *A Companion to Families in the Greek and Roman Worlds*, ed. Beryl Rawson (Chichester: Wiley-Blackwell, 2011), 349. Eva Cantarella also indicates that reciprocal obligations between the heir and his relatives were prominent in families in Athenian society (Eva Cantarella, "Greek Law and the Family," in *A Companion to Families in the Greek and Roman Worlds*, 338).

[66] Ada Cohen, "Picturing Greek Families," in *A Companion to Families in the Greek and Roman Worlds*, 469.

[67] Burke, *Adopted*, 63–4. Burke builds up his argument on Jeffers' investigation. See James S. Jeffers, *Conflict at Rome: Social Order and Hierarchy in Early Christianity* (Minneapolis: Fortress, 1991), 48.

[68] Judith Evans Grubbs, "Promoting Pietas through Roman Law," in *A Companion to Families in the Greek and Roman Worlds*, 377–92.

[69] Grubbs, 377. Therefore, Grubbs concurs with Richard Saller, "Pietas, Obligation and Authority in the Roman Family," in *Alte Geschichte und Wissenschaftsgeschichte, Festschrift für Karl Christ*, ed. Peter Kneissl and Volker Losemann (Darmstadt: Wissenschaftliche Buchgesellschaft, 1988), 399 (cited in Grubbs, 377).

[70] E.g. Cod. justin. 5.25.1 (Antoninus); 5.25.2 (Marcus Aurelius and Lucius Verus); 8.46.5 (Diocletian and Maximian) (see Grubbs, 382–3).

[71] Trevor J. Burke, "The Characteristics of Paul's Adoptive-Sonship (Huiothesia) Motif," *IBS* 17 (1995): 64.

relational status.[72] As can be seen in Rom. 8:12–17, it is the responsibility as "heirs" that occupies a significant portion of Paul's exhortation. Enduring suffering is the foremost responsibility that derives from the identity as heirs (cf. 8:17). On the other hand, in 8:32, Paul draws attention to the love of God who willingly provides all things (τὰ πάντα) for his children just as he has already sacrificed his own son for their sake. In this respect, Paul does not merely single out believers' obligation in the relationship with their father (God), but draws attention to the two-way interactions.[73] The presentation of the father-child relationship in the *Haustafel* of the other NT texts attributed to Paul correlates with our case in Romans 8 concerning the mutual responsibility between father and children (cf. Eph. 6:1–4; Col. 3:20–21). Carolyn Osiek also recognizes that the father-son relationships in both Ephesians and Colossians contain "mutual relationships of love and respect," pointing out the importance of an active role for a subordinate party (children) in the relationship.[74]

Thus, we can see that the terms related to the father-son relationship have a similar meaning with what the phrase αββα ὁ πατήρ implies. Paul emphasizes the importance of mutual commitment in the relationship with God, reminding believers of their special identity. In accordance with the expectations held for each family member in Paul's contemporary society, Paul highlights that mutual responsibility and affection in God's family should also be fulfilled, and believers' participation should not be overlooked as God continues showing his commitment for his dear children.

7.4.2.2 *The use of συν- compounds*

The necessity of mutual commitment in the "investment situation" in Romans 8 is also stressed in Paul's extensive use of συν- compounds in Rom. 8:16–28. These συν-compounds illustrate various types of mutual interactions aimed toward accomplishing the shared goal of the divine-human relationship, in which believers' active participation through enduring sufferings is indispensable. We will look at four types of alliances elaborated by the συν- compounds.

Firstly, several συν- compounds emphasize believers' unity with Christ. In 8:9–11, Paul has already emphasized this type of unity, defining believers as those who have the "spirit of Christ" (πνεῦμα Χριστοῦ). The συν- compounds in 8:17 also elaborate on the unity between believers and Christ. As "co-heirs" (συγκληρονόμοι) with Christ, believers ought to suffer with Christ (συμπάσχω) in order to be glorified with him

---

[72] Longenecker, *Romans*, 701; Robert B. Lewis, *Paul's "Spirit of Adoption" in its Roman Imperial Context* (London: Bloomsbury, 2016), 166–9. Lewis, suggesting the Roman imperial context (e.g. the adoption of Augustus by Julius Caesar) as a background of Paul's articulation of "the spirit of adoption" (8:15), argues that the language of adoption in this passage legitimates the new relational status of gentile believers "in distinction from the adoption of Roman Emperors as sons of God" ("the believer was not being protected by the *genius Augusti*, but by the Spirit of Christ"). See Lewis, 151; 177–85.

[73] Rabens, 214–15.

[74] Carolyn Osiek, "What We Do and Don't Know About Early Christian Families," in *A Companion to Families in the Greek and Roman Worlds*, 199.

(συνδοξάζω). In particular, believers' unity with Christ is important for managing the "investment situation," because the appropriateness of believers' mutual commitment (i.e. endurance throughout suffering) in the relationship with God derives from their unified identity with Christ,[75] who can be a model for them. In 8:29, Christ is depicted as "the firstborn among many brothers" (πρωτότοκον ἐν πολλοῖς ἀδελφοῖς), to whom believers should conform.[76] The fact that Christ died, was raised again and is seated at the right hand of God (8:34; cf. 1:4), recapitulates the sequence of investment and achievement, and such a pattern is applicable for believers who consequently must be mutually involved in the achievement of the goal by undergoing sufferings. The Greek concept ἀδελφός, which includes the ideal of "solidarity and identification," can also indicate the appropriateness of believers' conformity to Christ.[77] Therefore, the image of God's son (τῆς εἰκόνος τοῦ υἱοῦ αὐτου) being characterized by suffering and glorification (cf. 8:17) attests to the existence of family resemblance.[78]

Secondly, several συν- verbs (συστενάζω, συνωδίνω [8:22]) depict the cooperation between believers and non-human creation. Scholars have debated the identity of ἡ κτίσις in Romans 8. However, given the distinctive manner in which Paul addresses human agents as partners of God,[79] it is reasonable to see that Paul is indicating non-human creation with ἡ κτίσις.[80] Even though believers' cooperation with non-human creation might not directly affect the structure of the divine-human relationship, this type of collaboration ultimately facilitates believers' mutual engagement in the "investment situation."

We can see that "the revealing of the sons of God" (τὴν ἀποκάλυψιν τῶν υἱῶν τοῦ θεοῦ [8:19]) or "the freedom of the glory of the children of God" (τὴν ἐλευθερίαν τῆς δόξης τῶν τέκνων τοῦ θεου [8:21]) is vital for the liberation of creation from its "bondage to corruption" (τῆς δουλείας τῆς φθορᾶς [8:21]).[81] In other words, it is the fulfilment of the goal of the divine-human relationship that brings freedom to creation. For that purpose, all of creation also participates in believers' endurance. Both συστενάζω and συνωδίνω are *hapax legomena* in the NT, and they specify creation's

---

[75] Cf. Rabens, 236.
[76] Also, a cooperative aspect between Jesus and believers can be explicated with the Graeco-Roman background of ἀδελφός relationship, which is characterized by "love, harmony, concord and cooperation" (Paul Trebilco, *Self-designations and Group Identity in the New Testament* [Cambridge: Cambridge University Press, 2011], 18–21; 44–5). This quality is seen in Jesus' intercession for his "brothers" in 8:34. The term πρωτότοκος, which mainly reflects privilege, also has a similar function of unifying Christ's sonship and believers' sonship. Cf. Michael Peppard, "Adopted and Begotten Sons of God: Paul and John on Divine Sonship," *CBQ* 73.1 (2011): 101–2.
[77] Cf. Philip Harland, "Familial Dimensions of Group Identity," *JBL* 124.3 (2005): 491–513.
[78] Sylvia C. Keesmaat, "Crucified Lord or Conquering Saviour: Whose Story of Salvation?," *HBT* 26.2 (2004): 88.
[79] E.g. υἱῶν τοῦ θεοῦ (8:19); τέκνων τοῦ θεοῦ (8:21).
[80] Concerning this debate, see Kruse, 347; Duncan, 413–14.
[81] Inasmuch as Paul constantly employs familial nomenclatures to address believers throughout the universalized context of Romans 8, "the sons (children) of God" in 8:19-21 can be seen as primarily indicating the believers glorified with Christ. Thus, it is less probable to see that Paul's main focus here is Israel based on the Jewish background of the phrase, though the possibility that currently unbelieving Jews will be included in the group in the future exists (cf. Romans 9–11). *Pace* Susan Eastman, "Whose Apocalypse? The Identity of the Sons of God in Romans 8:19," *JBL* 121.2 (2002): 263–77. Cf. Kruse, 343.

cooperation with believers.⁸² Creation's activity of συστενάζω (8:22) can be linked with the στενάζω (8:23), which illustrates believers' activity of enduring sufferings for the sake of reaching the ultimate goal (cf. 2 Cor. 5:2-4). The expression οὐ μόνον, ἀλλὰ καὶ (8:23) also emphasizes the fact that the activity of believers in 8:23 is closely related to the creation's activity in 8:19-22. The image created by συνωδίνω is similar. The activity of child-birthing that the verb ὠδίνω points out is a laborious activity that causes groaning in pain and simultaneously requires waiting in patience (cf. 8:24-25). However, it is also a purposeful activity that results in a certain fruit ("childbirth").⁸³ In this sense, the creation's activity of συνωδίνω implies that creation also participates in believers' painful experience of the present, but in the hope of the forthcoming fruit.⁸⁴

Believers are not alone in experiencing and enduring sufferings, but all of creation also participates in such endurance through suffering.⁸⁵ This fact underlines again the cosmic significance of the divine-human relationship and its goal. The fact that creation is eagerly awaiting with their groaning and suffering together with believers shows how magnificent and important the glory about to be revealed is. Although not enough attention has been paid to the link between non-human creation and humanity by biblical scholars, as Horrell points out, we can hardly discount the significance of creation in Paul's cosmic vision.⁸⁶ Given that the liberation of creation is the element through which the human vocation in the cosmic vision is elaborated,⁸⁷ it is important to pay attention to what sort of activities creation is doing in the midst of the time of endurance throughout suffering.

Thirdly, Paul employs particular συν- compounds to refer to the cooperation between the Spirit and believers in 8:16 and 8:26. Συμμαρτυρέω in 8:16 is the activity that the Spirit performs together with believers' spirit (i.e. human spirit), and such an

---

[82] *Pace* Cranfield, 415 ("the sense must be 'together', 'with one accord'"). Jewett argues that "anaphoric reduplication of συν" makes the two verbs as "a rhetorically unified expression" (Jewett, *Romans*, 517). Cf. Cherryl Hunt, David G. Horrell and Christopher Southgate, "An Environmental Mantra? Ecological Interest in Romans 8:19-23 and a Modest Proposal for Its Narrative Interpretation," *JTS* 59.2 (2008): 565-6.

[83] Cf. Dunn, *Romans 1-8*, 472.

[84] Similar to Rom. 8:22, the use of ὠδίνω in Gal. 4:19 also implies that suffering (of Paul) the pain of childbirth is a purposeful activity, and the result of such an activity is fruitful (believers' conformity to Christ).

[85] Rehman, 77.

[86] David G. Horrell, "A New Perspective on Paul? Rereading Paul in a Time of Ecological Crisis," *JSNT* 33.1 (2010): 3-30. An exception, according to Horrell, is Brendan Byrne, "Creation Groaning: An Earth Bible Reading of Romans 8.18-22," in *Readings from the Perspective of Earth*, ed. Norman C. Habel (Sheffield: Sheffield Academic, 2000), 193-203.

[87] Cf. Horrell, "Rereading," 20 ("the assemblies of Christian believers, as they live out their new life in Christ and fulfil the responsibilities that that implies, play some part in the story of creation's liberation"). Therefore, Horrell not only elucidates the connection between transformation of believers and the liberation of creation (e.g. Yates, 153; Jackson, 150) but also asks about the significance of believers' role–especially their ethical responsibility–in this process of cosmic salvation. Similarly, Byrne also claims that given the possibility that the human action can influence the world, either positively or negatively, in the overlapping ages, "the future of the world [salvation] does to some extent lie in human hands," as "the prevailing power of God's grace" works "through human cooperation" (Byrne, "Ecological," 92-3). Similarly, Douglas J. Moo, "Creation and New Creation," *BBR* 20.1 (2010): 59-60 ("God, in his grace, is using our efforts to accomplish his own purpose").

activity aims to confirm believers' distinctive identity as children of God (τέκνα θεοῦ). Although the nuance of the prefix συν- in the verb συμμαρτυρέω appears weak in Rom. 2:15 and 9:1, 8:16 can be distinguished from these two occasions. In 8:16, the subject of the verb is the third-person, not the introspective self,[88] and the insertion of "our spirit" (πνεύματι ἡμῶν), coupled with "the Spirit" (πνεῦμα), suggests that συμμαρτυρέω in 8:16 depicts a joint activity between the two subjects. Accordingly, the dynamic between the Spirit and believers can be better understood if the etymological distinctiveness of the verb is taken into account.[89] Grant Macaskill also recognizes this point, acknowledging the active role of believers' cooperation with the Spirit:

> While to be led by the Spirit (8:14) may imply a passive state, συμμαρτυρεῖ ... implies co-agency. Clearly the fact that the Spirit "leads" ascribes to him a primary role, but the human partner is also identified as the acting subject of the verbs, through the συν- prefix.[90]

We can observe a similar point from συναντιλαμβάνομαι in 8:26. Both in Lk. 10:40 and Rom. 8:26, the two occasions in the NT where συναντιλαμβάνομαι appears, the verb does not explain an activity of one-sided helping alone, but describes a joint activity ("join in helping"[91]) or participation in other's work (cf. Exod. 18:22; Num. 11:17; Ps. 88:22 [LXX]).[92] Noting that "the sense of taking part in a responsibility or task" is implied in the word, Dunn provides a helpful illustration for understanding what συναντιλαμβάνομαι describes in Rom. 8:26: "the image of the Spirit shouldering the burden which our weakness imposes on us."[93] Wu also finds a sense of solidarity in this type of helping, extending the boundary of believers' solidarity to the solidarity with God.[94] As believers groan (with creation) the Spirit intercedes for believers with his own groans (στεναγμοῖς), which implies that the Spirit shares believers' distress in prayer. Such intercession is primarily for believers (ἐντυγχάνει ὑπὲρ ἁγίων [8:27]), but it is also done together with believers.[95] Believers' prayer can be effective even when they are in weakness (ἀσθενείᾳ), which includes their shortage of knowledge about what to pray,[96] because the Spirit who stands by believers also prays together with them, though it may not be physically audible (ἀλάλητος).[97] Enduring suffering is not

---

[88] Both in 2:15 and in 9:1, the reference to "conscience" (συνείδησις) reflects that συμμαρτυρέω in these cases is a sort of introspective activity.

[89] Pace Kruse, 339. Jewett also argues that "it is inappropriate to reduce the semantic range of συμμαρτυρέω for apologetic reasons," though his view of "our spirit" as "apportioned Spirit" is unlikely since Paul is clearly dealing with "us" as believers (Jewett, Romans, 500).

[90] Grant Macaskill, Union with Christ in the New Testament (Oxford: Oxford University Press, 2013), 240.

[91] Dunn, Romans 1–8, 476.

[92] Jewett, Romans, 521.

[93] Dunn, Romans 1–8, 477. Some scholars are reluctant to accept the specific implication of συν- prefix here (e.g. Cranfield, 421; Kruse, 351).

[94] Wu, 154.

[95] Cf. Dunn, Romans 1–8, 478 ("Paul clearly intends with στεναγμοῖς to link the thought back to vv. 22 and 23").

[96] Cranfield, 421.

[97] The immediate context does not allow us to see στεναγμοῖς ἀλαλήτοις as glossolalia. Pace Käsemann, Romans, 240–2.

merely a duty of believers; it is described as a kind of cooperative activity with the Spirit. Although the divine help is always decisive, believers' mutual engagement cannot be discounted. Rather, the divine help (e.g. the Spirit's help) complements the believers' activity (e.g. prayer), so that they can successfully play their part in the relationship in order to reach the goal.

Fourthly, συνεργέω in 8:28 deserves our special attention regarding the mutual engagement between God and believers. The meaning of 8:28 depends on who is understood to be the subject of συνεργέω. As several scholars have pointed out, the ὁ θεός after συνεργεῖ in some manuscripts (P⁴⁶, A, B, 81, sa) appears to be a later insertion because it is more natural for συνεργεῖ to take a personal subject.[98] However, it is still arguable whether πάντα can be an actual subject of συνεργεῖ. Cranfield is in favour of seeing πάντα as a real subject of συνεργεῖ. Thus, he argues that "the primary reference to πάντα is, no doubt, to 'the sufferings of the present time.'"[99] In contrast, a number of scholars consider πάντα as an accusative form, either accusative of respect,[100] or direct object of the verb,[101] assuming that an implied subject of συνεργεῖ may be either God[102] or the Spirit.[103] However, it is still unclear why there is no corresponding preposition if πάντα is used as an accusative of respect,[104] and as argued by several scholars, the verb συνεργέω does not usually take a direct object.[105] The various suggestions appear to be influenced to a degree by theological views. For instance, C.H. Dodd refuses to take πάντα as the subject because such an interpretation reflects "the evolutionary optimism of the nineteenth century."[106] Thus, given this ambiguity, it is necessary to find the meaning of συνεργεῖ by looking at the location of 8:28 within its surrounding context.

From Rom. 8:28, Paul recapitulates what has been indicated previously. Οἴδαμεν works as a sort of discourse marker, indicating that Paul is now rephrasing what has been said previously. There are several occasions in which οἴδαμεν introduces a summary and elaboration of the previous statements (cf. Rom. 3:19; 7:14; 2 Cor. 5:1). Gieniusz also indicates the function of 8:28-30 as reinforcing the previous argument, insisting that the passage cannot be regarded as a "self-standing, independent unit."[107]

---

[98] Cf. Bruce M. Metzger, *A Textual Commentary on the Greek New Testament: A Companion Volume to the United Bible Societies' Greek New Testament (Fourth Revised Edition)* (Stuttgart; New York: Deutsche Bibelgesellschaft; United Bible Societies, 1994), 458. See also Dunn, *Romans 1-8*, 466; Cranfield, 425-7; Jewett, *Romans*, 526; Fitzmyer, *Romans*, 523.

[99] Cranfield, 427. See also Dunn, *Romans 1-8*, 480; Käsemann, *Romans*, 243; Stuhlmacher, *Romans*, 136; Fitzmyer, *Romans*, 523.

[100] Andrzej Gieniusz, *Romans 8:18-30: "Suffering Does Not Thwart the Future Glory"* (Atlanta: Scholars, 1999), 427; Mark S. Gignilliat, "Working Together with Whom? Text-Critical, Contextual, and Theological Analysis of Συνεργεῖ in Romans 8,28," *Bib* 87 (2006): 513; Jewett, *Romans*, 526. Cf. RSV.

[101] Sanday and Headlam, 215; Gordon D. Fee, *God's Empowering Presence: The Holy Spirit in the Letters of Paul* (Peabody: Hendrickson, 1994), 588; Longenecker, *Romans*, 738.

[102] F.F. Bruce, *Romans* (London: IVP, 1974), 175-6; Ziesler, *Romans*, 225; Keck, 216; Kruse, 353-5. Seeing God as a subject of the intransitive verb, Mark Gignilliat argues that "cooperation" is made between God and the Spirit (Gignilliat, 514).

[103] Jewett, *Romans*, 526-7; Fee, 587-90.

[104] Cf. J. Gwyn Griffiths, "Romans Viii. 28," *ExpT* 49 (1938): 475; Cranfield, 426; Jewett, *Romans*, 526.

[105] Griffiths, 475-6; Cranfield, 426; Moo, *Romans*, 528; Gieniusz, *Romans 8*, 225.

[106] Dodd, *Romans*, 138-9.

[107] Gieniusz, *Romans 8*, 249.

According to Gieniusz's rhetorical analysis of 8:18–30, 8:18 and 8:19–27 work as *propositio* and *probatio*, respectively, and 8:28–30 can be understood as *conclusio*.[108]

In Rom. 8:28, what is recapitulated and elaborated is the two types of cooperation in 8:18–27 that revolve around the expressions of groaning:[109] 1) the cooperation between creation and believers and 2) the cooperation between the Spirit and believers. In both cases, believers constitute one of the mainstays of the collaboration, and in 8:28 those who work together with whoever is the subject of συνεργεῖ, are also believers. Although the two dative phrases in 8:28 (τοῖς ἀγαπῶσιν τὸν θεὸν and τοῖς κατὰ πρόθεσιν κλητοῖς οὖσιν) are frequently interpreted in a way that emphasizes believers' position as beneficiaries,[110] these phrases can also be understood as describing those who cooperate with the subject of συνεργεῖ.[111] James 2:22 is a good example that shows how the subject of συνεργέω (intransitive) associates with the agent in the dative phrase (ἡ πίστις συνήργει τοῖς ἔργοις αὐτοῦ).

Therefore, the subject of συνεργεῖ is an actor who is also influential on believers' cooperation with creation and the Spirit, and we find that God is also involved in the two types of cooperation. Unsurprisingly, it has been suggested by several scholars that the subject of συνεργεῖ is God. Given that an explicit reference to God is absent in Rom. 8:29–30 where Paul spells out God's activity, it seems natural that Paul is doing something similar in 8:28. Also, God has already been made known both in the dative phrase that precedes συνεργεῖ and in 8:27. Furthermore, God is actually present when both types of cooperation happen. In 8:20, God engages in the collaboration between creation and believers by subjecting creation to futility—the result of which is to make the creation groan together with believers who are in a similar situation.[112] In addition, God's presence is also observed when the Spirit cooperates with believers in prayer. In 8:27, God is depicted as the one who searches believers' hearts and who also knows the mind of the Spirit. Such activities are for maintaining the congruence between God and the Spirit, by means of which the Spirit's intercession for believers can be effective.[113]

Then, we can understand πάντα as an accusative of respect, and we can find that it is the two types of cooperation with believers to which πάντα points. As Gieniusz argues, πάντα can be used as an accusative of respect without a preposition.[114] First Corinthians 9:25, 10:33 and 11:2 show Paul's usage of πάντα as an accusative of respect to indicate the occasion in which what a main verb expresses happens. Given that Paul's main interest in Rom. 8:18–27 is not merely about sufferings per se, but about the collaborations to make believers successfully endure suffering, we need to broaden the

---

[108] Ibid., 285–7.
[109] Ibid., 250.
[110] For instance, Gignilliat argues that to understand believers in 8:28 as co-workers with God weakens "the beneficiary idea" along with "the theocentricity of Paul's thought" (Gignilliat, 514; Moo, *Romans*, 529 [n. 120]).
[111] In this respect, the translation of the dative phrases as "for (or to) those who" appears somewhat limited (cf. NRSV; NIV; ESV).
[112] Cf. Dunn, *Romans 1–8*, 470.
[113] Cf. 1 Cor. 2:10
[114] Gienisuz, *Romans 8*, 256.

range of meaning for πάντα in the final section. Thus, recapitulating 8:18–27 with a focus on the divine-human relationship, 8:28 states that God himself works together (συνεργεῖ) with believers—in their collaborations with creation and the Spirit indicated by πάντα, and this offers a more direct picture of how both God and believers are mutually committed in the "investment situation" for achieving their final goal. The aorist verbs in the rest of the summarizing section (8:29–30) support 8:28 by confirming the certainty of God's plan for believers.

Therefore, Romans 8:28 makes better sense with the following translation: "and we know that for those who love God, in all things [i.e. believers' cooperation with creation and the Spirit] he [God] works together for good, with those who are called according to [his] purpose."[115] In fact, the idea that believers are co-workers with God is not alien to Paul, as can be seen in 1 Cor. 3:9, 2 Cor. 6:4 and 1 Thess. 3:2.[116] This interpretation does not put forward simple synergism.[117] We do not need to undermine the diverse types of the asymmetric natures between the actors in order to speak of cooperation. By highlighting the presence of cooperation, we bring to the fore the cosmic significance of the goal and mutuality, a core element for the accomplishment of the goal, regardless of the effectiveness and originality of each actor's labours. Therefore, in talking about cooperation, it is not our aim to merely stress the human capacity. Rather, by indicating the fact that believers share in the responsibility of the ultimate cosmic vision, Paul achieves two different goals: 1) to underscore the responsibility of believers and 2) to encourage his recipients by informing them of the greatness of the cosmic glory and their privileged position as co-workers of God. All these elements were designed to help believers to endure sufferings successfully.

To summarize, we can recognize that Paul's use of συν- compounds is very purposeful. The συν- compounds that describe the various types of unity and collaborations highlight the necessity of mutual engagement of believers through enduring sufferings in the "investment situation" on different levels for the accomplishment of the ultimate goal.

---

[115] By translating the two dative phrases as "for" and "with" respectively, I intend to express both the cooperative and beneficiary aspects together. Jewett, *Romans*, 504 suggests a similar translation of the two dative phrases ("<u>for</u> those who love God … <u>with</u> those who are called according to a purpose"). Similarly, Susan Eastman, "Oneself in Another: Participation and the Spirit in Romans 8," in *"In Christ" in Paul: Explorations in Paul's Theology of Union and Participation*, ed. Michael J. Thate, Kevin J. Vanhoozer and Constantine R. Campbell (Tübingen: Mohr Siebeck, 2014), 115–16 ("in all things the Spirit works together <u>with and for</u> 'those who love him'"). Cf. RSV ("with those who love him, who are called according to his purpose").

[116] In 2 Cor. 6:1, Paul presents himself and his fellows as συνεργοῦντες (2 Cor. 6:1), and the parallel expression in 2 Cor. 6:4 (θεοῦ διάκονοι) enables us to see that it is God with whom they are working together (cf. NRSV ["we work together with him"]) for the gospel of reconciliation as ambassadors for Christ (cf. 2 Cor. 5:20). Similarly, whereas συνεργός is mostly used to refer to the relationship between fellow believers (cf. Rom. 16:3, 9, 21; 2 Cor. 1:24; 8:23; Phil. 2:25; 4:3; Phlm. 1, 24), the reference to θεοῦ in 1 Cor. 3:9 (θεοῦ γάρ ἐσμεν συνεργοί) and 1 Thess. 3:2 (συνεργὸν τοῦ θεοῦ) is distinctive. In the former case, συνεργοί might also refer to Paul and Apollos, but the context appears to support the idea that both Paul and Apollos are working with God (cf. 1 Cor. 3:6). Cf. C.K. Barrett, *A Commentary on the First Epistle to the Corinthians* (London: Black, 1968), 86; E. Earle Ellis, "Paul and His Co-Workers," *NTS* 17.4 (1971): 440. In the latter, it is relatively clear that Timothy is described as God's "co-worker" in the enterprise of preaching the gospel of Christ.

[117] Cf. Jewett, *Romans*, 527–8 (see especially n. 211).

7.5 Strategies for sustaining the relationship

We have noted that Paul highlights the significance of forgoing immediate interest and mutual commitment for the successful management of the "investment situation." Kelley et al. discuss several factors that can promote one's attempt to meet the two requirements of "investment," asking the reason for persistence or withdrawal in the "investment situation."[118] As we will see, the factors pointed out by scholars also provide helpful insights for understanding Paul's encouragement to believers to remain in the "investment situation" as well as aspects of the Spirit's empowerment of believers.[119]

7.5.1 Persistence objectively warranted by a goal (Rom. 8:26-27, 31-39)

According to Kelley et al., people basically tend to persist in the "investment situation" when it is likely that they can obtain good outcomes by doing so.[120] In particular, two conditions are significant to bring about "rich dividends" for the partner in the "investment situation": 1) the trustworthiness of the partner and 2) one's ability to offer the required investment.[121] In the "investment situation" in Romans 8, confirming that the two conditions are fulfilled is also essential for encouraging believers to persist in their relationship with God, because such fulfilment can increase the certainty that they will be rewarded with good outcomes as a result of their persistence. The trustworthiness of the partner has previously been confirmed by God's self-sacrificial act (i.e. Christ's death) in Romans 3 and 5, and it is accentuated again in 8:31-39 (especially 8:32).[122] In addition, the cooperation with the Spirit is a crucial means of empowering believers to make the necessary "investment," since believers are still weak (cf. 8:26). Therefore, given these conditions, there are good reasons for Paul to assure believers of the future glory that cannot be thwarted by present suffering.

7.5.2 Persistence promoted by proximity (Rom. 8:18)

However, there are some occasions when one may be willing to persist in the "investment situation" despite the lack of information about the situation that might cause latent risk.[123] Among such occasions, the belief that "the desired goal is closer" can promote persistence in spite of the fact that one does not possess in totality the information about the completion of the current relationship.[124] In this respect, we can

---

[118] Kelley et al., 288.
[119] For this section, I will roughly follow the order in Kelley et al., 288-301.
[120] Ibid., 288-9.
[121] Ibid.
[122] For the significance of trustworthiness, see especially Section 7.5.4. Tyler Stewart argues that 8:31-39 recapitulates "the whole logic of participation" throughout Romans 5-8 (i.e. "God puts to death those who participate in Jesus' cross as a means of freeing them from the Adam-age"), and what seems to be mainly recapitulated is God's faithfulness testified by the Christ-event spelt out in the previous chapters (Tyler A. Stewart, "The Cry of Victory: A Cruciform Reading of Psalm 44:22 in Romans 8:36," *JSPHL* 3.1 [2013]: 25-45 [see especially 39-40]).
[123] Kelley et al., 290.
[124] Ibid., 290-1.

think about the implications of Paul's emphasis on the proximity of the glory (τὴν μέλλουσαν δόξαν ἀποκαλυφθῆναι εἰς ἡμᾶς [8:18]). According to Dunn, μέλλω connotes both propinquity and certainty (cf. 8:13).[125] Although μέλλω can simply signify a future event, this does not necessarily exclude proximity.[126] Rather, proximity is one of the modes of the future.[127] Furthermore, the atmosphere of the cosmic picture in Romans 8, which is strongly imbued with feelings of tension—e.g. the picture of labouring together (cf. 8:22)—implies that the approaching future is quite near (cf. 13:11). Therefore, the fact that they will receive the ultimate reward not too far from now can encourage believers to endure present sufferings with positive expectations.

7.5.3 Persistence promoted by mounting exit costs (Rom. 8:6, 13)

Persistence can also be promoted by the high cost of exiting the relationship. One of the most prominent factors that increase the exit cost is the decrease in the quality of alternative partners.[128] In Romans 8, Paul forcefully emphasizes the fact that the obvious outcome of maintaining the alternative relationship with Sin is death (cf. 8:6, 13). Death does not merely mean physical death, but rather it is fundamentally antithetical to eternal life (ζωή αἰώνιος) (cf. 6:22–23). Therefore, because of such a high exit cost, it is much more beneficial for believers not to exit the current relationship with God, which means that they ought to continue to make investments there. It is by this logic that Paul exhorts believers to live according to the Spirit and not according to the flesh (8:13).

7.5.4 Persistence promoted by trust and commitment (Rom. 8:31–39)

IT suggests that trust and commitment are the most important qualities that can lead the "investment situation" to a successful completion.[129] According to Kelley et al., trust "facilitates the ability of interactants to confidently pursue a remote goal, single-mindedly suffering direct costs and forgoing tempting alternatives."[130] Trust can also reduce uncertainty in the relationship, and promotes confidence in a partner's attitude toward one's own well-being and prior promises.[131]

When it comes to Romans 8, we can observe that Paul highlights God's trustworthiness to believers in times of suffering. Romans 8:31–39 is one of the most emphatic passages where Paul dramatically spells out God's trustworthiness to his human partners. Much like in Rom. 5:6–11, Paul asserts in 8:32 that God's giving up his Son for all humanity (ὑπὲρ ἡμῶν πάντων παρέδωκεν αὐτόν) is the most obvious evidence that testifies his trustworthiness. In 8:39, God's trustworthiness is elaborated

---

[125] Dunn, *Romans 1–8*, 467.
[126] *Pace* Jewett, *Romans*, 510; Esler, *Romans*, 260. Moo also recognizes that the imminence of the glory is an option, though he thinks that the best alternative is "a nuance of certainty" (Moo, *Romans*, 512 [see n. 19]).
[127] Cf. Käsemann, 232 ("imminent expectation comes to expression here").
[128] Kelley et al., 289.
[129] Ibid., 296.
[130] Ibid.
[131] Ibid.

as "the love of God in Christ Jesus our Lord" (τῆς ἀγάπης τοῦ θεοῦ τῆς ἐν Χριστῷ Ἰησοῦ τῷ κυρίῳ ἡμῶν).[132] It is notable that when Paul speaks of the divine love he usually exemplifies God's self-sacrificial saving action for humanity (cf. 5:5, 8).[133] The love is not simply an emotional quality, but is expressed in a concrete form, and thus it can be considered as vivid evidence of trustworthiness.[134] Therefore, believers' trust can be augmented by bringing to mind God's "willingness to forgo his direct self-interest" as revealed in Christ's death.[135] Such trust also takes away the fear of the possibility of the relationship's dissolution by the partner, and upholds the confidence that God will give "all things" (τὰ πάντα) to support their endurance.[136]

In addition, Paul's exhortation in Rom. 8:31–39 can militate in favour of encouraging believers' commitment to the "investment situation." Commitment in a dyadic relationship is expressed by "intent to persist, psychological attachment to the partner (i.e. concern with their well-being), and long-term orientation (i.e. the inclination to consider future implications of present actions)."[137] Thus, partners in strong commitment often exhibit prosocial actions, maintaining a positive attitude toward each other and risking cost.[138] In this respect, to increase mutual commitment is one key to the successful management of the "investment situation."

Kelley et al. summarize three main elements that increase commitment: 1) a high degree of satisfaction level, 2) the poor quality of alternatives and 3) the size of past and current investments.[139] We have already discussed the implications of 1) and 2) (see 7.5.3). The third element is not directly relevant to our case; however, the fact that God has paid a considerable cost for his partners can show that God is strongly committed to his relationship with humanity. Accordingly, this can be another ground on which believers can risk themselves in the "investment situation."

As in IT, trust and commitment are important factors that facilitate the achievement of the goal of the divine-human relationship. God's demonstration of his trustworthiness to his partners increases their trust. As a response to God's prosocial act, believers are expected to "make themselves vulnerable by becoming more dependent on their partner, forgoing tempting alternatives."[140] Consequently, believers' increased dependence will lead them to make a strong commitment to their relationship, exhibiting prosocial behaviours for the partner and bearing the costs (e.g. suffering).[141] In this respect, it is also true in Romans 8 that "trust and commitment influence one another in a reliable feedback loop."[142]

---

[132] Cf. Rom. 8:35.
[133] In 5:5, God's love is specified in relation to the indwelling of the Spirit, while in 5:8, Christ's sacrificial death surfaces more explicitly for demonstrating the love of God.
[134] Moo, *Romans*, 543 ("gracious action on our behalf").
[135] Kelley et al., 296. Cf. Jennifer Wieselquist et al., "Commitment, Pro-Relationship Behavior, and Trust in Close Relationships," *JPSP* 77.5 (1999): 942–66.
[136] Cf. Moo, *Romans*, 541 ("all those blessings —spiritual and material—that we require on the path toward that final salvation").
[137] Kelley et al., 296.
[138] Ibid.
[139] Ibid.
[140] Ibid., 297.
[141] Ibid.
[142] Ibid.

7.5.5 Relationship maintenance mechanisms (Rom. 8:14-17)

Kelley et al. point out that in ongoing relationships partners tend to develop various types of "maintenance mechanisms"[143] that are "the specific means by which partners sustain long-term, well-functioning relationships."[144] Maintenance mechanisms can be classified into two types: 1) behavioural maintenance acts that deal with aspects of behavioural shifts (e.g. accommodations; willingness to sacrifice; forgiveness); and 2) cognitive maintenance acts that engage in "cognitive restructuring" (e.g. derogation of alternatives; positive illusion; cognitive interdependence).[145]

The notion of "maintenance mechanisms" is useful for comprehending the implication of mutual interactions between God and humanity. On God's side, we can observe that what God has done for his human partners is very close to the aim of "behavioural maintenance mechanisms." In terms of "behavioural maintenance mechanisms" epitomized by the accommodation of the partner's weakness and faults (e.g. forgiveness), God's sacrificial act in Christ's death can be seen as a manifestation of his commitment, which is the deciding factor in his forgiving his partner's betrayal.

On the human side, the strategy of creating "cognitive interdependence" is also in operation when Paul utilizes familial terms to designate believers' identity. Rusbult, Arriaga and Agnew observe that "cognitive interdependence" can be revealed according to a specific understanding of the actor's identity.[146] For instance, if one deploys such a maintenance mechanism, they restructure the self-identity in relation to the partner, for instance "we, us, our rather than I, me, mine."[147] In this respect, believers' redefined identity in Rom. 8:14–17 functions to promote solidarity between God and believers as one family. This solidarity can "facilitate movement toward a remote yet desirable goal,"[148] promoting a pro-relationship attitude.[149] The goal is not only for "me" or "you," but rather becomes for "us."

7.5.6 Increasing locomotion (Rom. 8:13-14, 18, 24-25)

From the IT point of view, the help of the Spirit can be interpreted as an attempt to increase believers' "locomotion." Kelley et al. explain that "'locomotion' involves the drives relevant to achieving movement from state to state, including effort expenditure and the application of other resources toward goal attainment."[150]

The function of locomotion is particularly important when one needs to exert self-control in a condition that requires forgoing both immediate interests and promising alternatives.[151] To put it differently, "locomotion" can be viewed as the "willpower" to

---

[143] Ibid.
[144] Rusbult, Arriaga and Agnew, 377. Cf. Kelley et al., 297.
[145] Rusbult, Arriaga and Agnew, 378. Cf. Kelley et al., 297.
[146] Rusbult, Arriaga and Agnew, 381.
[147] Agnew et al. characterize this mechanism as "inclusion of other in the self." Christopher R. Agnew et al., "Cognitive Interdependence: Commitment and the Mental Representation of Close Relationships," *JPSP* 74.4 (1998): 942.
[148] Kelley et al., 297.
[149] Rusbult, Arriaga and Agnew, 381.
[150] Kelley et al., 298.
[151] Ibid., 298-9.

persist in the relationship.[152] On the basis of this IT concept, putting to death the deeds of the body becomes one example of exercising willpower or strong locomotion for forgoing immediate interests. Paul's use of an instrumental dative in 8:13 (πνεύματι ["by the Spirit"]) and the passive voice of ἄγονται in 8:14 (πνεύματι θεοῦ ἄγονται ["to be led by the Spirit of God"]) implies that the help of the Spirit is essential for this practice.[153] The Spirit's help in prayer can also be a complement to believers' "locomotion" in prayer (cf. 8:26–27).

Paul's exhortation can also be considered as an attempt to encourage his hearers' "locomotion" for overcoming a conventional estimation of the "investment situation." Kelley et al. indicate that those who have "strong locomotion tendencies" are likely to experience "transformation processes that result in 'irrational' investment."[154] In fact, believers' persistence in the "investment situation" can be seen as irrational from a conventional point of view, because of the nature of the cost and the invisible nature of the goal. However, Paul's counter-intuitive prospect of the "investment situation" stimulates believers to transform the conventional frame of mind into the same disposition by which Paul reconceptualizes the present situation. For instance, Paul encourages his hearers by insisting on the surpassing value of the glory over current sufferings (cf. 8:18). Also, Paul relativizes "visible hope" (ἐλπὶς βλεπομένη), emphasizing the superiority of the hope that cannot be seen (ὃ οὐ βλέπομεν) (cf. 8:24–25). Therefore, although believers' investment may be viewed as irrational in the current situation, such motivation can strengthen believers' "locomotion" so that they can keep pursuing the goal, perpetuating the affiliation with God their partner.

7.6 Conclusion

In conclusion, we have examined the role of believers as God's partners for the achievement of the eschatological and cosmic goal described in Rom. 8:12–39. In Romans 8, it is the endurance throughout suffering that characterizes believers' active participation in the divine-human relationship. On the one hand, believers' endurance is an expression of fidelity to their partner, who was the first to demonstrate love and faithfulness. On the other hand, endurance is considered as an investment toward the future goal. In order to obtain the future glory, believers must make an investment. With the help of studies on the "investment situation" by IT, we have observed that in order to reach the long-term goal, believers have to forgo immediate interests, which usually involves the temptation of an alternative option. Mutual commitment is also one of the vital conditions for successfully accomplishing the goal. Paul's employment of some distinctive terms (i.e. familial language and συν- compounds) reflects the significance of mutual engagement between God and believers—and it is this mutuality that constitutes the structure of "interdependence" in terms of outcomes. Furthermore, there are several strategies for sustaining the relationship that are at work in the text. In

---

[152] Ibid., 298.
[153] Cf. Rabens, 214–15.
[154] Kelley et al., 298.

some cases, we have seen these strategies in Paul's exhortation, while in other cases, we have interpreted the help of the Spirit in terms of the IT framework.

We have noted that while the fundamental possibility of the relationship is dependent upon God's initiative, this does not necessarily exclude the necessity of believers' mutual participation in managing the relationship toward achieving the goal. As Barclay argues, since believers' lives hang upon "the resurrection life of Christ,"[155] it would be misguided to understand the diversity of believers' active participation as self-generated.[156] Rather, human agents, as active and responsible partners of God, are restored and sustained by the divine actions. Thus, it is equally unhelpful "to play the agency of the believer off against the agency of Christ/the Spirit."[157] In this respect, Romans 8:12–39 reflects the multidimensional nature of the divine-human relationship, elaborating on the dynamics between God and human beings (and even including non-human creation).[158]

---

[155] Barclay, *Gift*, 581.
[156] Cf. ibid., 493.
[157] Ibid., 518.
[158] Barclay argues that "his [Paul's] paraenesis points simultaneously to divine- and believer-agency, as the expression and realization of the good news" (Barclay, *Gift*, 442. See also John M.G. Barclay, "Grace and the Transformation of Agency in Christ," in *Redefining First-Century Jewish and Christian Identities*, ed. Fabian E. Udoh [Notre Dame: University of Notre Dame Press, 2008], 372–89). Similarly, Wells, 237–8.

8

Conclusion

This study has sought to explicate the geography of the divine-human relationship in Romans 1–8 for the purpose of arguing that although the relationship is fundamentally contingent upon God's initiative, the mutual engagement of human beings as God's partners is also an indispensable factor that upholds and develops the relationship. Paul's depiction of the divine-human relationship in Romans 1–8 is dynamic, since the relationship goes through changes and developments, with each stage possessing its own characteristics. Furthermore, the fact that the divine-human relationship has a shared goal is also significant for understanding the reason for the changes and developments in the relationship. Keeping these two points in mind, we have attempted to explain the divine-human relationship portrayed throughout Romans 1–8, focusing on several characteristic phases of the relationship. We have identified the key stages as betrayal (Rom. 1:18–3:20), forgiveness and reconciliation (3:21–26; 5:1–11), non-voluntary dependence (5:12–8:11) and investment for the future (8:12–39).

8.1 Summary of the study

In order to deal with the series of relational situations in a consistent manner, we have adopted a social psychological framework that specializes in diagnosing the relational structures of a dyadic relationship, i.e. "interdependence theory" (IT). IT explains the implications of the various interactions between partners with reference to the relational structure that has been shaped by expectations of outcomes, addressing why a certain pattern of behaviour arises at some times and not at others. To our knowledge, our study is the first attempt to deploy IT for biblical interpretation. Therefore, we have scrutinized the validity of IT for our project. The result of such an investigation has directed the manner in which we have utilized IT for our study. In terms of historical appropriateness, we have shown that the focus of IT on the interaction between individuals is still valid, since in antiquity the individual was regarded as a self-conscious and active agent. Also, we have identified that ancient thinkers, including Paul, also considered the concept of outcome as an influential factor on human behaviour in the form of self-interest. What is more, both these ancient thinkers and IT acknowledge the possibility that on some occasions, people do not act in the pursuit of direct self-interest. We have also discussed how IT is relevant for the theological nature of our topic. We have noted that what provides the foundation for our approach is the fact that in Romans, Paul frequently speaks "in a human way" (κατὰ ἄνθρωπον) in order to illustrate aspects of the divine-human relationship, much like the OT writers and other ancient thinkers did. This strategy of expression also supports our undertaking, along with the inclusiveness of the core concepts of IT that enables us to utilize even textual data.

On the basis of methodological considerations, we have traced the changes and developments in the divine-human relationship throughout Romans 1–8. The first stage in the relationship that Paul mentions is the situation that can be characterized as betrayal (1:18–3:20). Referring to what IT explicates about betrayal, we have illustrated that the human sinfulness described in 1:18–32 (mainly in the case of the Gentiles) represents aspects of betrayal in two points: the subversion of the relational order and animosity against the partner. Furthermore, we have noted that the betrayal marks the transference from the relationship with God to an alternative partner, namely, Sin as a personified cosmic force whose identity is subsequently uncovered (cf. 5:12–21). We have also indicated that the law and circumcision function as "social norms," and that the unfaithfulness of Paul's interlocutor (a representative of Jewish people) to God is characterized by the perversion of those "social norms" (2:1–3:8). Our diagnosis reveals that the problem of human sinfulness according to Paul's description is mainly a relational one.

Therefore, it is not strange that Paul explains the meaning of the solution by the Christ-event in a relational way, by using some relational images that point to the moment of forgiveness and reconciliation. In 3:21–26, in discussing the relational significance of Jesus' death, we have focused on Paul's description of Jesus as ἱλαστήριον. In order to navigate our way among multiple suggestions for the meaning of ἱλαστήριον, we have referred to the process of forgiveness from the IT perspective. Our IT framework makes much of the perpetrator's role of making amends for the process of forgiveness, to show that the perpetrator must exhibit willingness to take responsibility for their act of betrayal. Likewise, we have also identified that in ancient Graeco-Roman society, the offender's role of making reparation was a crucial element to turn away the victim's wrath and to work toward reconciliation. Our application of the IT framework has shown that Jesus as ἱλαστήριον works as the "amends" for the forgiveness of the human partners' betrayal. Although such "amends" have an unusual origin (i.e. from the victim, not the offender), the "amends" can still function as normal when the "amends" are received and offered through the human partners' faith (διὰ πίστεως). In this sense, mutuality has been an important element from the beginning of the restoration of the divine-human relationship, and it develops further as the relationship goes on to a deeper level. Our reading also suggests that several different interpretations of ἱλαστήριον (i.e. expiation, propitiation and the mercy seat) can successfully coexist within the concept of "amends," each illumining a specific facet of the function of "amends."

By scrutinizing Paul's detailed representation about Christ's death for reconciliation in another passage that centres on the moment of restoration of the divine-human relationship (5:1–11), we have attempted to understand in what way the human response for reconciliation becomes available. Employing the processes of transformation and communication in IT, we have proposed that God's self-giving act in Christ as his "self-presentation" works as an essential factor that elicits the human faith by demonstrating his trustworthiness to his partners. Such "self-presentation" has the power to change the human partners' cognition, emotion and habit to gain a prosocial orientation, and the resulting changes can be summarized in the comprehensive concept of faith. It is in this respect that we can observe the divine origin of faith. The lifestyle of commitment that has been shaped by such faith is one type of proper response towards God's positive expectations that are inherent in his self-giving act. Paul's characterization of the Christ-event as χάρις also indicates the importance of the human partners' proper response to God.

We have also discussed the impact of the Christ-event, particularly Christ's death, on the Sin-human relationship (5:12–8:11). The Sin-human relationship that had been initiated by the human betrayal made all humanity to be under Sin's oppression. Humanity was not able to escape from the bondage of Sin despite the recognition of the miserable outcomes. We have attempted to understand this particular situation and the meaning of Christ's death as the solution while referencing the "non-voluntary dependence" in an abusive relationship from the IT perspective. What enables us to apply such a framework is Paul's characterization of the Sin-human relationship as slavery under a malicious master, in which non-voluntariness constitutes the backbone of the relational structure. On the basis of the IT framework, we have suggested that the reason that the "I," who is a representative of all humanity, was bound to Sin's exploitation is because of the substantial cost (i.e. death) for an alternative choice. Christ's death on behalf of human beings, in this respect, enables them to return to God, since it brings about a significant change to this relational structure by removing the unrealistic cost to human beings. The freedom to return to God is a key determinant that facilitates the mutual interaction between God and humanity. Through our reading, we have also suggested a solution to an exegetical crux of the point in time of the situation of the "I." In the absence of a plausible alternative option, we have argued that the monologue of "I" represents the human condition before the Christ-event.

The climactic stage of the divine-human relationship is found in Paul's portrayal of the eschatological and cosmic vision in 8:12–39. We have attempted to elucidate aspects of "interdependence" between God and believers, focusing on the human role for the fulfilment of the ultimate goal of the relationship. We have recognized that endurance throughout suffering epitomizes believers' active participation toward the completion of the goal. Believers' endurance is the effort to keep their fidelity to God. Also, in the light of the IT framework on the "investment situation," believers' endurance can be seen as 1) an effort to forgo immediate interests and 2) an expression of mutual commitment. In particular, the emphasis on mutual engagement in the divine-human relationship is detected in Paul's use of familial terms and the several συν– compounds that describe different types of believers' collaborations (e.g. with Christ, creation, the Spirit and God). We have also observed that various strategies to sustain the divine-human alliance are operating in Paul's exhortations as well as in the help of the Spirit. Our findings in 8:12–39 indicate that for the successful completion of the eschatological and cosmic goal of the divine-human relationship, not only is God's initiative essential but so is active human participation—this last factor marks the most advanced stage of the divine-human relationship.

8.2 Implications of the study

Our study challenges a static and partial understanding of the divine-human relationship through the investigation of Romans 1–8. Instead of focusing on a specific stage of the relationship, we have considered several characteristic junctures together; as a result, we have shown that the divine-human relationship according to Paul's understanding carries a dynamic character. The result of our study also offers several suggestions to the important strands of Pauline studies that we surveyed at the beginning. For the issue of agency, our study suggests that the divine and human agencies are not competing against one another. Divine empowerment does not remove human agency, but rather transforms it so that believers will actively participate in the relationship with God.

Although we do concur with the "apocalyptic Paul" school's emphasis on the cosmic dimension of Paul's gospel, our study complements this particular reading by providing an alternative view on the role of humanity in the cosmic warfare. Once liberated by God's cosmic invasion, believers by divine empowerment overcome suffering and temptations from the hostile power, thereby maturing to become active agents in the pursuit of the ultimate goal.

In terms of the study of the Pauline concept of χάρις (gift), our investigation similarly signifies the importance of mutual interactions between God and human beings. Although the studies of χάρις reach that point by investigating the ancient concept of χάρις, we have taken a different approach to understanding the content of χάρις with IT. Just as the studies of χάρις have challenged the modern notion of gift/grace in Paul—which does not accept the significance of returning from a recipient—our study has also highlighted the expectations embedded in what God has done for his human partners. Nevertheless, we have endeavoured to go beyond the realm of the studies of χάρις by extending further our focus on the divine-human relationship to before and after the Christ-event.

The trajectory of the studies on χάρις is also instructive for our further project. As the studies of χάρις have advanced by focusing on two different aspects of χάρις in Paul—divine χάρις and human χάρις respectively—it will be our next task to apply the IT framework to various relational issues between human beings, in particular, within the community of believers. Romans 12–16 will be the most relevant material for this future research, since by investigating these chapters we will be able to see how our findings concerning the divine-human relationship in Romans 1–8 are meaningful for the understanding of human-to-human interactions. Interactions between members of one body (12:3–8), the relationship between the weak and the strong (14:1–15:13) and the relationship between Paul and the Roman believers (15:14–16:27) are topics that can be discussed from the IT perspective. In addition, the relationship between Jews and Gentiles in Romans 9–11 with regard to salvation is another intriguing issue that can be viewed from the IT framework, and the study of these chapters will also show how the divine-human relationship in Romans 1–8 is contextualized in accordance with the particular interest of Romans 9–11.

Although we acknowledge the ingenuity of Wright's covenantal framework for his narrative progression of the divine-human relationship, our study suggests that we do not need to adhere to connecting Paul strictly to the OT story of Israel in order to understand certain aspects of the divine-human relationship in Romans. Rather, Paul appears free in his use of various cultural elements (e.g. the Graeco-Roman context) to explain key stages of the divine-human relationship. In this sense, our approach has the advantage in identifying the core relational feature of the divine-human relationship, by adopting an inclusive framework with which we can handle different contextual layers together. However, on the other hand, Wright's approach illumines how our reading, which is based on the relational framework, can contribute to the field of Pauline studies. Much like Wright's attempts to embrace various perspectives on Paul with his covenantal framework, our study can suggest that a relational reading can set up the ground on which the diverse emphases in Paul can be explicated. The forensic, participatory, apocalyptic, salvation historical, anthropological, transformational dimensions are elements that each explicate a specific phase of the single narrative of the divine-human relationship.

Such a benefit partly originates from our employment of a consistent framework, i.e. "interdependence theory." As noted at the beginning of the present study, one of the expected contributions of this study is to test the usefulness of and suggest the application of IT for biblical interpretation. Once its validity and usefulness is demonstrated, IT can be adopted to discuss various relational issues in different types of texts such as how "social identity theory" is now widely employed in the field of biblical studies.[1] In particular, there are several interesting relational issues in Pauline letters that we may deal with using IT, such as situations of conflict and unity in a community (cf. 1 Cor. 8–10; 11:17–13:13; Gal. 5:13–6:10; Phil. 2:1–4) or between communities (cf. 2 Cor. 8–9 [see Rom. 15:25–27; 1 Cor. 16:1–4]), Paul's (and his co-workers') relationships with specific communities (cf. 2 Cor. 7:2–16; 11:1–12:21; Gal. 4:12–20; Phil. 4:10–20; 1 Thess. 2–3) or individuals (Philemon) along with the communal concerns in Romans 12–15. How do we characterize Paul's attempt to solve the conflicts between sub-groups in one community? How does Paul define his relationship with his followers? How do we understand Paul's appeal and reasoning to Philemon? Since we have been able to propose solutions to several interpretative cruxes in Romans with IT (e.g. the meaning of ἱλαστήριον [3:21–26]; the issue of the "I" [7:7–25]), we can expect that IT will provide us with creative frameworks and approaches for further study of these diverse relational issues.

Finally, our study can also be applicable to other theological discourses, just as a number of Pauline interpretations have been. By examining the divine-human relationship in Romans 1–8, we can speak of the dynamic and open nature of the divine-human relationship, but from a different starting point. Downing's observation

---

[1] See *T&T Clark Handbook to Social Identity in the New Testament*, ed. by Coleman A. Baker and J. Brian Tucker (London: Bloomsbury, 2014).

of the prominence of a relational framework (i.e. the friendship framework) in the concept of the Trinity and the divine-human relationship in modern theological works as well as in the early church fathers' thoughts implies that there are some points in which our reading of Paul can interact with later theological conceptions of the divine-human relationship.[2]

---

[2] For instance, Kathryn Tanner, *Economy of Grace* (Minneapolis: Fortress, 2005); the Cappadocian Fathers. See F. Gerald Downing, "Friends in God: A Foundational Motif in Classical Reflections on the Divine Economy," *AThR* 97.3 (2015): 490–4.

Bibliography

Adams, Edward. *Constructing the World: A Study in Paul's Cosmological Language.* Edinburgh: T&T Clark, 2000.
Agnew, Christopher R., Paul A. M. Van Lange, Caryl E. Rusbult and Christopher A. Langston. "Cognitive Interdependence: Commitment and the Mental Representation of Close Relationships." *JPSP* 74.4 (1998): 939–54.
Bailey, Daniel P. "Jesus as the Mercy Seat: The Semantics and Theology of Paul's Use of Hilasterion in Romans 3:25." *TynB* 1.51 (2000): 155–8.
Barclay, John M.G. "Apocalyptic Allegiance and Disinvestment in the World: A Reading of 1 Corinthians 7:25–35." In *Paul and the Apocalyptic Imagination*, edited by Ben C. Blackwell, John K. Goodrich and Jason Maston, 257–74. Minneapolis: Fortress, 2016.
———. "Believers and the 'Last Judgment' in Paul: Rethinking Grace and Recompense." In *Eschatologie-Eschatology*, 195–208. Tübingen: Mohr Siebeck, 2011.
———. "Benefiting Others and Benefit to Oneself: Seneca and Paul on 'Altruism'." In *Paul and Seneca in Dialogue*, edited by Joseph R. Dodson and David E. Briones, 109–26. Leiden: Brill, 2017.
———. "'By the Grace of God I Am What I Am': Grace and Agency in Philo and Paul." In *Divine and Human Agency in Paul and His Cultural Environment*, edited by John M.G. Barclay and Simon J. Gathercole, 140–57. London: T&T Clark, 2006.
———. "Grace and the Transformation of Agency in Christ." In *Redefining First-Century Jewish and Christian Identities*, edited by Fabian E. Udoh, 372–89. Notre Dame: University of Notre Dame Press, 2008.
———. "Introduction." In *Divine and Human Agency in Paul and His Cultural Environment*, edited by John M.G. Barclay and Simon J. Gathercole, 1–8. London: T&T Clark, 2006.
———. *Obeying the Truth: Paul's Ethics in Galatians.* Vancouver: Regent College Publishing, 2005.
———. "Paul And Philo on Circumcision: Romans 2.25–9 in Social and Cultural Context." *NTS* 4.44 (1998): 536–56.
———. *Paul and the Gift.* Grand Rapids: Eerdmans, 2015.
———. "Paul, Philemon and the Dilemma of Christian Slave-Ownership." *NTS* 37.02 (1991): 161–86.
———. *Pauline Churches and Diaspora Jews.* Tübingen: Mohr Siebeck, 2011.
———. "Paul's Story: Theology as Testimony." In *Narrative Dynamics in Paul: A Critical Assessment*, edited by Bruce W. Longenecker, 133–56. Louisville: WJK, 2002.
———. "Pure Grace? Paul's Distinctive Jewish Theology of Gift." *ST* 68.1 (2014): 4–20.
———. "Review: Paul and the Faithfulness of God." *STJ* 68.2 (2015): 235–43.
———. "Under Grace: The Christ-Gift and the Construction of a Christian Habitus." In *Apocalyptic Paul: Cosmos and Anthropos in Romans 5–8*, edited by Beverly Roberts Gaventa, 59–76. Waco: Baylor University Press, 2013.
———. "Why the Roman Empire Was Insignificant to Paul." In *Pauline Churches and Diaspora Jews*, 363–87. Tübingen: Mohr Siebeck, 2011.
Barrett, C.K. *A Commentary on the First Epistle to the Corinthians.* London: Black, 1968.

———. *The Epistle to the Romans*. London: A&C Black, 1991.
Barth, Karl. *The Epistle to the Romans*. Translated by Edwyn C. Hoskyns. Sixth Edition. Oxford: Oxford University Press, 1933.
Barton, Stephen C. "Social-Scientific Criticism." In *A Handbook to the Exegesis of the New Testament*, edited by Stanley E. Porter, 277–89. Leiden: Brill, 1997.
Bassler, Jouette M. *Navigating Paul: An Introduction to Key Theological Concepts*. Louisville: WJK, 2007.
Baumeister, R.F., A. Stillwell and T.F. Heatherton. "Personal Narratives About Guilt: Role in Action Control and Interpersonal Relationships." *BASP* 17.1–2 (1995): 173–98.
Baumeister, R.F., A. Stillwell and S.R. Wotman. "Victim and Perpetrator Accounts of Interpersonal Conflict: Autobiographical Narratives about Anger." *JPSP* 59.5 (1990): 994–1005.
Bell, Richard H. *No One Seeks for God: An Exegetical and Theological Study of Romans 1.18–3.20*. Tübingen: Mohr Siebeck, 1998.
———. "Sacrifice and Christology in Paul." *JTS* 1.53 (2002): 1–27.
Berger, Klaus. *Identity and Experience in the New Testament*. Translated by Charles Muenchow. Minneapolis: Fortress, 2003.
Berkley, Timothy W. *From a Broken Covenant to Circumcision of the Heart: Pauline Intertextual Exegesis in Romans 2:17–29*. Atlanta: SBL, 2000.
Black, Matthew. *Romans*. London: Oliphants, 1973.
Blackwell, Ben C. *Christosis: Pauline Soteriology in Light of Deification in Irenaeus and Cyril of Alexandria*. Tübingen: Mohr Siebeck, 2011.
———. "The Greek Life of Adam and Eve and Romans 8:14–39: (Re-)creation and Glory." In *Reading Romans in Context: Paul and Second Temple Judaism*, edited by Ben C. Blackwell, John K. Goodrich and Jason Maston, 108–14. Grand Rapids: Zondervan, 2015.
Blackwell, Ben C., John K. Goodrich and Jason Maston, eds. "Paul and the Apocalyptic Imagination: An Introduction." In *Paul and the Apocalyptic Imagination*, 3–21. Minneapolis: Fortress, 2016.
Blanton, Thomas R. "The Benefactor's Account-Book: The Rhetoric of Gift Reciprocation According to Seneca and Paul." *NTS* 59.3 (2013): 396–414.
Blau, Peter M. *Exchange and Power in Social Life*. New York: Wiley, 1964.
de Boer, Martinus C. "Apocalyptic as God's Eschatological Activity in Paul's Theology." In *Paul and the Apocalyptic Imagination*, edited by Ben C. Blackwell, John K. Goodrich and Jason Maston, 45–63. Minneapolis: Fortress, 2016.
———. "N.T. Wright's Great Story and Its Relationship to Paul's Gospel." *JSPHL* 4.1 (2014): 49–57.
———. "Paul's Mythologizing Program in Romans 5–8." In *Apocalyptic Paul*, edited by Beverly Roberts Gaventa, 1–20. Waco: Baylor University Press, 2013.
———. *The Defeat of Death: Apocalyptic Eschatology in 1 Corinthians 15 and Romans 5*. Sheffield: JSOT Press, 1988.
Bourdieu, Pierre. *Outline of a Theory of Practice*. Cambridge: Cambridge University Press, 1977.
Bradley, Keith. "Animalizing the Slave: The Truth of Fiction." *JRS* 90 (2000): 110–25.
Breytenbach, Cilliers. "'Christus Starb Für Uns'. Zur Tradition Und Paulinischen Rezeption Der Sogenannten 'Sterbeformeln.'" *NTS* 49.4 (2003): 447–75.
———. "Forgiveness in Early Christian Tradition." In *Grace, Reconciliation, Concord: The Death of Christ in Graeco-Roman Metaphors*, 279–95. Leiden: Brill, 2010.

———. "Salvation of the Reconciled (with a Note on the Background of Paul's Metaphor of Reconciliation)." In *Grace, Reconciliation, Concord: The Death of Christ in Graeco-Roman Metaphors*, 171–86. Leiden: Brill, 2010.

———. "The 'For Us' Phrases in Pauline Soteriology: Considering Their Background and Use." In *Grace, Reconciliation, Concord: The Death of Christ in Graeco-Roman Metaphors*, 59–81. Leiden: Brill, 2010.

———. *Versöhnung: Eine Studie zur paulinischen Soteriologie*. Neukirchen-Vluyn: Neukirchener Verlag, 1989.

Briones, David E. "Mutual Brokers of Grace: A Study in 2 Corinthians 1.3-11." *NTS* 56.4 (2010): 536–56.

———. *Paul's Financial Policy: A Socio-Theological Approach*. London: Bloomsbury, 2013.

Bruce, F.F. *Romans*. London: IVP, 1974.

———. "The Romans Debate – Continued." *BJRL* 64 (1981): 334–59.

Buchanan, George Wesley. "The Day of Atonement and Paul's Doctrine of Redemption." *NovT* 32.3 (1990): 236–49.

Bultmann, Rudolf. "New Testament and Mythology." In *Kerygma and Myth: A Theological Debate*, edited by Hans Werner Bartsch, translated by Reginald H. Fuller. New York: Harper & Row, 1961.

———. "Romans 7 and the Anthropology of Paul." In *Existence and Faith: Shorter Writings of Rudolf Bultmann*, edited by S.M. Ogden, 147–57. London: Hodder & Stoughton, 1961.

Burke, Trevor J. *Adopted into God's Family: Exploring a Pauline Metaphor*. Nottingham: Apollos, 2006.

———. "The Characteristics of Paul's Adoptive-Sonship (Huiothesia) Motif." *IBS* 17 (1995): 62–74.

Burnett, Gary W. *Paul and the Salvation of the Individual*. Leiden: Brill, 2001.

Byrne, Brendan. "An Ecological Reading of Rom. 8.19-22: Possibilities and Hesitations." In *Ecological Hermeneutics: Biblical, Historical and Theological Perspectives*, edited by David G. Horrell, Cherryl Hunt, Christopher Southgate and Francesca Stavrakopoulou, 83–93. London: T&T Clark, 2010.

———. "Creation Groaning: An Earth Bible Reading of Romans 8.18-22." In *Readings from the Perspective of Earth*, edited by Norman C. Habel, 193–203. Sheffield: Sheffield Academic, 2000.

———. *Romans*. Collegeville: Liturgical Press, 1996.

Byron, John. "Paul and the Background of Slavery: The Status Quaestionis in New Testament Scholarship." *CBR* 3.1 (2004): 116–39.

———. *Slavery Metaphors in Early Judaism and Pauline Christianity: A Traditio-Historical and Exegetical Examination*. Tübingen: Mohr Siebeck, 2003.

Campbell, Douglas A. *The Deliverance of God: An Apocalyptic Rereading of Justification in Paul*. Grand Rapids: Eerdmans, 2009.

———. *The Rhetoric of Righteousness in Romans 3.21–26*. Sheffield: Sheffield Academic, 1992.

———. "The Story of Jesus in Romans and Galatians." In *Narrative Dynamics in Paul: A Critical Assessment*, edited by Bruce W. Longenecker, 97–124. Louisville: WJK, 2002.

Cantarella, Eva. "Greek Law and the Family." In *A Companion to Families in the Greek and Roman Worlds*, edited by Beryl Rawson, 333–45. Chichester: Wiley-Blackwell, 2011.

Catchpole, David. "Who and Where Is the 'Wretched Man' of Romans 7, and Why Is 'She' Wretched?" In *The Holy Spirit and Christian Origins: Essays in Honor of James D.G. Dunn*, edited by Graham N. Stanton, Bruce W. Longenecker and Stephen C. Barton, 168–80. Grand Rapids: Eerdmans, 2004.

Chang, Hae-Kyung. "The Christian Life in a Dialectical Tension? Romans 7:7–25 Reconsidered." *NovT* 49 (2007): 257–80.
Clarke, Andrew D. *Secular and Christian Leadership in Corinth: A Socio-Historical and Exegetical Study of 1 Corinthians 1–6.* Leiden: Brill, 1993.
Clarke, Andrew D. and J. Brian Tucker. "Social History and Social Theory in the Study of Social Identity." In *T&T Clark Handbook to Social Identity in the New Testament*, edited by J. Brian Tucker and Coleman A. Baker, 41–58. London: Bloomsbury, 2014.
Cohen, Ada. "Picturing Greek Families." In *A Companion to Families in the Greek and Roman Worlds*, edited by Beryl Rawson, 465–87. Chichester: Wiley-Blackwell, 2011.
Combes, I.A.H. *The Metaphor of Slavery in the Writings of the Early Church: From the New Testament to the Beginning of the Fifth Century.* Sheffield: JSOT Press, 1998.
Cranfield, C.E.B. *A Critical and Exegetical Commentary on the Epistle to the Romans.* Edinburgh: T&T Clark, 1975.
Crook, Zeba A. "Critical Notes: Reflections on Culture and Social-Scientific Models." *JBL* 124.3 (2005): 515–20.
———. *Reconceptualising Conversion: Patronage, Loyalty, and Conversion in the Religions of the Ancient Mediterranean.* Berlin: de Gruyter, 2004.
Dahl, N.A. "Two Notes on Romans 5." *ST* 5.1 (1951): 37–48.
Das, A. Andrew. *Solving the Romans Debate.* Minneapolis: Fortress, 2007.
Davies, J.P. "What to Expect When You're Expecting: Maternity, Salvation History, and the 'Apocalyptic Paul.'" *JSNT* 38.3 (2016): 301–15.
Deissmann, Adolf. *Bible Studies.* Translated by Alexander Grieve. Second Edition. Edinburgh: T&T Clark, 1909.
deSilva, David. "Grace, the Law, and Justification in 4 Ezra and the Pauline Letters: A Dialogue." *JSNT* 37.1 (2014): 25–49.
———. *Honor, Patronage, Kinship & Purity: Unlocking New Testament Culture.* Downers Grove: IVP Academic, 2000.
———. "'We Are Debtors': Grace and Obligation in Paul and Seneca." In *Paul and Seneca in Dialogue*, edited by Joseph R. Dodson and David E. Briones, 150–78. Leiden: Brill, 2017.
Dinkler, E. *Eirēnē: Der Urchristliche Friedensgedanke.* Heidelberg: Winter, 1973.
Dodd, Brian J. *Paul's Paradigmatic "I": Personal Example as Literary Strategy.* Sheffield: Sheffield Academic, 1999.
Dodd, C.H. *The Epistle of Paul to the Romans.* New York: Harper & Row, 1932.
———. "Ἱλάσκεσθαι, Its Cognates, Derivatives and Synonyms in the Septuagint." *JTS* 32 (1931): 352–60.
Dodson, Joseph R. *The "Powers" of Personification: Rhetorical Purpose in the "Book of Wisdom" and the Letter to the Romans.* Berlin: de Gruyter, 2008.
Donfried, Karl P., ed. *The Romans Debate.* Peabody: Hendrickson, 1991.
Downing, F. Gerald. "Friends in God: A Foundational Motif in Classical Reflections on the Divine Economy." *AThR* 97.3 (2015): 483–94.
———. "Person in Relation." In *Making Sense in (and of) the First Christian Century*, 43–61. Sheffield: Sheffield Academic, 2000.
Duncan, John. "The Hope of Creation: The Significance of Ἐφ᾿ Ἐλπίδι (Rom 8.20c) in Context." *NTS* 61.3 (2015): 411–27.
Dunn, James D.G. "Paul's Understanding of the Death of Jesus." In *Reconciliation and Hope: New Testament Essays on Atonement and Eschatology Presented to L.L. Morris on His 60th Birthday*, 125–41. Exeter: Paternoster, 1974.
———. *Romans 1–8.* Dallas: Word Books, 1988.

———. *The New Perspective on Paul*. Grand Rapids: Eerdmans, 2007.
———. *The Theology of the Paul the Apostle*. Grand Rapids: Eerdmans, 1998.
Dunson, Ben C. "Faith in Romans: The Salvation of the Individual or Life in Community?" *JSNT* 34.1 (2011): 19–46.
———. *Individual and Community in Paul's Letter to the Romans*. Tübingen: Mohr Siebeck, 2012.
———. "The Individual and Community in Twentieth- and Twenty-first-Century Pauline Scholarship." *CBR* 9.1 (2010): 63–97.
Eastman, Susan. "Apocalypse and Incarnation: The Participatory Logic of Paul's Gospel." In *Apocalyptic and the Future of Theology: With and Beyond J. Louis Martyn*, edited by Joshua B. Davis and Douglas Harink, 165–82. Eugene: Cascade, 2012.
———. "Oneself in Another: Participation and the Spirit in Romans 8." In *"In Christ" in Paul: Explorations in Paul's Theology of Union and Participation*, edited by Michael J. Thate, Kevin J. Vanhoozer and Constantine R. Campbell, 103–26. Tübingen: Mohr Siebeck, 2014.
———. "Whose Apocalypse? The Identity of the Sons of God in Romans 8:19." *JBL* 121.2 (2002): 263–77.
Elliott, Neil. *The Rhetoric of Romans: Argumentative Constraint and Strategy and Paul's Dialogue with Judaism*. Sheffield: JSOT Press, 1990.
Ellis, E. Earle. "Paul and His Co-Workers." *NTS* 17.4 (1971): 437–52.
Engberg-Pedersen, Troels. *Cosmology and Self in the Apostle Paul: The Material Spirit*. Oxford: Oxford University Press, 2010.
———. "Gift-Giving and Friendship: Seneca and Paul in Romans 1–8 on the Logic of God's Χάρις and Its Human Response." *HTR* 101.01 (2008): 15–44.
———. *Paul and the Stoics*. Louisville: WJK, 2000.
Esler, Philip F. *Conflict and Identity in Romans: The Social Setting of Paul's Letter*. Minneapolis: Fortress, 2003.
———. *Galatians*. London: Routledge, 1998.
———. "Models in New Testament Interpretation: A Reply To David Horrell." *JSNT* 22.78 (2000): 107–13.
Espy, John M. "Paul's 'Robust Conscience' Re-Examined." *NTS* 31 (1985): 161–88.
Fee, Gordon D. *God's Empowering Presence: The Holy Spirit in the Letters of Paul*. Peabody: Hendrickson, 1994.
Finkel, Eli J., Caryl E. Rusbult, Madoka Kumashiro and Peggy A. Hannon. "Dealing with Betrayal in Close Relationships: Does Commitment Promote Forgiveness?" *JPSP* 82.6 (2002): 956–74.
Finlan, Stephen. *The Background and Content of Paul's Cultic Atonement Metaphors*. Leiden: Brill, 2004.
Fitzgerald, John T. "Paul and Paradigm Shifts: Reconciliation and Its Linkage Group." In *Paul Beyond the Judaism/Hellenism Divide*, edited by Troels Engberg-Pedersen, 241–62. Louisville: WJK, 2001.
Fitzmyer, Joseph A. "Reconciliation in Pauline Theology." In *To Advance the Gospel: New Testament Studies*, Second Edition, 162–85. Grand Rapids: Eerdmans, 1998.
———. *Romans: A New Translation with Introduction and Commentary*. New Haven: Yale University Press, 2008.
Forman, Mark. *The Politics of Inheritance in Romans*. Cambridge: Cambridge University Press, 2011.
Freedman, Suzanne. "Forgiveness and Reconciliation: The Importance of Understanding How They Differ." *CV* 42.3 (1998): 200–216.

Fryer, Nico S. L. "The Meaning and Translation of Hilastērion in Romans 3:25." *EQ* 59.2 (1987): 99–116.
Furnish, Victor Paul. "Living to God, Walking in Love: Theology and Ethics in Romans." In *Reading Paul's Letter to the Romans*, edited by Jerry L. Sumney, 187–202. Atlanta: SBL, 2012.
———. *Theology and Ethics in Paul*. Louisville: WJK, 2009.
Garlington, Don B. *The Obedience of Faith*. Tübingen: Mohr Siebeck, 1991.
Garrett, Susan R. "Sociology of Early Christianity." In *The Anchor Bible Dictionary*. Vol. 6, 89–98. New York: Doubleday, 1996.
Gathercole, Simon J. "A Law unto Themselves: The Gentiles in Romans 2.14-15 Revisited." *JSNT* 85 (2002): 27–49.
———. *Defending Substitution: An Essay on Atonement in Paul*. Grand Rapids: Baker Academic, 2015.
———. "Sin in God's Economy: Romans 1 and 7." In *Divine and Human Agency in Paul and His Cultural Environment*, edited by John M.G. Barclay and Simon J. Gathercole, 158–72. London: T&T Clark, 2008.
———. *Where Is Boasting?: Early Jewish Soteriology and Paul's Response in Romans 1–5*. Grand Rapids: Eerdmans, 2002.
Gaventa, Beverly Roberts. "Neither Height nor Depth: Discerning the Cosmology of Romans." *STJ* 64.3 (2011): 265–78.
———. *Our Mother Saint Paul*. Louisville: WJK, 2007.
———. "The Cosmic Power of Sin in Paul's Letter to the Romans." *Int* 58.3 (2004): 229–40.
———. "The Rhetoric of Violence and the God of Peace in Paul's Letter to Romans." In *Paul, John, and Apocalyptic Eschatology: Studies in Honour of Martinus C. de Boer*, edited by Jan Krans, L. J. Lietaert Peerbolte, Peter-Ben Smit and Arie Zwiep, 61–75. Leiden: Brill, 2012.
———. "The Shape of the 'I': The Psalter, the Gospel, and the Speaker in Romans 7." In *Apocalyptic Paul*, edited by Beverly Roberts Gaventa, 77–92. Waco: Baylor University Press, 2013.
———. "Which Humans? What Response? A Reflection on Pauline Theology." *ExAud* 30 (2014): 50–64.
Gieniusz, Andrzej. "'Debtors to the Spirit' in Romans 8.12? Reasons for the Silence." *NTS* 59.1 (2013): 61–72.
———. *Romans 8:18-30: "Suffering Does Not Thwart the Future Glory."* Atlanta: Scholars, 1999.
Gignilliat, Mark S. "Working Together with Whom? Text-Critical, Contextual, and Theological Analysis of Συνεργεῖ in Romans 8,28." *Bib* 87 (2006): 511–15.
Goede, Hendrik. "Constructing Ancient Slavery as Socio-Historic Context of the New Testament." *HTS Teologiese Studies/Theological Studies* 69.1 (2013): 1–7.
Goodrich, John K. "Sold under Sin: Echoes of Exile in Romans 7:14-25." *NTS* 59.4 (2013): 476–95.
Gorman, Michael J. *Becoming the Gospel: Paul, Participation, and Mission*. Grand Rapids: Eerdmans, 2015.
———. *Inhabiting the Cruciform God: Kenosis, Justification, and Theosis in Paul's Narrative Soteriology*. Grand Rapids: Eerdmans, 2009.
———. *The Death of the Messiah and the Birth of the New Covenant: A (Not So) New Model of the Atonement*. Eugene: Cascade, 2014.
Griffiths, J. Gwyn. "Romans Viii. 28." *ExpT* 49 (1938): 474–6.
Grubbs, Judith Evans. "Promoting Pietas through Roman Law." in *A Companion to Families in the Greek and Roman Worlds*, edited by Beryl Rawson, 377–92. Chichester: Wiley-Blackwell, 2011.

Gundry, Robert H. "The Moral Frustration of Paul before His Conversion: Sexual Lust in Romans 7:7–25." In *Pauline Studies: Festschrift for F.F. Bruce*, 228–45. Exeter: Paternoster, 1980.
Gundry Volf, Judith M. *Paul and Perseverance: Staying in and Falling Away*. Louisville: WJK, 1990.
Gupta, Nijay K. "Towards a Set of Principles for Identifying and Interpreting Metaphors in Paul: ΠΡΟΣΑΓΩΓΗ (Romans 5:2) as a Test Case." *ResQ* 3.51 (2009): 169–81.
———. "Which 'Body' Is a Temple (1 Corinthians 6:19)? Paul beyond the Individual/Communal Divide." *CBQ* 72 (2010): 518–36.
———. *Worship That Makes Sense to Paul a New Approach to the Theology and Ethics of Paul's Cultic Metaphors*. Berlin: de Gruyter, 2010.
Haacker, Klaus. *The Theology of Paul's Letter to the Romans*. Cambridge: Cambridge University Press, 2003.
Hagen, Jeanette M. "Faith as Participation: An Exegetical Study of Some Key Pauline Texts." PhD Thesis, Durham University, 2016.
Hägerland, Tobias. *Jesus and the Forgiveness of Sins: An Aspect of His Prophetic Mission*. Cambridge: Cambridge University Press, 2011.
Hahne, Harry Alan. *The Corruption and Redemption of Creation: Nature in Romans 8:19-22 and Jewish Apocalyptic Literature*. London: T&T Clark, 2006.
Hannon, Peggy A., Caryl E. Rusbult, Eli J. Finkel and Madoka Kamashiro. "In the Wake of Betrayal: Amends, Forgiveness, and the Resolution of Betrayal." *PR* 17.2 (2010): 253–78.
Harland, Philip. "Familial Dimensions of Group Identity." *JBL* 124.3 (2005): 491–513.
Harrill, J. Albert. "Paul and Slavery." In *Paul in the Greco-Roman World: A Handbook*, edited by J. Paul Sampley, 575–607. Harrisburg: Trinity Press International, 2003.
———. "Slavery." In *DNTB*, 1124–8. Downers Grove: IVP, 2000.
———. "Slavery and Inhumanity: Keith Bradley's Legacy on Slavery in New Testament Studies." *BibInt* 21 (2013): 506–14.
———. *Slaves in the New Testament: Literary, Social, and Moral Dimensions*. Minneapolis: Fortress, 2006.
Harris, Murray J. *The Second Epistle to the Corinthians*. Grand Rapids: Eerdmans, 2005.
Harrison, James R. "Paul, Eschatology and the Augustan Age of Grace." *TynB* 1.50 (1999): 79–91.
———. *Paul's Language of Grace in Its Graeco-Roman Context*. Tübingen: Mohr Siebeck, 2003.
Hay, David M. "Paul's Understanding of Faith as Participation." In *Paul and His Theology*, edited by Stanley E. Porter, 45–76. Leiden: Brill, 2006.
———. "Pistis as 'Ground for Faith' in Hellenized Judaism and Paul." *JBL* 108.3 (1989): 461–76.
Hays, Richard B. *The Moral Vision of the New Testament: A Contemporary Introduction to New Testament Ethics*. Edinburgh: T&T Clark, 1997.
———. "Paul's Hermeneutics and the Question of Truth." *ProEccl* 16 (2007): 126–33.
———. *The Faith of Jesus Christ: The Narrative Substructure of Galatians 3:1–4:11*. Second Edition. Grand Rapids: Eerdmans, 2002.
———. "Πίστις and Pauline Christology: What Is at Stake?" In *The Faith of Jesus Christ: The Narrative Substructure of Galatians 3:1–4:11*, Second Edition, 272–97. Grand Rapids: Eerdmans, 2002.
Herbert, A. Gabriel. "'Faithfulness' and 'Faith.'" *Theology* 58 (1955): 373–9.
Higgins, E.T. "Beyond Pleasure and Pain." *APsy* 52 (1997): 1280–1300.
Hilborn, David. "A Response to Campbell's 'Connecting the Dots.'" In *Beyond Old and New Perspectives on Paul*, edited by Chris Tilling, 114–27. Cambridge: James Clarke & Co, 2014.

Hill, David. *Greek Words and Hebrew Meanings: Studies in the Semantics of Soteriological Terms*. Cambridge: Cambridge University Press, 1967.

Holmberg, Bengt. *Paul and Power: The Structure of Authority in the Primitive Church as Reflected in the Pauline Epistles*. Lund: Gleerup, 1978.

Holmes, John G. "The Benefits of Abstract Functional Analysis in Theory Construction: The Case of Interdependence Theory." *PSPR* 8.2 (2004): 146–55.

Hooker, Morna D. "Adam in Romans 1." In *From Adam to Christ: Essays on Paul*, 73–84. Cambridge: Cambridge University Press, 1990.

———. "Another Look at Πίστις Χριστοῦ." *STJ* 69.1 (2016): 46–62.

———. "Interchange and Atonement." In *From Adam to Christ: Essays on Paul*, 26–41. Cambridge: Cambridge University Press, 1990.

———. "Paul and 'Covenantal Nomism.'" In *From Adam to Christ: Essays on Paul*, 155–64. Cambridge: Cambridge University Press, 1990.

———. "Πίστις Χριστοῦ." In *From Adam to Christ: Essays on Paul*, 165–86. Cambridge: Cambridge University Press, 1990.

Horrell, David G. "A New Perspective on Paul? Rereading Paul in a Time of Ecological Crisis." *JSNT* 33.1 (2010): 3–30.

———. "Models and Methods in Social-Scientific Interpretation: A Response To Philip Esler." *JSNT* 22.78 (2000): 83–105.

———. "Paul's Narratives or Narrative Substructure?: The Significance of 'Paul's Story.'" In *Narrative Dynamics in Paul*, 157–71. Louisville: WJK, 2002.

———. "Social-Scientific Interpretation of the New Testament: Retrospect and Prospect." In *Social-Scientific Approaches to New Testament Interpretation*, edited by David G. Horrell, 3–28. Edinburgh: T&T Clark, 1999.

———. *The Social Ethos of the Corinthian Correspondence: Interests and Ideology from 1 Corinthians to 1 Clement*. Edinburgh: T&T Clark, 1996.

———. "Wither Social-Scientific Approaches to New Testament Interpretation? Reflections on Contested Methodologies and the Future." In *After the First Urban Christians: The Social-Scientific Study of Pauline Christianity Twenty-Five Years Later*, edited by David G. Horrell and Todd D. Still, 6–20. London: Continuum, 2010.

Hultgren, Arland J. *Paul's Gospel and Mission: The Outlook from His Letter to the Romans*. Philadelphia: Fortress, 1985.

Hunt, Cherryl, David G. Horrell and Christopher Southgate. "An Environmental Mantra? Ecological Interest in Romans 8.19-23 and a Modest Proposal for Its Narrative Interpretation." *JTS* 59.2 (2008): 546–79.

Jackson, T. Ryan. *New Creation in Paul's Letters: A Study of the Historical and Social Setting of a Pauline Concept*. Tübingen: Mohr Siebeck, 2010.

Jeffers, James S. *Conflict at Rome: Social Order and Hierarchy in Early Christianity*. Minneapolis: Fortress, 1991.

Jervis, L. Ann. "Divine Retribution in Romans." *Interpretation* 69.3 (2015): 323–37.

———. "'The Commandment Which Is for Life' (Romans 7.10): Sin's Use of the Obedience of Faith." *JSNT* 27.2 (2004): 193–216.

Jewett, Robert. *Paul's Anthropological Terms: A Study of Their Use in Conflict Settings*. Leiden: Brill, 1971.

———. *Romans: A Commentary*. Minneapolis: Fortress, 2007.

Johnson, L.T. "Rom 3:21-26 and the Faith of Jesus." *CBQ* 1.44 (1982): 77–90.

Joubert, Stephan. "Coming to Terms with a Neglected Aspect of Ancient Mediterranean Reciprocity: Seneca's Views on Benefit-Exchange in De Beneficiis as the Framework for a Model of Social Exchange." In *Social Scientific Models for Interpreting the Bible: Essays by the Context Group in Honor of Bruce J. Malina*. edited by John J. Pilch, 47–63. Leiden: Brill, 2001.

———. *Paul as Benefactor: Reciprocity, Strategy and Theological Reflection in Paul's Collection*. Tübingen: Mohr Siebeck, 2000.

Judge, E.A. "The Social Identity of the First Christians: A Question of Method in Religious History." *JRH* 11 (1980): 201–17.

Käsemann, Ernst. *Commentary on Romans*. Translated by Geoffrey W. Bromiley. Grand Rapids: Eerdmans, 1980.

———. "On Paul's Anthropology." In *Perspectives on Paul*, translated by Margaret Kohl, 1–31. London: SCM, 1971.

———. "Some Thoughts on the Theme 'The Doctrine of Reconciliation in the New Testament'." In *The Future of Our Religious Past: Essays in Honour of Rudolf Bultmann*, edited by James M. Robinson, translated by Charles E. Carlston and Robert. P. Scharlemann, 49–64. London: SCM, 1971.

———. "'The Righteousness of God' in Paul." In *New Testament Questions of Today*, translated by W.J. Montague, 168–82. London: SCM, 1969.

———. "The Saving Significance of the Death of Jesus in Paul." In *Perspectives on Paul*. Translated by Margaret Kohl, 32–59. London: SCM, 1971.

Keck, Leander E. *Romans*. Nashville: Abingdon, 2005.

Keener, Craig S. *The Mind of the Spirit: Paul's Approach to Transformed Thinking*. Grand Rapids: Baker Academic, 2016.

Keesmaat, Sylvia C. "Crucified Lord or Conquering Saviour: Whose Story of Salvation?" *HBT* 26.2 (2004): 69–93.

———. *Paul and His Story: (Re)Interpreting the Exodus Tradition*. Sheffield: Sheffield Academic, 1999.

Kelley, Harold H. "The Theoretical Description of Interdependence by Means of Transition Lists." *JPSP* 47.5 (1984): 956–82.

Kelley, Harold H., John G. Holmes, Norbert L. Kerr, Harry T. Reis, Caryl E. Rusbult and Paul A.M Van Lange. *An Atlas of Interpersonal Situations*. Cambridge: Cambridge University Press, 2003.

Kelley, Harold H. and John W. Thibaut. *Interpersonal Relations: A Theory of Interdependence*. New York: Wiley, 1978.

———. "Self-Interest, Science, and Cynicism." *JSCP* 3.1 (1985): 26–32.

Khobnya, Svetlana. *The Father Who Redeems and the Son Who Obeys*. Cambridge: James Clarke & Co, 2014.

King, Justin. "Rhetorical Chain-Link Construction and the Relationship between Romans 7.1–6 and 7.7–8.39: Additional Evidence for Assessing the Argument of Romans 7–8 and the Identity of the Infamous 'I'." *JSNT* 39.3 (2017): 258–78.

Kruse, Colin G. *Paul's Letter to the Romans*. Nottingham: Apollos, 2012.

Kümmel, Werner G. *Römer 7 Und Die Bekehrung Des Paulus*. Leipzig: J.C. Hinrichs, 1974.

Lakoff, George and Mark Johnson. *Metaphors We Live By*. Chicago: Univ. of Chicago Press, 1980.

Lawrence, Louise J. *An Ethnography of the Gospel of Matthew*. Tübingen: Mohr Siebeck, 2002.

Leary, Mark R., Carrie Springer, Laura Negel, Emily Ansell and Kelly Evans. "The Causes, Phenomenology, and Consequences of Hurt Feelings." *JPSP* 74.5 (1998): 1225–37.

Lee, Michelle V. *Paul, the Stoics, and the Body of Christ*. Cambridge: Cambridge University Press, 2006.

Lewin, Kurt. *Resolving Social Conflicts: Selected Papers on Group Dynamics.* Edited by Gertrud Weiss Lewin. New York: Harper & Row, 1948.

Lewis, Robert B. *Paul's "Spirit of Adoption" in Its Roman Imperial Context.* London: Bloomsbury, 2016.

Lincoln, Andrew T. *Ephesians.* Dallas: Word, 1990.

Lindsay, Hugh. "Adoption and Heirship in Greece and Rome." In *A Companion to Families in the Greek and Roman Worlds,* edited by Beryl Rawson, 346–60. Chichester: Wiley-Blackwell, 2011.

Linebaugh, Jonathan A. *God, Grace, and Righteousness in Wisdom of Solomon and Paul's Letter to the Romans: Texts in Conversation.* Leiden: Brill, 2013.

List, Christian and Kai Spiekermann. "Methodological Individualism and Holism in Political Science: A Reconciliation." *APSR* 107.04 (2013): 629–43.

Longenecker, Bruce W. "Sharing in Their Spiritual Blessings? The Stories of Israel in Galatians and Romans." In *Narrative Dynamics in Paul: A Critical Assessment,* edited by Bruce W. Longenecker, 58–84. Louisville: WJK, 2002.

———. "ΠΙΣΤΙΣ in Romans 3.25: Neglected Evidence for the 'Faithfulness of Christ'?" *NTS* 39.3 (1993): 478–80.

Longenecker, Richard N. *Introducing Romans: Critical Issues in Paul's Most Famous Letter.* Grand Rapids: Eerdmans, 2011.

———. *The Epistle to the Romans.* Grand Rapids: Eerdmans, 2016.

Luce, Robert D. and Howard Raiffa. *Games and Decisions: Introduction and Critical Survey.* New York: Wiley, 1957.

Macaskill, Grant. *Union with Christ in the New Testament.* Oxford: Oxford University Press, 2013.

MacIntyre, Alasdair. *After Virtue: A Study in Moral Theory.* Third Edition. Notre Dame: University of Notre Dame Press, 2007.

Malina, Bruce J. *The New Testament World: Insights from Cultural Anthropology.* Third Edition. Louisville: WJK, 2001.

Malina, Bruce J. and Jerome H. Neyrey. *Portraits of Paul: An Archaeology of Ancient Personality.* Louisville: WJK, 1996.

Manson, T.W. "ΙΛΑΣΤΗΡΙΟΝ." *JTS* 46 (1945): 1–10.

Marshall, I. Howard. *Jesus the Saviour: Studies in New Testament Theology.* London: SPCK, 1990.

———. "The Development of the Concept of Redemption in the New Testament." In *Jesus the Saviour,* 239–57. London: SPCK, 1990.

Martin, Dale B. *Slavery as Salvation: The Metaphor of Slavery in Pauline Christianity.* New Haven: Yale University Press, 1990.

Martin, Ralph P. *Reconciliation: A Study of Paul's Theology.* Atlanta: John Knox, 1981.

———. "Reconciliation: Romans 5:1–11." In *Romans and the People of God,* edited by Sven K. Soderlund and N.T. Wright, 36–48. Grand Rapids: Eerdmans, 1999.

Martyn, J. Louis. "A Personal Word about Ernst Käsemann." In *Apocalyptic and the Future of Theology: With and Beyond J. Louis Martyn,* edited by Joshua B. Davis and Douglas Harink, xiii–xv. Eugene: Cascade, 2012.

———. "Afterword: The Human Moral Drama." In *Apocalyptic Paul: Cosmos and Anthropos in Romans 5–8,* edited by Beverly Roberts Gaventa, 157–66. Waco: Baylor University Press, 2013.

———. "Epilogue: An Essay in Pauline Meta-Ethics." In *Divine and Human Agency in Paul and His Cultural Environment,* edited by John M.G. Barclay and Simon J. Gathercole, 173–83. London: T&T Clark, 2008.

———. "The Apocalyptic Gospel in Galatians." *Int* 54.3 (2000): 246–66.

———. *Theological Issues in the Letters of Paul.* Edinburgh: T&T Clark, 1997.

Maston, Jason. *Divine and Human Agency in Second Temple Judaism and Paul: A Comparative Study*. Tübingen: Mohr Siebeck, 2010.
McCullough, Michael E., Everett L. Worthington and Kenneth C. Rachal. "Interpersonal Forgiving in Close Relationships." *JPSP* 73.2 (1997).
McFarland, Orrey. *God and Grace in Philo and Paul*. Leiden: Brill, 2016.
McGinn, Sheila E., ed. *Celebrating Romans: Template for Pauline Theology: Essays in Honor of Robert Jewett*. Grand Rapids: Eerdmans, 2004.
McLean, B. Hudson. *The Cursed Christ: Mediterranean Expulsion Rituals and Pauline Soteriology*. Sheffield: Sheffield Academic, 1996.
Meggitt, Justin J. *Paul, Poverty and Survival*. Edinburgh: T&T Clark, 1998.
Metzger, Bruce M. *A Textual Commentary on the Greek New Testament: A Companion Volume to the United Bible Societies' Greek New Testament (Fourth Revised Edition)*. Stuttgart; New York: Deutsche Bibelgesellschaft; United Bible Societies, 1994.
Meyer, Paul W. "The Worm at the Core of the Apple: Exegetical Reflections on Romans 7." In *The Word in This World: Essays in New Testament Exegesis and Theology*, edited by John T. Carroll, 57–77. Louisville: WJK, 2004.
Milbank, John. *Theology and Social Theory: Beyond Secular Reason*. Second Edition. Oxford: Blackwell, 2006.
Miller, Colin D. *The Practice of the Body of Christ: Human Agency in Pauline Theology after MacIntyre*. Cambridge: James Clarke & Co, 2014.
Moo, Douglas J. "Creation and New Creation." *BBR* 20.1 (2010): 39–60.
———. *The Epistle to the Romans*. Grand Rapids: Eerdmans, 1996.
Moore, Richard K. "N. T. Wright's Treatment of 'Justification' in *The New Testament for Everyone*." *ExpT* 125.10 (2014): 483–6.
———. *Paul's Concept of Justification: God's Gift of a Right Relationship*. Eugene: Wipf & Stock, 2015.
Morgan, Teresa. *Roman Faith and Christian Faith: Pistis and Fides in the Early Roman Empire and Early Churches*. Oxford: Oxford University Press, 2015.
Morris, Leon. *The Apostolic Preaching of the Cross*. Grand Rapids: Eerdmans, 1965.
———. *The Epistle to the Romans*. Grand Rapids: Eerdmans, 1988.
Mott, Stephen C. and Gerald F. Hawthorne. "The Power of Giving and Receiving: Reciprocity in Hellenistic Benevolence." In *Current Issues in Biblical and Patristic Interpretation*, 60–72. Grand Rapids: Eerdmans, 1975.
Myers, David G. *Social Psychology*. New York: McGraw-Hill, 2010.
Neyrey, Jerome H. "Prayer, in Other Words: New Testament Prayers in Social Science Perspective." In *Social Scientific Models for Interpreting the Bible: Essays by the Context Group in Honor of Bruce J. Malina*, 349–80. Leiden: Brill, 2001.
———. *Render to God: New Testament Understandings of the Divine*. Minneapolis: Fortress, 2004.
Oakes, Peter. *Philippians: From People to Letter*. Cambridge: Cambridge University Press, 2001.
———. *Reading Romans in Pompeii: Paul's Letter at Ground Level*. London: SPCK, 2009.
Osiek, Carolyn. "What We Do and Don't Know About Early Christian Families." In *A Companion to Families in the Greek and Roman Worlds*, edited by Beryl Rawson, 198–213. Chichester: Wiley-Blackwell, 2011.
Patterson, Orlando. *Slavery and Social Death: A Comparative Study*. Cambridge: Harvard University Press, 1982.
Peppard, Michael. "Adopted and Begotten Sons of God: Paul and John on Divine Sonship." *CBQ* 73.1 (2011): 92–110.
Pilch, John J. and Bruce J. Malina, eds. *Handbook of Biblical Social Values*. Peabody: Hendrickson, 1998.

Porter, Stanley E. *Καταλλάσσω in Ancient Greek Literature, with Reference to the Pauline Writings*. Cordoba: Ediciones el Almendro, 1994.
———. "Paul's Concept of Reconciliation, Twice More." In *Paul and His Theology*, edited by Stanley E. Porter, 131–52. Leiden: Brill, 2006.
Powers, Daniel G. *Salvation through Participation*. Leuven: Peeters, 2001.
Rabens, Volker. *The Holy Spirit and Ethics in Paul: Transformation and Empowering for Religious-Ethical Life*. Tübingen: Mohr Siebeck, 2013.
Rajak, Tessa. "The Individual and the Word in Hellenistic Judaism: Cases in Philo and Josephus." In *The Individual in the Religions of the Ancient Mediterranean*, 298–314. Oxford: Oxford University Press, 2013.
Rehman, Luzia S. "To Turn the Groaning into Labor: Romans 8.22-23." In *A Feminist Companion to Paul*, edited by Amy-Jill Levine and Marianne Blickenstaff, 74–84. Cleveland: Pilgrim, 2004.
Rüpke, Jörg. "Individualization and Individuation as Concepts for Historical Research." In *The Individual in the Religions of the Ancient Mediterranean*, edited by Jörg Rüpke, 3–38. Oxford: Oxford University Press, 2013.
Rusbult, Caryl E. "Interdependence Theory." In *Encyclopedia of Psychology*, edited by Alan E. Kazdin. Vol. 4, 330–1. Oxford: American Psychological Association; Oxford University Press, 2000.
Rusbult, Caryl E., Ximena B. Arriaga and Christopher R. Agnew. "Interdependence in Close Relationships." In *Blackwell Handbook of Social Psychology: Interpersonal Processes*, edited by Garth J.O. Fletcher and Margaret S. Clark. Oxford: Blackwell, 2003.
Rusbult, Caryl E. and John M. Martz. "Remaining in an Abusive Relationship: An Investment Model Analysis of Nonvoluntary Dependence." *PSPB* 21.6 (1995): 558–71.
Rusbult, Caryl E., Madoka Kumashiro, Shevaun L. Stocker, Jeffrey L. Kirchner, Eli J. Finkel and Michael K. Coolsen. "Self Processes in Interdependent Relationships: Partner Affirmation and the Michelangelo Phenomenon." *IntS* 6.3 (2005): 375–91.
Rusbult, Caryl E. and Paul A.M. Van Lange. "Interdependence, Interaction, and Relationships." *ARP* 54.1 (2003): 351–75.
———. "Why We Need Interdependence Theory." *SPPC* 2.5 (2008): 2049–70.
Saller, Richard. "Pietas, Obligation and Authority in the Roman Family." In *Alte Geschichte Und Wissenschaftsgeschichte, Festschrift Für Karl Christ*, edited by Peter Kneissl and Volker Losemann, 393–410. Darmstadt: Wissenschaftliche Buchgesellschaft, 1988.
Sanday, William and Arthur C. Headlam. *A Critical and Exegetical Commentary on the Epistle to the Romans*. Tenth Edition. New York: Charles Scribner's Sons, 1905.
Sanders, E.P. *Paul and Palestinian Judaism: A Comparison of Patterns of Religion*. Philadelphia: Fortress, 1977.
Schlatter, Adolf. *Gottes Gerechtigket. Ein Kommentar Zum Römerbrief*. Stuttgart: Calwer, 1935.
Schliesser, Benjamin. *Abraham's Faith in Romans 4*. Tübingen: Mohr Siebeck, 2007.
Schreiber, Stefan. "Das Weihegeschenk Gottes: Eine Deutung Des Todes Jesu in Röm 3,25." *ZNW* 97 (2006): 88–110.
———. "Weitergedacht: Das Versöhnende Weihegeschenk Gottes in Röm 3,25." *ZNW* 106.2 (2015): 201–15.
Scott, James M. *Adoption as Sons of God*. Tübingen: Mohr Siebeck, 1992.
Seeley, David. *The Noble Death: Graeco-Roman Martyrology and Paul's Concept of Salvation*. Sheffield: JSOT Press, 1989.
Seifrid, Mark A. "The Subject of Rom 7:14-25." *NovT* 34.4 (1992): 313–33.
Sellars, John. *Stoicism*. Berkeley: University of California Press, 2006.

Shaw, David A. "Apocalyptic and Covenant: Perspectives on Paul or Antinomies at War?" *JSNT* 36.2 (2013): 155-71.
Siegert, Folker. "Philo and the New Testament." In *The Cambridge Companion to Philo*, edited by Adam Kamesar, 175-209. Cambridge: Cambridge University Press, 2009.
Siikavirta, Samuli. *Baptism and Cognition in Romans 6-8*. Tübingen: Mohr Siebeck, 2015.
Southall, David J. *Rediscovering Righteousness in Romans*. Tübingen: Mohr Siebeck, 2008.
Sprinkle, Preston M. *Paul and Judaism Revisited: A Study of Divine and Human Agency in Salvation*. Downers Grove: IVP Academic Press, 2013.
———. "The Afterlife in Romans: Understanding Paul's Glory Motif in Light of the Apocalypse of Moses and 2 Baruch." In *Lebendige Hoffnung - Ewiger Tod?!: Jenseitsvorstellungen Im Hellenismus, Judentum Und Christentum*, edited by Michael Labahn and Manfred Lang, 201-33. Leipzig: Evangelische Verlagsanstalt, 2007.
Stendahl, Krister. *Paul among Jews and Gentiles, and Other Essays*. Philadelphia: Fortress, 1976.
———. "The Apostle Paul and the Introspective Conscience of the West." In *Paul among Jews and Gentiles*, 78-96. Philadelphia: Fortress, 1976.
Stephens, William O. *Stoic Ethics: Epictetus and Happiness as Freedom*. London: Continuum, 2007.
Stewart, Tyler A. "The Cry of Victory: A Cruciform Reading of Psalm 44:22 in Romans 8:36." *JSPHL* 3.1 (2013): 25-45.
Stowers, Stanley K. *A Rereading of Romans: Justice, Jews, and Gentiles*. New Haven: Yale University Press, 1994.
———. "Paul and Self-Mastery." In *Paul in the Greco-Roman World: A Handbook*, edited by J. Paul Sampley, 524-50. Harrisburg: Trinity Press International, 2003.
Stökl Ben Ezra, Daniel. *The Impact of Yom Kippur on Early Christianity*. Tübingen: Mohr Siebeck, 2003.
Stuhlmacher, Peter. *Paul's Letter to the Romans: A Commentary*. Louisville: WJK, 1994.
———. "Recent Exegesis on Romans 3:24-26." In *Reconciliation, Law, & Righteousness: Essays in Biblical Theology*, 94-109. Philadelphia: Fortress, 1986.
Tabb, Brian J. "Paul and Seneca on Suffering." In *Paul and Seneca in Dialogue*, edited by Joseph R. Dodson and David E. Briones, 88-108. Leiden: Brill, 2017.
Tannehill, Robert C. *Dying and Rising with Christ: A Study in Pauline Theology*. Berlin: Töpelmann, 1967.
Tanner, Kathryn. *Economy of Grace*. Minneapolis: Fortress, 2005.
Theissen, Gerd. *Psychological Aspects of Pauline Theology*. Philadelphia: Fortress, 1987.
Thibaut, John W. and Harold H. Kelley. *The Social Psychology of Groups*. New York: Wiley, 1959.
Thiessen, Matthew. *Paul and the Gentile Problem*. Oxford: Oxford University Press, 2016.
Thiselton, Anthony C. *Discovering Romans: Content, Interpretation, Reception*. London: SPCK, 2016.
Thorsteinsson, Runar. *Paul's Interlocutor in Romans 2: Function and Identity in the Context of Ancient Epistolography*. Eugene: Wipf & Stock, 2015.
———. *Roman Christianity and Roman Stoicism: A Comparative Study of Ancient Morality*. Oxford: Oxford University Press, 2010.
Tiwald, Markus. "Christ as Hilasterion (Rom 3:25). Pauline Theology on the Day of Atonement in the Mirror of Early Jewish Thought." In *The Day of Atonement: Its Interpretations in Early Jewish and Christian Traditions*, edited by Thomas Hieke and Tobias Nicklas, 189-209. Leiden: Brill, 2012.
Tolstoy, Leo. *Family Happiness*. Translated by D. Bondar. London: Bath, Sir Isaac Pitman & Sons, 1945.

Trebilco, Paul. *Self-Designations and Group Identity in the New Testament*. Cambridge: Cambridge University Press, 2011.

Van Kooten, George H. *Paul's Anthropology in Context*. Tübingen: Mohr Siebeck, 2008.

Versnel, Henk S. "Making Sense of Jesus' Death: The Pagan Contribution." In *Deutungen Des Todes Jesu Im Neuen Testament*, edited by Jörg Frey and Jens Schröter, 213–96. Tübingen: Mohr Siebeck, 2005.

Wallach, Michael A. and Lise Wallach. *Psychology's Sanction for Selfishness: The Error of Egoism in Theory and Therapy*. San Francisco: W.H. Freeman, 1983.

Walters, James C. "Paul, Adoption, and Inheritance." In *Paul in the Greco-Roman World: A Handbook*, edited by J. Paul Sampley, 42–76. Harrisburg: Trinity Press International, 2003.

Wasserman, Emma. "Paul among the Philosophers: The Case of Sin in Romans 6–8." *JSNT* 30.4 (2008): 387–415.

———. *The Death of the Soul in Romans 7*. Tübingen: Mohr Siebeck, 2008.

Watson, Francis. "Constructing an Antithesis: Pauline and Other Jewish Perspectives on Divine and Human Agency." In *Divine and Human Agency in Paul and His Cultural Environment*, edited by John M.G. Barclay and Simon J. Gathercole, 99–116. London: T&T Clark, 2006.

———. *Paul and the Hermeneutics of Faith*. Second Edition. London: Bloomsbury, 2016.

———. *Paul, Judaism, and the Gentiles: Beyond the New Perspective*. Grand Rapids: Eerdmans, 2007.

———. "Review of The Deliverance of God." *EC* 1.1 (2010): 179–85.

Way, David. *The Lordship of Christ: Ernst Käsemann's Interpretation of Paul's Theology*. Oxford: Clarendon, 1991.

Wedderburn, A.J.M. *The Reasons for Romans*. London: T&T Clark, 2004.

Weima, Jeffery A.D. "The Function of the Law in Relation to Sin: An Evaluation of the View of H. Räisänen." *NovT* 32.3 (1990): 219–35.

———. "The Reason for Romans: The Evidence of Its Epistolary Framework (1:1–15; 15:14–16:27)." *R&E* 100 (2003): 17–33.

Wells, Kyle B. *Grace and Agency in Paul and Second Temple Judaism: Interpreting the Transformation of the Heart*. Leiden: Brill, 2015.

Westerholm, Stephen. "Paul's Anthropological 'Pessimism' in Its Jewish Context." In *Divine and Human Agency in Paul and His Cultural Environment*, edited by John M.G. Barclay and Simon J. Gathercole, 71–98. London: T&T Clark, 2008.

Wiefel, Wolfgang. "The Jewish Community in Ancient Rome and the Origins of Roman Christianity." In *The Romans Debate*, edited by Karl P. Donfried, 85–101. Peabody: Hendrickson, 1991.

Wieselquist, Jennifer, Caryl E. Rusbult, Craig A. Foster and Christopher R. Agnew. "Commitment, Pro-Relationship Behavior, and Trust in Close Relationships." *JPSP* 77.5 (1999): 942–66.

Williams, Jarvis. *Christ Died for Our Sins: Representation and Substitution in Romans and Their Jewish Martyrological Background*. Cambridge: James Clarke & Co, 2015.

Williams, Sam K. *Jesus' Death as Saving Event: The Background and Origin of a Concept*. Missoula: Scholars, 1975.

———. "The 'Righteousness of God' in Romans." *JBL* 99.2 (1980): 241–90.

Windsor, Lionel J. *Paul and the Vocation of Israel: How Paul's Jewish Identity Informs His Apostolic Ministry, with Special Reference to Romans*. Berlin: de Gruyter, 2014.

Witherington III, Ben. *Paul's Letter to the Romans: A Socio-Rhetorical Commentary*. Grand Rapids: Eerdmans, 2004.

Wolter, Michael. *Paul: An Outline of His Theology*. Translated by Robert L. Brawley. Waco: Baylor University Press, 2015.
Worthington, Everett L. *Handbook of Forgiveness*. New York: Routledge, 2005.
Wright, N.T. "Apocalyptic and the Sudden Fulfillment of Divine Promise." In *Paul and the Apocalyptic Imagination*, edited by Ben C. Blackwell, John K. Goodrich and Jason Maston, 111–34. Minneapolis: Fortress, 2016.
———. *Jesus and the Victory of God*. Minneapolis: Fortress, 1996.
———. *Paul and the Faithfulness of God*. London: SPCK, 2013.
———. *Paul: In Fresh Perspective*. Minneapolis: Fortress, 2005.
———. "Romans and the Theology of Paul." In *Pauline Theology*, edited by David M. Hay and E. Elizabeth Johnson, Volume III, 30–67. Minneapolis: Fortress, 1995.
———. *The Climax of the Covenant: Christ and the Law in Pauline Theology*. Edinburgh: T&T Clark, 1991.
———. "The Law in Romans 2." In *Paul and the Mosaic Law*, edited by James D.G. Dunn, 131–50. Tübingen: Mohr Siebeck, 1996.
———. *The Resurrection of the Son of God*. Minneapolis: Fortress, 2003.
———. "Translating Δικαιοσύνη: A Response." *ExpT* 125.10 (2014): 487–90.
Wu, Siu Fung. *Suffering in Romans*. Eugene: Pickwick Publications, 2015.
Yates, John W. *The Spirit and Creation in Paul*. Tübingen: Mohr Siebeck, 2008.
Yinger, Kent L. *Paul, Judaism, and Judgment According to Deeds*. Cambridge: Cambridge University Press, 1999.
Young, Frances M. "Understanding Romans in the Light of 2 Corinthians." *STJ* 43.4 (1990): 433–46.
Young, Norman H. "C. H. Dodd, 'Hilaskesthai' and His Critics." *EQ* 2.48 (1976): 67–78.
Ziesler, John A. *Paul's Letter to the Romans*. London: SCM Press, 1989.
———. *The Meaning of Righteousness in Paul: A Linguistic and Theological Enquiry*. Cambridge: Cambridge University Press, 1972.
———. "The Role of the Tenth Commandment in Romans 7." *JSNT* 33 (1988): 41–56.

Index of References

OLD TESTAMENT/HEBREW BIBLE

Genesis
1	61
1–3	60, 133
1:2	60
1:20–25	60
1:26–27	60
2–3	61
3	61
3:4	60
3:19	124
15:6	3, 79
18:17	47
32:20	80
50:15–21	74

Exodus
4:22	142
15	82
18:22	146
20:3–17	65
25:22 (LXX)	89
32	56
32:14	81

Leviticus
16:2 (LXX)	89
16:14–17	89
16:30	82
18:5	4
26:41	67

Numbers
7:89	89–90
11:17	146

Deuteronomy
5:7–21	65
10:16	67
14:1–2	142
28	65
30:1–10	67
30:6	67
32:5–6	47

1 Samuel
6:3	81
13:13	56
16:7	48

2 Samuel
7:14–15	47

1 Kings
8:42	48

2 Kings
17:15	56
24:4	81

1 Chronicles
2:18	56

Psalm
17:28	57
31:1 (LXX)	76
33:9	47
51:1–2	82
68:5	47
88:11	57
88:22 (LXX)	146
89:26	47
93:2	57
94:9	47
95:12–13 (LXX)	107
96:1–2 (LXX)	107
97:9 (LXX)	107
98:4–5 (LXX)	107
100:5	57
103:13	47
105:30	81
119:21	57

Proverbs		Hosea	
3:34	57	2:1	142
15:25	57	2:18	134
16:14	80	11:1	142

Isaiah		Habakkuk	
1:2	47	2:5	57
1:4	47		
2:12	57	Zephaniah	
11:6–9	134	3:6	57
13:11	57		
43:19–21	134	Zechariah	
49:15	47	7:2	81
50:1	47	8:12	134
52:5	65	8:22	81
54:5–8	47		
55:12–13	134	Malachi	
62:5	47	1:9	81
64:8	47		
66:13	47		

NEW TESTAMENT

Matthew	
5:28	34
20:28	86

Jeremiah			
2:5	56	Mark	
3:1	47	7:20–23	34
3:4	47	10:45	86
3:7–8	57	14:36	141
3:8	47		
3:10–11	57	Luke	
3:19	47	1:51	57
3:20	47	10:40	146
3:22	47	12:34	34
4:4	67		
9:25	67	Acts	
31:20	47	8:1	135
31:22	47	10:43	94
31:33 (38:33 [LXX])	66, 67	13:50	135

Ezekiel		Romans	
16:32	47	1	60
16:35–43	47	1–3	114
34:25–31	134	1–5	60
36	134	1–8	18, 157
36:24–28	66	1–11	16
36:25–26	67	1:1	112
36:26–27	66	1:3–4	141
44:7	67		
44:9	67		

1:4	128, 141, 144	2:5	66, 83, 87
1:6	112	2:6–16	37, 65
1:7	112	2:7	62, 65
1:9	108	2:7–10	133
1:13–14	37	2:8	41, 59, 66, 87
1:15	1	2:8–9	61
1:16	37, 53	2:9	59
1:16–17	9, 36, 45, 54, 115	2:10	62
		2:14–15	66
1:16–3:20	12	2:14–19	37
1:17	53, 68, 79	2:15	37, 146
1:18	53, 78, 83, 87	2:16	34
1:18–32	19, 44, 60–1, 65, 69, 109, 115	2:17	64–5
		2:17–25	37, 45
1:18–3:8	65, 68	2:17–29	64, 67, 120
1:18–3:20	2, 19, 51, 53, 54, 69, 81, 140, 157, 158	2:18	65
		2:19	65
		2:20	65
1:18–3:26	5	2:21–22	65
1:19–23	54	2:21–23	66
1:20	45, 60, 61	2:23	65, 66
1:21	56, 57, 58, 61, 62, 110	2:23–24	65
		2:24	65, 68
1:21–22	59	2:25–26	66
1:21–23	56	2:25–29	66
1:21–27	56, 57	2:26–27	66–7
1:21–32	56	2:26–29	37
1:22	58	2:28–29	67, 120
1:23	56, 60, 133	2:29	67
1:24	59, 120	3:1–2	66
1:24–32	116	3:1–9	37
1:25	56, 60	3:3	91
1:26	56	3:3–5	88
1:26–27	59	3:4	68
1:27	61	3:5	83, 87
1:28	44, 57, 108, 109	3:9	37, 54, 65, 68, 115
1:28–31	56		
1:29–31	59	3:9–18	44
1:32	57, 59, 61	3:9–20	68
2	64	3:10	68
2:1	45	3:10–18	68
2:1–5	64–5	3:10–20	37
2:1–16	54, 67	3:11	58, 69
2:1–3:8	19, 54, 63, 68, 69, 158	3:12	69
		3:18	58, 69
2:3	45	3:19	147
2:4	58	3:21	71, 79
2:4–5	88	3:21–22	9

3:21–26	2, 19, 51, 71, 77–80, 82, 84, 88, 91–4, 132, 157, 158, 161	5:6–11	10, 13, 45, 46, 103, 151
		5:7	46
		5:8	99, 100, 105, 152
3:21–4:25	94		
3:21–5:21	109	5:9	66, 78, 83, 87, 88, 105
3:22	91, 92		
3:23–24	5	5:9–10	99
3:24	78, 79, 80, 85, 109	5:9–11	102
		5:10	78
3:24–26	88	5:10–11	76
3:25	76, 78, 80, 81, 82, 83, 89, 90, 91, 93	5:11	78, 98
		5:12	114
		5:12–14	61
3:26	78, 79, 80, 91	5:12–21	9, 37, 60, 61, 102, 114, 119, 123, 125, 128, 134, 158
3:27	93		
3:27–31	92		
4	17		
4:2–5	5	5:12–8:11	2, 19, 51, 113, 114, 115, 157, 158
4:5–8	37		
4:7	76		
4:11	66	5:12–8:13	114
4:11–12	37	5:13	114
4:13	131	5:14	117
4:13–14	131	5:15	109
4:16	37	5:15–19	141
4:16–25	131	5:16	7, 109
4:17	68	5:17	7, 98, 109, 117, 123
4:23–25	37, 79		
4:24	103	5:18	7
4:24–25	92	5:18–19	92
5	97, 98	5:19	15, 141
5–8	15, 114, 119	5:20	109, 114
5:1	90, 97, 103	5:21	109, 114, 117, 124
5:1–2	90, 133		
5:1–11	2, 12, 19, 44, 46, 51, 71, 78, 90, 97–9, 102, 132, 157, 158	6	106, 108
		6–7	46, 117–18
		6–8	6, 7, 116, 129, 139
5:2	90, 109, 133	6:1–11	6, 127
5:3	135	6:2	124, 127
5:3–4	105, 133	6:3–5	127
5:3–5	104	6:4	127
5:5	12, 105, 127, 152	6:4–11	127
		6:6	105
5:6	78, 102	6:6–7	124, 127
5:6–8	104	6:10–11	127
5:6–9	5	6:11	116, 124, 126–8
5:6–10	78	6:11–13	139

6:12	105, 114	7:24	124
6:12–13	106	7:25	108, 117, 126, 128
6:12–23	6, 15		
6:13	106, 108, 116, 127	8	17, 109, 119, 133–4
6:14–15	124	8:1–11	126–8
6:15–23	117	8:1–13	5, 6, 136
6:16	108	8:1–17	138
6:16–23	114	8:2	126
6:19	106, 108, 116, 117	8:3	126, 127
		8:3–4	12
6:19–21	125	8:4–8	128
6:19–23	105	8:6	128, 151
6:22–23	151	8:7	139
6:23	117	8:9	128
7	19, 36, 113, 118–19	8:9–11	143
		8:10	136
7:1–3	123	8:11	128
7:1–6	123–6	8:12	128, 142
7:4	124, 127	8:12–13	138, 139
7:4–6	124	8:12–17	138–40, 143
7:5	106, 128	8:12–25	142
7:6	117	8:12–30	137–8
7:7	119, 124	8:12–39	2, 19, 51, 129, 131–2, 155, 157, 158
7:7–13	118		
7:7–21	37		
7:7–25	4, 24, 45, 113, 118–20, 125, 161	8:13	5, 128, 132, 151, 154
	123, 124	8:13–14	13, 140, 153
7:8	123, 124	8:14	128, 141, 146, 154
7:8–9	114		
7:8–10	123	8:14–17	138, 139, 141, 153
7:9–11	124		
7:11	114, 117, 124	8:14–19	46
7:12	124	8:15	117, 141
7:13	124	8:15–16	128, 132
7:14	123, 128, 147	8:16	142, 145, 146
7:14–20	118	8:16–28	143
7:14–25	118	8:17	131, 132, 135, 141, 142, 143, 144
7:15	120, 124		
7:16	124		
7:17	114	8:17–18	132–5
7:18	128	8:17–30	12
7:18–19	123, 124	8:18	134, 148, 150–1, 153, 154
7:19	120, 124		
7:20	114	8:18–27	148–9
7:21	123, 124	8:18–30	15, 140–9
7:22	123	8:18–39	17, 133
7:23	106, 108	8:19	144

8:19–21	144	12:1–3	109
8:19–22	131, 145	12:2	108, 109
8:19–27	148	12:3	10
8:20	148	12:3–8	106, 160
8:21	117, 133, 141, 144	12:10	106
		12:14	136
8:22	144, 145, 151	12:14–21	106
8:23	132, 133, 141, 145	13:8	67
		13:8–10	106
8:24–25	135, 145, 153, 154	13:11	151
		13:13–14	139
8:26	128, 145, 146, 150	14:1–2	10
		14:1–6	109
8:26–27	132, 150, 154	14:1–15:13	160
8:27	146, 148	14:5	108
8:28	112, 134, 148–9	14:6	110
		14:7	106
8:28–30	147	14:7–8	106, 108, 120
8:29	141, 144	14:7–9	109
8:29–30	148, 149	14:9	109
8:31	136	14:13	106
8:31–39	135, 150, 151–2	14:17	120
		14:18	108, 109
8:32	143, 150, 151	14:19	106
8:33	136	14:23	106, 120
8:34	136, 144	15:1	10
8:35	105, 135, 152	15:1–2	106
8:35–36	135	15:1–3	108
8:36	68	15:3	68
8:38	136	15:7	106
8:39	105, 139	15:7–12	17
9–11	2, 161	15:9	68
9:1	146	15:14–16:27	160
9:13	68	15:21	68
9:33	68	15:22–24	1
10:9	9	15:25–27	161
10:13	9	15:30	105
10:15	68	16	37
11:8	68	16:3	149
11:21–22	14	16:9	149
11:26	9, 68	16:17	69
11:32	9	16:17–20	115
11:33–36	45	16:21	149
11:34	108		
12	37	*1 Corinthians*	
12–15	2, 67, 106, 161	1:1	112
12–16	160	1:10	108
12:1	106, 108	1:31	68
12:1–2	108, 109	2:6	136

2:8	136	5:2–4	145
2:9	68	5:7	91
2:16	108	5:9	108
3:6	149	5:11–21	46
3:9	149	5:14–15	105
3:16–17	37	5:14–21	209
4:5	34	5:15	109, 136
4:6–16	109	5:18–20	76
5:5	115	5:20	97, 98, 149
6:19	37	6:1	149
6:19–20	37	6:4	133, 149
6:20	85	6:13	61
7:5	115, 139	6:14	115
7:10–16	135	6:18	46
7:11	46	7:2–16	161
7:23	85	7:4	133
7:26	140	8–9	161
8–10	161	8:1–2	133
9:25	148	8:1–6	111
10:21	115	8:15	68
10:33	148	8:23	149
11:1	109	9:9	68
11:2	148	11:1–12:21	161
11:17–13:13	161	11:14	115
14:14	108	12:7	115
14:15	34, 108	12:10	135
14:19	108	12:20	41, 59
15:20–28	114		
15:56	114	Galatians	
16:1–4	161	1:15	112
		2:16	91
2 Corinthians		3:13	85, 86
1:1	112	3:26–4:7	46
1:4	133	3:29	141
1:4–5	133	4:1	141
1:8	133	4:1–7	142
1:24	149	4:3	86
2:4	133	4:4	141
2:11	115	4:5	85
3:6	67	4:6	141
4:4	115	4:7	141
4:7–12	136	4:12–20	161
4:14	136	4:19	145
4:17	133, 135, 136	5	139
4:17–18	135	5:13–6:10	161
4–5	136	5:17	139
5	97	5:19–21	139
5:1	147	5:20	41, 59
5:1–5	136	5:23	39

Ephesians
1:7	86
2:18	90
3:12	90
5:6	87
5:10	108
6:1–4	143

Philippians
1:1	112
1:17	59
1:21–25	41
1:29	133
2:1–4	161
2:3	59
2:3–4	41
2:4	41
2:6–8	141
2:6–11	92, 141
2:7–8	141
2:8	141
2:9–11	141
2:12–13	4
2:14–15	46
2:25	149
3:3	67
3:6	119
3:9	91
3:17	109
3:20–21	141
4:3	149
4:7	108
4:10–20	161
4:14	133
4:17	41
4:18	108

Colossians
1:14	86
1:15–17	141
3:6	87
3:20	108
3:20–21	143

1 Thessalonians
1:6	133
1:10	88
2–3	161
2:16	87
2:18	115
3:2	149
3:3	133
3:5	115
3:7	133
5:9	88

2 Thessalonians
1:4	135

1 Timothy
2:6	86

2 Timothy
3:11	135

Titus
2:9	108

Philemon
1	149
24	149

Hebrews
9:5	80
9:11–28	80
9:15	86
12:9	47

James
2:22	148
3:14	59
3:16	59
4:6	57

1 Peter
1:5	57
3:18	90

APOCRYPHA
2 Maccabees
1:5	46
7:18	75
7:33	46
7:37–38	75
8:28	46
8:29	75

Sirach	
4:10	142
35:21	57
45:23	81

PSEUDEPIGRAPHA

Apocalypse of Baruch (2 Baruch)
29:1–8	134

1 Enoch
Apocalypse of Weeks
(93:1–10; 91:11–17)	134
Books of Parables (31–71)	134

4 Ezra
8:51–54	134

Jubilees 134
1:24–25	142

Life of Adam and Eve
10–12	134
24	134
39:1–3	134

4 Maccabees 4
17:22	89

Psalms of Solomon
2:31	57
17:26–27	142

NEW TESTAMENT APOCRYPHA AND PSEUDEPIGRAPHA

Pseudo-Clementines

Homilies
1.12	57

DEAD SEA SCROLLS

4QMMT	4

PHILO

De confusione linguarum
144	47
170	47
175	47

De ebrietate
74	47

De fuga et invention
84	47
177	47
197	47

De migratione Abrahami
34–9	35
46	47
135	47
195	47

De mutatione nominum
29	47
45	47
127	47
129	47

De opificio mundi
7	47
72	47

De plantatione
130	110

De posteritate Caini
33–39	110

De somniis
1.237	47
2.175–7	100

De specialibus legibus
2.234	110

De vita contemplativa
75–8	35
86	35

Legatio ad Gaium
118	110

Legum allegoriae
1.18	47
3.27	47

Quis rerum divinarum heres sit

62	47
98	47
110	47
200	47
205	47
236	47

Quod deterius potiori insidari soleat

97	34

Quod Deus sit immutabilis

31	47

JOSEPHUS

Contra Apionem

2.196–7	35

Jewish Antiquities

6.143	46

Jewish War

3.350–4	36

CLASSICAL LITERATURE

Cicero

Paradoxa Stoicorum

17	34

Codex justinianus

5.25.1	142
5.25.2	142
8.46.5	142

Epictetus

Diatribai

1.12	119
1.19.11–12	39
1.19.12–13	39
1.29	34
1.4	34
1.4.1–12	34
2.6.24–29	39
2.22.15–16	39
2.22.18–19	39

3.1–40	34
3.2	34
3.2.13	34
3.3.2	34
3.4.10	34
4.5.34	34

Euripides

Iphigenia aulidensis

1157–58	75

Homer

Iliad

1.224–9	35
9.496f	74
11.477–8135	

Plato 53

Respublica

8.566E	75

Plutarch

Pelopidas

26.2	74

Polybius

21.16.9	74

Seneca

De beneficiis

1.1.9	100
1.6.1	40
2.2.2	40
2.22	51
4.1.3	40
4.12.3	40
4.14.2–4	40
4.14.3	40
4.14.4	40
4.22.2–3	40
4.25.3	40
6.5.1–2	40
6.13.1–2	41

Epistulae morales
47.17	116
124.23	34

Tacitus

Annales
14.42–45	116

Vita Aesopi
2.100	75

Xenophon

Cyropaedia
7.5.45	90

APOSTOLIC FATHERS

1 Clement
35.5	57

2 Clement
1.3	61
9.7	61
11.6	61
15.2	61

PAPYRI

Oxyrhynchus papyri (P.Oxy.)
104	46, 75

P.Mich. (Michigan Papyri)
VIII.502, 7–8	74

Index of Authors

Adams, Edward 133, 135, 136
Agnew, Christopher R. 153

Bailey, Daniel P. 82–3
Baker, Coleman A. and Tucker, J. Brian 161
Barclay, John M.G. 3, 11, 14–15, 16–17, 38, 40, 41, 51, 67, 93, 98, 100, 106, 108, 110, 117, 133, 136, 140, 155
Barrett, C.K. 66, 82, 87, 149
Barth, Karl 91
Barton, Stephen C. 45, 48
Bassler, Jouette M. 107
Baumeister, R.F., Stillwell, A. and Heatherton, T.F. 74
Baumeister, R.F., Stillwell, A. and Wotman, S.R. 74
Bell, Richard H. 66, 86, 90
Berger, Klaus 33
Berkley, Timothy W. 66, 67
Blackwell, Ben C. 105, 134
Blackwell, Ben C., Goodrich, John K. and Maston, Jason 7, 133
Blackwell, Matthew 81
Blanton, Thomas R. 110
Blau, Peter M. 22
Bourdieu, Pierre 106
Bradley, Keith 117
Breytenbach, Cilliers 46, 76, 77, 78, 100
Briones, David E. 40, 41, 110, 111
Bruce, F.F. 2, 147
Buchanan, George Wesley 77
Buechsel, Friedrich 46
Bultmann, Rudolf 4, 115, 118
Burke, Trevor J. 142
Burnett, Gary W. 34–5, 36–7, 44, 107
Byrne, Brendan 133, 145
Byron, John 116, 117, 126

Campbell, Douglas A. 8–9, 15, 77, 79, 92, 103
Cantarella, Eva 142
Catchpole, David 132

Chang, Hae-Kyung 119
Clarke, Andrew D. 33
Clarke, Andrew D. and Tucker, J. Brian 38
Cohen, Ada 142
Combes, I.A.H. 117, 125
Cranfield, C.E.B. 65, 66, 68, 81, 98, 114, 118, 124, 142, 145, 146, 147
Crook, Zeba A. 47, 48

Dahl, N.A. 103
Das, A. Andrew 2
Davies, J.P., 16
de Boer, Martinus C. 17, 115, 129
Deissmann, Adolf 81, 83
deSilva, David 13–14, 105, 107, 110, 112
Dinkler, E. 97
Dodd, Brian J. 38, 119
Dodd, C.H. 77, 80–1, 97, 147
Dodson, Joseph R. 61, 115, 116
Donfried, Karl P. 2
Downing, F. Gerald 34, 35, 162
Duncan, John 133, 144
Dunn, James D.G. 2, 16, 37, 58, 59–60, 66, 68, 76, 79, 82, 83, 86, 88, 92, 93, 114, 116, 118, 120, 124, 127, 133, 135, 145, 146, 147, 148, 151
Dunson, Ben C. 34, 36, 37, 39, 44, 45, 106

Eastman, Susan 129, 144, 149
Elliott, Neil 97
Ellis, E. Earle 149
Engberg-Pedersen, Troels 12–13, 106, 110, 114, 139, 140
Esler, Philip F. 32, 33, 49, 51, 63, 67, 151
Espy, John M. 119

Fee, Gordon D. 147
Finkel, Eli J. 54–5, 64, 72, 73
Finlan, Stephen, 81, 82, 83, 85, 87, 92
Fitzgerald, John T. 74–6

Fitzmyer, Joseph A. 60, 61, 77, 78, 114, 124, 147
Forman, Mark 131
Freedman, Suzanne 74
Fryer, Nico S.L. 82
Furnish, Victor Paul 108

Garlington, Don B. 16
Garrett, Susan R. 32, 38
Gathercole, Simon J. 46, 66, 68, 100, 114
Gaventa, Beverly Roberts 9, 114, 115, 119, 131, 132
Gieniusz, Andrzej 86, 147–8
Gignilliat, Mark S. 147, 148
Goede, Hendrik 116
Goodrich, John K. 118
Gorman, Michael J. 53, 93, 95
Griffiths, J. Gwyn 147
Grubbs, Judith Evans 142
Gundry, Robert H. 118
Gundry Volf, Judith M. 132
Gupta, Nijay K. 37, 90, 108

Haacker, Klaus 2, 53
Hagen, Jeanette M. 93
Hahne, Harry Alan 133, 134
Hannon, Peggy A. 72–4, 85–9, 93
Harland, Philip 144
Harrill, J. Albert 116, 117, 119
Harris, Murray J. 136
Harrison, James R. 10–11
Hay, David M. 93, 94, 98, 106, 107
Hays, Richard B. 4, 91, 92, 109
Hägerland, Tobias 94
Higgins, E.T. 31
Hilborn, David 9
Hill, David 81
Herbert, A. Gabriel 91
Holmberg, Bengt 33
Holmes, John G. 42
Hooker, Morna D. 16, 54, 60, 93
Horrell, David G. 21, 31–2, 38, 43, 45, 48, 51, 108, 145
Hultgren, Arland J. 83
Hunt, Cherryl, Horrell, David G. and Southgate, Christopher 145

Jackson, T. Ryan 134, 136, 145
Jeffers, James S. 142

Jervis, L. Ann 88, 119
Jewett, Robert 53, 65, 66, 67, 82, 85, 86, 97, 100, 107, 108, 117, 118, 119, 120, 123, 124, 126, 128, 133, 136, 141, 142, 145, 146, 147, 149, 151
Johnson, L.T. 91, 92
Joubert, Stephen 22, 110–11
Judge, E.A. 32, 33

Käsemann, Ernst 14, 54, 62, 76, 78, 80, 86, 90, 105, 106, 118, 119, 136, 146, 147, 151
Keck, Leander E. 126, 147
Keener, Craig S. 109
Keesmaat, Sylvia C. 136, 144
Kelley, Harold H. 21, 22, 24, 28, 42, 50, 55, 73, 101, 137, 138, 139, 140, 150, 151–2, 153–4
Kelley, Harold H. and Thibaut, John W. 21–9, 42–3, 49–50, 51, 58, 100
Khobnya, Svetlana 92
King, Justin 124
Kruse, Colin G. 65, 68, 71, 118, 119, 141, 144, 146, 147
Kümmel, Werner G. 119

Lakoff, George and Johnson, Mark 84
Lawrence, Louise J. 43
Leary, Mark R. 72
Lee, Michelle V. 139
Lewin, Kurt 22
Lewis, Robert B. 143
Lincoln, Andrew T. 90
Lindsay, Hugh 142
Linebaugh, Jonathan A. 53, 84, 87
List, Christian and Spiekermann, Kai 44
Longenecker, Bruce W. 79, 86, 91
Longenecker, Richard N. 2, 83, 91, 97, 118, 119, 141, 143, 147
Luce, Robert D. and Raiffa, Howard 22

Macaskill, Grant 146
McCullough, Michael E., Worthington, Everett L. and Rachal, Kenneth C. 73
McFarland, Orrey 47, 100, 110, 111
McGinn, Sheila E. 2
MacIntyre, Alasdair 6
McLean, B. Hudson 77, 81
Malina, Bruce J. 33, 34, 48

Malina, Bruce J. and Neyrey, Jerome H. 33
Manson, T.W. 82
Marshall, I. Howard 75, 76, 86, 97
Martin, Dale B. 116
Martin, Ralph P. 53, 66, 88, 97, 98, 99, 103
Martyn, J. Louis 7–8, 10, 114
Maston, Jason 4–5, 119
Meggitt, Justin J. 35
Metzger, Bruce M. 147
Meyer, Paul W. 118
Milbank, John 45
Miller, Colin D. 6, 114
Moo, Douglas J. 36, 56, 71, 97, 99, 114, 115, 118, 119, 133, 134, 135, 145, 147, 148, 151, 152
Moore, Richard K., 79
Morgan, Teresa 92, 93, 104, 107
Morris, Leon 54, 81, 85
Mott, Stephen C. and Hawthorne, Gerald F. 111
Myers, David G. 22, 49

Neyrey, Jerome H. 47–8, 69

Oakes, Peter 18, 81, 116, 117, 141
Osiek, Carolyn 143

Patterson, Orlando 117, 125, 127
Peppard, Michael 144
Pilch, John J. and Malina, Bruce J. 33
Porter, Stanley E. 75, 76
Powers, Daniel G. 77, 93, 105

Rabens, Volker 139, 140, 141, 142, 143, 144, 154
Rajak, Tessa 35–6
Rehman, Luzia S. 132, 145
Rusbult, Caryl E. 22, 29, 31, 137
Rusbult, Caryl E., Arriaga, Ximena B. and Agnew, Christopher R. 22, 23, 26–30, 43, 55–6, 57, 58, 59, 63–4, 99–101, 105, 121, 153
Rusbult, Caryl E. and Martz, John M. 121, 126, 127
Rusbult, Caryl E. and Van Lange, Paul A.M. 21, 22, 24–31, 43, 44, 63, 64, 102–4, 105, 106, 120, 121, 126
Rüpke, Jörg 35

Saller, Richard 142
Sanday, William and Headlam, Arthur C. 97, 124, 147
Sanders, E.P. 16, 53, 119, 125
Schlatter, Adolf 131
Schliessler, Benjamin 94
Schreiber, Stefan 81
Scott, James M. 141, 142
Seeley, David 77
Seifrid, Mark A. 118
Sellars, John 39
Shaw, David A. 16
Siegert, Folker 47
Siikavirta, Samuli 127
Southall, David J. 117
Sprinkle, Preston M. 5–6, 133, 134
Stendahl, Krister 76, 119
Stephens, William O. 39
Stewart, Tyler A. 150
Stowers, Stanley K. 64, 77, 114, 118, 119, 139
Stökl Ben Ezra, Daniel 82
Stuhlmacher, Peter 67, 82, 88, 118, 126, 141, 147

Tabb, Brian J. 133
Tannehill, Robert C. 93
Tanner, Kathryn 162
Theissen, Gerd 45, 119
Thibaut, John W. and Kelley, Harold H. 21, 25, 30, 44, 64, 120–1
Thiessen, Matthew 64
Thiselton, Anthony S. 87, 135
Thorsteinsson, Runar 64, 65, 66
Tiwald, Markus 84, 89
Tolstoy, Leo 49
Trebilco, Paul 144

Van Kooten, George H. 109
Versnel, Henk S. 100

Wallach, Michael A. and Wallach, Lise 42
Walters, James C. 131, 142
Wasserman, Emma 114, 118
Watson, Francis 3–4, 8, 98, 119
Way, David 63
Wedderburn, A.J.M. 2

Weima, Jeffery A.D. 1, 123
Wells, Kyle B. 67, 155
Westerholm, Stephen 114, 115
Wiefel, Wolfgang 83, 120
Wieselquist, Jennifer 152
Williams, Jarvis 77, 89
Williams, Sam K. 77, 91
Windsor, Lionel J. 65, 67
Witherington III, Ben 64, 124
Wolter, Michael 84, 89
Worthington, Everett L. 72

Wright, N.T. 16–17, 36, 66, 67, 79, 98, 103, 118, 129, 131, 133
Wu, Siu Fung 133, 146

Yates, John W. 134, 145
Yinger, Kent L. 16
Young, Frances M. 136
Young, Norman 82

Ziesler, John A. 79, 82, 85, 86, 87, 119, 124, 126, 147

www.ingramcontent.com/pod-product-compliance
Lightning Source LLC
Chambersburg PA
CBHW070636300426
44111CB00013B/2133